Reconciling with the Past

Are countries truly reconciled after successful conflict resolution? Are only resource-rich regions capable of reconciliation, while supposedly resource-poor ones are condemned to recurring conflicts?

This book examines the availability of various resources for political reconciliation, and explores how they are utilized in overcoming particular obstacles during the process. While the existing literature focuses on themes such as justice, apology and resentment, the analysis here is centred on resources in terms of ideas, memory cultures, master narratives, economic incentives, civil society initiatives and object lessons.

The research and comparative research in this volume are conducted by renowned regional experts from South Africa to the Asia-Pacific, thus providing multidisciplinary perspectives and new insight on the subject.

Annika Frieberg is Assistant Professor at San Diego State University. She studied Modern and Central European History at the University of North Carolina-Chapel Hill. She has taught courses in 19th and 20th century European and East European history. Her research and teaching interests centre on war and genocide, conflict resolution, media, national, and transnational questions in Central Europe. She has published several articles, including "Reconciliation Remembered. Early Activists and the Polish-German Relations" in *Re-Mapping Polish-German Memory*, which was published by Indiana University Press in 2011. Dr. Frieberg is currently working on her book manuscript, *Costly Reconciliation: Transnational Networks and Media in post-war Polish-German Relations.*

C. K. Martin Chung is Assistant Professor in the Department of Government and International Studies at Hong Kong Baptist University. Previously he was Research Assistant Professor of the European Union Academic Programme Hong Kong, and Lecturer at the University of St. Joseph (Macau). He holds a PhD from the University of Hong Kong (2014) and conducts research on political reconciliation and "coming to terms with the past" in Europe (Cornell University Press; Vandenhoeck & Ruprecht) and East Asia (Franz Steiner Verlag; Nomos).

Routledge Advances in International Relations and Global Politics

124 Apology and Reconciliation in International Relations
The importance of being sorry
Edited by Christopher Daase, Stefan Engert, Michel-André Horelt, Judith Renner, Renate Strassner

125 The United States and Turkey's Path to Europe
Hands across the table
Armağan Emre Çakır

126 Western Muslim Reactions to Conflicts Abroad
Conflict spillovers to diasporas
Juris Pupcenoks

127 U.S. Security Cooperation with Africa
Political and policy challenges
Robert J. Griffiths

128 Russia's Relations with Kazakhstan
Rethinking post-communist transitions in the emerging world system
Yelena Nikolayevna Zabortseva

129 Reinventing Regional Security Institutions in Asia and Africa
Power shifts, ideas, and institutional change
Kei Koga

130 Sincerity in Politics and International Relations
Edited by Sorin Baiasu and Sylvie Loriaux

131 Neutrality in International Law
From the sixteenth century to 1945
Kentaro Wani

132 Reconciling with the Past
Resources and Obstacles in a Global Perspective
Edited by Annika Frieberg and C. K. Martin Chung

Reconciling with the Past
Resources and Obstacles in a
Global Perspective

Edited by Annika Frieberg and
C. K. Martin Chung

LONDON AND NEW YORK

First published 2017
by Routledge
2 Park Square, Milton Park, Abingdon, Oxon OX14 4RN

and by Routledge
711 Third Avenue, New York, NY 10017

Routledge is an imprint of the Taylor & Francis Group, an informa business

© 2017 selection and editorial matter, Annika Frieberg and C.K. Martin Chung; individual chapters, the contributors

The right of Annika Frieberg and C.K. Martin Chung to be identified as the authors of the editorial material, and of the authors for their individual chapters, has been asserted in accordance with sections 77 and 78 of the Copyright, Designs and Patents Act 1988.

All rights reserved. No part of this book may be reprinted or reproduced or utilised in any form or by any electronic, mechanical, or other means, now known or hereafter invented, including photocopying and recording, or in any information storage or retrieval system, without permission in writing from the publishers.

Trademark notice: Product or corporate names may be trademarks or registered trademarks, and are used only for identification and explanation without intent to infringe.

British Library Cataloguing-in-Publication Data
A catalogue record for this book is available from the British Library

Library of Congress Cataloging-in-Publication Data
A catalog record for this book has been requested

ISBN: 978-1-138-65172-2 (hbk)
ISBN: 978-1-315-62463-1 (ebk)

Typeset in Galliard
by Apex CoVantage, LLC

Contents

Contributors	vii
Acknowledgements	x

Introduction: Resources for political reconciliation   1
C. K. MARTIN CHUNG AND ANNIKA FRIEBERG

PART I
Reconciliation resources and obstacles   13

1   South Africa's reconciliation process: Tools, resources and
obstacles in the journey to deal with its atrocious past   15
JEREMY SARKIN

2   Amity symbolism as a resource for conflict resolution: The
case of Franco-German relations   29
MATHIAS DELORI

3   Forget and forgive?: Central European memory cultures,
models of reconciliation and Polish-German relations   41
ANNIKA FRIEBERG

4   Apology and confession: Comparing Sino-Japanese and
German-Jewish intellectual resources for reconciliation   54
C. K. MARTIN CHUNG

5   Ruist traditions of revenge and alternative resources for
Ruist-inspired reconciliation   69
LAUREN F. PFISTER

vi *Contents*

6 Repentance as a post-philosophical stance: Tanabe Hajime
and the road to reconciliation   83
DERMOTT J. WALSH

PART II
Regional experience and comparison   95

7 Reconciliation theories and the East Asian peace   97
ALAN HUNTER

8 Challenges of teaching international reconciliation in Japan
and Korea: A comparative perspective   110
SEUNGHOON EMILIA HEO

9 Altered states of consciousness: Identity politics and
prospects for Taiwan-Hong Kong-mainland reconciliation   122
EDWARD VICKERS

10 Wrestling with the past: Reconciliation, apology and
settling history in Australia and New Zealand   138
GISELLE BYRNES

11 Comparing Polish-German and Polish-Russian
reconciliation efforts   148
STANISŁAW BIELEŃ AND KRZYSZTOF ŚLIWIŃSKI

12 France and Algeria: Conflict, cooperation and conciliation   161
PHILLIP C. NAYLOR

Index   175

Contributors

Stanisław Bieleń is a professor at the Institute of International Relations, University of Warsaw, a political scientist specializing in issues of international relations, especially relating to the foreign policy of Russia. In 1999–2014 he was the editor-in-chief of the quarterly *Stosunki Międzynarodowe-International Relations*. His books include *Tożsamość międzynarodowa Federacji Rosyjskiej* (2006); *Polityka w stosunkach międzynarodowych* (2010); *Poland's Foreign Policy in the 21st Century* (ed., 2011); *Negocjacje w stosunkach międzynarodowych* (2013); *Pamięć i polityka historyczna w stosunkach polsko-rosyjskich* (co-edit., 2016).

Giselle Byrnes is an internationally recognized New Zealand historian who has published widely on aspects of settler colonial and indigenous histories. She has been a Fulbright scholar teaching New Zealand Studies at Georgetown University, Washington DC, and has served as President of the New Zealand Historical Association. Giselle has worked for the Waitangi Tribunal and held academic and senior university management roles in both New Zealand and Australia. She has recently been appointed Assistant Vice-Chancellor Research, Academic and Enterprise at Massey University, New Zealand and is working on a transnational history of apology.

C. K. Martin Chung is an assistant professor in the Department of Government and International Studies at Hong Kong Baptist University. Previously he was a research assistant professor of the European Union Academic Programme Hong Kong, and a lecturer at the University of St. Joseph (Macau). He holds a PhD from the University of Hong Kong (2014) and conducts research on political reconciliation and "coming to terms with the past" in Europe (Cornell University Press; Vandenhoeck & Ruprecht) and East Asia (Franz Steiner Verlag; Nomos).

Mathias Delori is research professor at Bordeaux University, France. After obtaining his PhD from the University of Grenoble (2008) he worked as a post-doctoral fellow at the European University Institute of Florence and at the University of Montréal. Mathias has been working since 2001 as a research professor (chargé de recherche CNRS) at the Centre Emile Durkheim of Sciences Po Bordeaux. His research interests straddle the fields of epistemology of the social sciences (Presses Universitaires de Rennes, 2009), Franco-German reconciliation (Peter Lang 2016), and critical war studies (Myriapode 2015).

viii *Contributors*

Originally from Sweden, Annika Frieberg is an assistant professor at San Diego State University. She studied Modern and Central European History at the University of North Carolina-Chapel Hill. She has taught courses in 19th and 20th century European and East European history. Her research and teaching interests centre on war and genocide, conflict resolution, media, national, and transnational questions in Central Europe. She has published several articles, including "Reconciliation Remembered. Early Activists and the Polish-German Relations" in *Re-Mapping Polish-German Memory*, which was published by Indiana University Press in 2011. Dr. Frieberg is currently working on her book manuscript, "Costly Reconciliation: Transnational Networks and Media in post-war Polish-German Relations."

Seunghoon Emilia Heo is an associate professor of global studies and international relations at Ritsumeikan Asia Pacific University and the author of *Reconciling Enemy States in Europe and Asia* (Palgrave Macmillan, 2012). Her current research focuses on artists, intellectuals, and youth in processes of reconciliation beyond national borders. She is working on a book project on comparing youth narratives about World War II in Germany, Poland, Japan, and South Korea. A graduate of Seoul National University, Emilia specialized first in European studies in France before earning her PhD in international history and politics from the Graduate Institute in Geneva, Switzerland. She has a career background in diplomatic service and regularly lectures in the Korean Parliament.

Alan Hunter studied modern Chinese at the University of Leeds and Fudan University Shanghai; and has a PhD in Religious Studies and a DLitt (Higher Doctorate) for his work on religion, peace and human security. From 2008 to 2012 he served as Director of the Centre for Peace and Reconciliation Studies at Coventry University, where he is also Professor of Asian Studies. His publications include Peace Studies in the Chinese Century, Human Security Challenges, and (with KK Chan) 'Religion, Culture and Confucius Institutes in China's Foreign Policy' in Kavalski (ed.) Research Companion to Chinese Foreign Policy.

Phillip C. Naylor is a professor of history at Marquette University. He is also a co-editor-in-chief of the *Journal of North African Studies*. He has authored *France and Algeria: A History of Decolonization and Transformation; The Historical Dictionary of Algeria;* and *North Africa: A History from Antiquity to the Present*. He also published "Bishop Pierre Claverie and the Risks of Religious Reconciliation," *Catholic Historical Review* 96, no. 4 (October 2010): 720–42 and has contributed to Oxford Islamic Studies Online. His current research includes a study of the life and ideas of the renowned Algerian intellectual, Malik Bennabi (1905–73).

Lauren F. Pfister 費樂仁 is a professor in the Religion and Philosophy Department and Director of the Centre for Sino-Christian Studies at Hong Kong Baptist

University, he has lived and worked in Hong Kong since 1987. Since 2011, he was made a Founding Fellow of the Hong Kong Academy of the Humanities, and serves now on its Executive Committee. Being an Associate Editor for the *Journal of Chinese Philosophy* since 1997, he pursues research in 19th and 20th century Ruist philosophy, the history of sinology, hermeneutics as well as comparative philosophical and comparative religious studies.

Jeremy Sarkin has undergraduate and postgraduate law degrees from South Africa, a Master of Laws from Harvard Law School and a Doctor of Laws degree on comparative and international law. He is admitted to practice as attorney in the USA and South Africa. He practiced at the New York bar during 1988 and 1989. He then spent time working at the International Commission of Jurists in Geneva, Switzerland. He is a Professor of Law at the University of South Africa (UNISA) and Distinguished Visiting Professor of Law at Nova University in Lisbon Portugal. He is a member, and was Chairperson-Rapporteur (2009–2012), of the United Nations Working Group on Enforced or Involuntary Disappearances. He served as an acting judge in 2002 and 2003 in South Africa.

Krzysztof Śliwiński (PhD University of Warsaw) is an associate professor at the Department of Government and International Studies of Hong Kong Baptist University. He holds regular lectures on European Integration, Security Studies, International Relations and Political Science. His main research interests include security and strategic issues, foreign and security policies of Great Britain, Poland and EU, non-traditional security issues. His most recent publications include: 'Moving Beyond the European Union's Weakness as a Cyber-security Agent', *Contemporary Security Policy*, 2014, 35, 3, In Smith, M. A. (ed.) European Security. Critical Concepts in Military, Strategic and Security Studies, (468–86). 2016, Routledge.

Edward Vickers is Professor of Comparative Education at Kyushu University, Japan. He has published extensively on education, political socialization and identity politics in mainland China, Hong Kong and Taiwan. His books include *In Search of an Identity: the Politics of History as a School Subject in Hong Kong, 1960s-2002* (2003), *History Education and National Identity in East Asia* (2005), *Imagining Japan in Post-War East Asia* (2013) and *Constructing Modern Asian Citizenship* (2015) (all published by Routledge). With Zeng Xiaodong he is currently co-authoring *Education and Society in Post-Mao China* (forthcoming with Routledge).

Dermott J. Walsh is a PhD candidate in Buddhist studies at the University of California, Los Angeles. He received a BA in Philosophy from Trinity College Dublin and an MA in Japanese studies from Leiden University. His dissertation research explores the importance of precepts in the early development of Japanese Zen. Dermott is also interested in broader questions concerning doctrinal and philosophical conceptions of morality within East Asian Buddhist thought.

Acknowledgements

This edited volume is based on two conferences organized in Hong Kong: the first at The University of Hong Kong (HKU) in January 2011, and the second at Hong Kong Baptist University in June 2014 (HKBU). The editors would like to acknowledge the sponsors of these conferences: the School of Modern Languages and Cultures at HKU, the Department of Government and International Studies and the Faculty of Social Sciences at HKBU, European Union Academic Programme Hong Kong (EUAPHK), Konrad-Adenauer-Stiftung and the French Centre for Research on Contemporary China.

The book project has also benefited tremendously from the initial inputs of Daqing Yang of George Washington University. We appreciate greatly the proactive and supportive editorship of Simon Bates at Taylor & Francis. To all the conference participants and the many other individuals who have contributed to this project, including Dr. Beatrice Cabau, Prof. Jean-Pierre Cabestan and Prof. Dr. H. Werner Hess at GIS, Martin Ho and Doris Lee at EUAPHK, we would like to express our gratitude.

Introduction
Resources for political reconciliation

C. K. Martin Chung and
Annika Frieberg

> After all, forgiveness, reconciliation, reparation were not the normal currency in political discourse [. . .] consequently spiritual resources were appropriately brought to bear on our task.
>
> – Desmond Tutu (1999, 80–82)

> I'm well aware of how problematic it is for me, a German, to speak of reconciliation here [in front of a Jewish audience]. But everything that the Jewish religion and Jewish philosophy have taught us is precisely also for reconciliation, for justice, wisdom and human love.
>
> – Willy Brandt (1961, 16)[1]

This book is concerned with reconciliation in the political and collective dimension. It grew out of two conferences held in Hong Kong between 2011 and 2014, dedicated to the extraction of intellectual resources for reconciliation from regional experiences, historical examples and philosophical traditions. Multidisciplinary in method, this volume thus contributes to peace and reconciliation studies through its conceptual focus on "resources".

Past injustice and atrocities between and within nations are never "over" even after successful conflict resolution. They continue to overshadow the present. In extreme cases, they threaten to undo or reverse peace processes. Even more troubling, they often become part of nation-building efforts, historical memory and the fabric of society itself. Political reconciliation involves a transition from precarious and wrongful to stable and just post-atrocity relationships. While peace studies, historical dialogues and research on collective memory have long explored theories and "models" of reconciliation, our collection, which includes essays by historians as well as political scientists, philosophers and area specialists focuses on the *cultural, economic* or *political assets and structures* one can use to overcome the unreconciled past.

The idea of reconciliation resources is not new. In cases spanning between South America, East Asia and Europe, scholars have concluded that studying and analyzing conflict resolution and conflict transformation from a political perspective is simply insufficient in terms of understanding long-term change (Iwabuchi 1997, 3; Liu and Lin 2002). By interrogating post-conflict relations in multiple

2   C. K. Martin Chung and Annika Frieberg

societies and cases, models and theories of reconciliation in light of inherent and available resources, we bring the question of such resources into a sharper analytical focus.

Definitions, obstacles, opportunities and the will to reconcile

The definitions of reconciliation are numerous, spanning from "thin" to "thick", spiritual to political, and from individual to collective realms (e.g. Galtung 2001, 3; Bar-Siman-Tov 2004, 4; Skaar, Gloppen and Suhrke 2005, 4). In this discussion, the concept of reconciliation is closely connected to healing and restoration of relationships damaged by the wrongful acts of one or many. These have left – as James Young put it – a "self-inflicted void" (Young 1998) in relationships between nations, ethnic groups and societies as a negative legacy to later generations. This void can be observed in its many guises: grievances and contempt for one another, ignorance and negative stereotyping, antipathy if not all-out enmity, a "negative 'climate of opinion'" (He 2009, 34) and the inability to resume neutral to positive sociability or political relations.[2] Building upon this understanding of reconciliation, we raise the question of "resources": with what resources can one fill this relational void and in which ways can they help rebuild damaged relationships? What do the "solutions" of healing require as constituent elements? A "resource" understood in this sense is itself also a metaphor: reconciliation, like any (re)construction, needs tools and assets. These include cultural, human and (where economic injustice is part of the problem) also financial factors. Some of these are "inherent", that is already available in the relational context. Social actors need only the will and the ability to do the extraction and application of them. Others need to be "transferred" from elsewhere. In this volume, we explore such resources in terms of philosophical and religious traditions; narratives of reconciliation, forgiveness, and related concepts; memory cultures and shared identities; existing or emerging economic cooperation; and democratic institutions.

The volume pays attention not only to the opportunities but also the cultural, political and historical *obstacles* to reconciliation. Obstacles might include (geo) political advantages to cultivating an atmosphere of antagonism, or fear towards a neighbouring country. In addition, traditional concepts and perceptions of conflict may be a central aspect of historical nation building in a given national or ethno-national group. Therefore, political and social elites may consider dispensing with such perceptions of conflict a threat to national identity. Third, as in the case of post-colonial Algerian-French relations described by Phillip Naylor in this volume, continued economic disparities may function as obstacles to political and moral efforts to reach reconciliation. Some of the chapters address these intellectual, often historically founded, hurdles and their present-day manifestations. They challenge us to pose probing questions concerning historical, national and intellectual heritage and whether it is possible to surmount the obstacles found in the regions under the influence of embedded cultural prejudices, hostilities and resistance to closer relations. Obstacles are equally significant to understand and analyze since they affect the ability of actors to utilize inherent as well as transferred resources for reconciliatory purposes.

A functional approach to cultural, intellectual or spiritual traditions based on their potential value as reconciliation resources or obstacles could easily turn into sheer comparative value judgements. However, this does not have to be the case. At the very least, the relative abundance or dearth of intellectual resources for political reconciliation may simply reflect the relative emphasis on this particular problem, not the difference in terms of intellectual ability or quality. One only needs to recall the Hegelian notion of *Versöhnung* and how far removed it is from the concerns of political reconciliation (i.e. to reconcile subjects in reality, not ideas or arguments metaphorically!) in order to appreciate the fact that what is called "reconciliation" in any tradition is not necessarily a resource for political reconciliation – that is the healing of collective relationships in its various "layers", communal, national and international (Daly and Sarkin 2007, 42) – and vice versa. Accordingly, the contributors to this volume endeavour to bear in mind this open-ended nature of reconciliation resources.

Likewise, there is no direct and simple relationship between economic resources and peace building. It is incorrect to assume that resource-rich regions are predestined to reconcile, while resource-poor ones are doomed to recurring conflicts and mutual victimization. For this reason, peace is not built merely by resolving existing economic disagreements and inequalities between post-conflict societies. Each conflict is set in a unique social, political and cultural context that shapes the "journey" towards reconciliation. At the same time, as Phillip Naylor's and Giselle Byrnes's contributions in particular show, economic considerations cannot be disregarded. In an increasingly globalized world, extractions, borrowing and import of reconciliation resources but also inherent cultural assets and opportunities are significant aspects and useful tools in initiating change, precisely where the idea of nemesis and cross-generational vengeance (*shichou* in Chinese) seems to reign. In this sense, it is the volume's analytical aim to engage in comparatively broader and more in-depth conversations between disciplines and regions about the resources that lead to or deter reconciliation. Through such conversations, we hope to enhance the *capability* of social actors to make use of such resources (or to first locate their equivalents where they are not readily available) in the attempt to achieve reconciliation in their own collective relational settings or to identify obstacles as they attempt to import or make use of existing models and approaches. Like any resources, those useful for political reconciliation remain dormant reserves until discovered and employed by willing communities and individual partners in their reconciliation work.

Methodology and historiography

Whereas the existing literature on reconciliation has focused on themes such as justice, apology and resentment in relation to reconciliation (e.g. Hirsch 2012; Togo 2013; Llewellyn and Philpott 2014), fewer volumes historicize

4 *C. K. Martin Chung and Annika Frieberg*

reconciliation or consider the resources employed in these processes. However, activists as well as analysts have recognized resources as crucial to success in conflict resolution also when they did not use these terms. The Final Report of South Africa's Truth and Reconciliation Commission mentioned "healing and restorative truth" alongside factual, narrative and dialogical truths as aspects of a successful process of reconciliation, recognizing truth as a culturally situated concept (1998, 114). It denotes the kind of truth that puts facts of atrocities and memories of suffering into some kind of *perspective* and endows these with a certain sense of *purpose*. The Report singled out South Africa's "Judeo-Christian tradition and African traditional values" as containing "strong sources of communal healing and restoration" (1998, 127). Likewise, Aleida Assmann, the preeminent scholar on European, especially German, *Erinnerungskultur*, or culture of remembrance, pointed to the cultural foundation of reconciliation attempts and coming to terms with the past in the German-Jewish context (Assmann and Frevert 1999, 91; Chung 2015). In Latin America, the use of Psalm 85 by the Nicaraguan "conciliators" was analyzed by John Paul Lederach as a resource not only in praxis but also in its theoretical contribution to understanding the tensions within reconciliation itself (Lederach 1997). In East Asia, literary scholars have long bemoaned the lack of attention to appropriate "intellectual resources" for the confession of guilt and facing the past (Iwabuchi 1997, 3; Liu and Lin 2002).[3] In turn, contemporary regional examples of (perceived) "successes" also serve as a role model and inspiration for those seeking to learn to do historical reflection and collective reconciliation in other regional contexts (He 2009; Hansen 2011). To accomplish reconciliation is difficult – hence, participants need a variety of inroads to overcome specific challenges and obstacles. While the few examples of relative success in Africa and in Europe are often singled out for emulation (e.g. Rigby 2001; Rothfield, Fleming and Komesaroff 2008), the question of comparability and transferability has never been answered satisfactorily, hence undermining the utility of model-based approaches to conflict resolution.

The complementary potential of the alternative resource-based approach can be glimpsed from examining He Yinan's comparative works on reconciliation as an example. As an International Relations expert, He largely avoids factoring in religious elements into her discussions on reconciliation, nor does she seem greatly focused on moral and spiritual aspects of reconciliation efforts as displayed in Archbishop Desmond Tutu's efforts in South Africa or in the Catholic dialogue in Poland and Germany. Her approach to international relations goes beyond an exclusively rational model but does not necessarily stray into idealism. However, much of the more idealistic literature on reconciliation is spiritual and moral in nature (Baum 1997), particularly the discussions about apology and forgiveness as a central aspect of reconciliation. Researchers focusing on conflict resolution frequently struggle to determine whether, if at all, apology and forgiveness work can actually have collective, concrete, political and long-lasting effects on relations between peoples. Elizabeth Dahl, for example argues that apologies are not as positively received in East Asia as in other cultures and can, therefore, not be considered useful political gestures (2008). A resource-centred perspective,

Introduction 5

which does not subscribe to any essentialist cultural theories, can contribute to these debates by highlighting the resources employed by social actors to prevail over the cognitive, emotional, social and political opposition – such as the problem of "national mythmaking" He rightly points out (He 2009, 10) – to reconciliatory movements. This way of looking at the problem of reconciliation still does not offer any one-size-fits-all solution – if there is any such universal panacea to begin with. But the utility of such a perspective is to help other social actors identify, locate and, if necessary, import the resources for a lasting reconciliation.

Structure of the book

The present volume is divided into two parts: the first is dedicated to the analysis of specific resources and obstacles in political reconciliation, with case studies ranging from South Africa to western and central Europe to East Asia, exploring identities, memory cultures, concepts of apology, revenge and repentance as elements facilitating or hindering reconciliation processes. This section addresses the question of resources and obstacles as such, whether these arise from various philosophical and religious traditions or are situated in related conceptual frameworks such as "processes" and "models".

The second part of the book includes chapters of original historical accounts and political analyses of reconciliation in particular post-colonial, post-communist, post-reunification and other "past-burdened" relationships. The resource perspective is adopted throughout these chapters to highlight the challenges – including theoretical and pedagogical ones – to political reconciliation. The second section offers, on a global comparative level, examples of how resources for reconciliation have functioned within specific politico-cultural or historical settings. Together, the two sections contribute to further the readers' understanding of the nuts and bolts of "reconciliation resources".

Chapter synopsis

A few international relations events have frequently been used as models and inspiration for global reconciliation efforts after World War II. These include, for example West German chancellor Willy Brandt's genuflection for German war crimes before the Warsaw Ghetto Monument in 1970, or other aspects of Polish-German and French-German relations, such as the historical textbook commissions, youth exchanges, and other public gestures of goodwill and/or remorse (Schneider 2006, 2008; He 2009). Another foundational model of reconciliation involves so-called Truth and Reconciliation Commissions in the aftermath of civil war, atrocities and internal conflict, most famously the South African Truth and Reconciliation Commission, founded in the 1990s after the end of Apartheid (Long and Brecke 2003).[4] Many of the contributions to this volume are concerned with whether, and to which extent, such models can be used, adapted and imported between different politico-cultural contexts. Imported reconciliation "tools" might constitute one type of resources in post-conflict international

6 C. K. Martin Chung and Annika Frieberg

relations. However, as many of the contributions indicate, borrowed models never work in a vacuum. Other significant resources draw from the cultural, historical, religious and philosophical traditions inherent to those specific post-conflict relations whether it is French-Algerian or Australian post-colonial apologies to indigenous populations. At times, local contexts and traditions hinder or even render certain reconciliatory models impossible to implement.

Even the supposed foundational cases of reconciliation were, upon closer investigation, complex developments, featuring partial successes and dependent on multiple factors. The first part of this volume engages with such cases and with deep-level transferrable intellectual, cultural or philosophical resources. Jeremy Sarkin, who was intimately involved with the process of South Africa's post-Apartheid reconstruction, describes the learned experiences from working with the South African Truth and Reconciliation Commission and provides a larger perspective on South African reconstruction in his contribution. According to Sarkin, the reconciliation process in South Africa greatly benefited from the participation of key political actors and from the simultaneous process of nation building but also from larger geopolitical developments such as the fall of communism in the late 1980s. In terms of cultural and intellectual resources, reconciliation drew on the use of markers and symbolism as well as of a multiplicity of national tools, including sports events, in overcoming the antagonisms of the past. Sarkin also emphasizes the importance of media in broadening the process to a national level.

Other widely recognized examples of reconciliation were post-war Franco-German and Polish-German relations in the aftermath of the two World Wars. Mathias Delori analyzes and re-emphasizes idealism and symbolism as significant aspects of French-German relations. He particularly focuses on the Elysée Treaty of 1963, arguing that moral and symbolic dimensions as well as the wide-reaching youth exchanges contributed to a semiotic shift in the French-German relationship towards reconciliation in the sense of re-establishment of harmony between the two countries. Other resources central to the development was the participants' drawing on a mutual mythical past. Annika Frieberg takes a different approach, interrogating the particular challenges of building reconciliation between reconstituted and divided states in the aftermath of multiple population movements and ethnic cleansings. She points out that a borderland background, ethnic pluralism and multilingualism might create obstacles in apologies as well as hindering truthful discourses about the past. On the other hand, they can also become resources in reconciliation. Finally, she makes the point that amnesia, at times, also serves as a short-term stabilizing tool in deep reconciliation. In the French-German as well as Polish-German case, economic incentives, geopolitical motivations and individual agency played equally crucial roles to the improvement of relations.

Meanwhile, drawing from classical texts, Martin Chung focuses on the different understandings of "apology" and "confession" in Asian and European intellectual traditions as potential resources or obstacles in contemporary political reconciliation. On the one hand, apologies primarily concerned with "hierarchical

Introduction 7

trespasses" can actually present an obstacle to reconciliation where a moral response is required for an atrocious past. On the other hand, Chung also asserts that state apologies can still have moral meaning when they are addressed to individual, actual victims instead of the state supposedly representing them. The more promising path, however, lies in "co-confessing" as a resource drawn from Judaism. Chung's and Frieberg's texts problematize apologies as reconciliation resources by considering their meanings and discursive power within distinct cultural, geographic or intellectual settings.

In other cases, culture-specific philosophical traditions can become a resource to help lay a foundation for long-term conflict transformation. Lauren Pfister argues that certain classical texts centred on revenge in Ruism present a considerable but surmountable challenge for hermeneutics to arrive at a reinterpretation towards a conciliatory response to mistreatment, cruelty or crime. Meanwhile, Dermott Walsh discusses the post-war Japanese philosopher Tanabe Hajime's understanding of the Buddhist concept "zange" or radical repentance and the Pure Land Buddhist concept of "other-power" as an experiential and transformative type of repentance rather than a rational and intellectual concept. Situating Tanabe in the historical context of Japan's role in World War II, Walsh discusses Tanabe's linking of the philosophical with the concrete and existential and its bearing on reconciliatory processes involving Japan.

As a whole, these texts indicate the ambivalence of top-down reconciliation tools as applied to existing intellectual traditions, nation- and memory-construction and historical interpretations. They are culturally embedded tools that, in the hands of reconciliation-oriented actors, may become incredibly significant and powerful. As Chung, Pfister and Walsh all point out, the interpretive context can present opportunities but also obstacles to reconciliation. For example, Walsh writes in Chapter 5 (p. 92) about "zange" that

> the suggestion that somehow this repentance comes from outside of us, from "other-power", may provide an obstacle to reconciliation. We expect repentance to follow a period of soul searching, of actively acquiring a corrected moral vision. For Tanabe, it is simply a case of waiting for other-power to act upon you, thus absolving the guilty of the need to repent and take personal responsibility.

Reconciliation never emerges in a cultural or historical vacuum. Each case has to take into consideration and draw upon existing resources and cultural tropes and local participants in order to be successful.

The second part of the volume introduces comparative efforts to introduce reconciliation elements into post-conflict relations in case studies ranging from Japan, Korea, Taiwan and Hong Kong via Australia and New Zealand to Algeria, France, Poland, Germany and Russia. Alan Hunter applies reconciliation theory broadly to the East Asian context. He argues that such initiatives in many cases have been unsuccessful on the basis of specific cultural and political factors. While the shared cultural aspects between the Asian cultures should aid reconciliatory

8   *C. K. Martin Chung and Annika Frieberg*

developments, prevailing obstacles such as national mythmaking, geopolitical concerns and memory politics have prevented viable reconciliation processes. Hunter claims that in the Asian case, reconciliation is a misleading term since it suggests "a restoration of an intimate relationship that suffered a rupture of some kind," while, in reality, such a relationship may never have existed in the first place (Chapter 7, p. 97). Hunter as well as Philip Naylor introduce the possibility of maintaining neighbourly relations and stability in a region *without* engaging in a reconciliation process. Hunter proposes that in light of "inherited animosities", "informal pragmatism" may be the more appropriate, short-term and realistic road for conflict prevention, cooperation and stability between China and Japan in particular.

Several chapters use the comparative focus to interrogate the use and significance of various reconciliatory actions or approaches in post-conflict and post-colonial settings. Edward Vickers describes in more detail the way in which identity politics in Taiwan, China and Hong Kong – particularly different interpretations of "Chineseness" function as obstacles to reconciliation. In this sense, the chapter highlights elements of, and difficulties in, achieving a lasting sense of connection, that which Yinan He termed "deep reconciliation" between antagonistic societies (He 2009, 3).

Giselle Byrnes compares the way in which apology processes work in Australian and New Zealand post-colonial relations between white settler societies and indigenous groups. In these cases, the focus has become claims processes and "settlements" rather than more open-ended reconciliation processes. Byrnes cautions, with an eye to cultural differences, that in these cases the legal emphasis has had the potential of moving the focus away from indigenous cultures.

In terms of top-down reconciliatory efforts, apologies and political initiatives, Polish-German relations can fruitfully be compared to Polish-Russian relations. Stanisław Bieleń and Krzysztof Śliwiński investigate how cultural and political efforts towards forgiveness and positive change have performed in the Polish-Russian compared to the Polish-German case. According to Bieleń and Śliwiński, the positive changes in Polish-German Cold War relations were brought about by the presence of charismatic individuals willing to engage in conciliatory processes, in the involvement of the media and the investment of the churches broadly but also in political needs of West Germany and in its diversity of dialogue after the war. The lack of corresponding developments in Polish-Russian relations might be attributed to the lack of such engaged personalities, the Russian disinterest in such processes and finally the Polish media's and broader public's firm anti-Russian position.

French-German reconciliatory efforts were sometimes used as a model for French-Algerian relations. However, the post-colonial relationship between the two states drastically changed the dynamic in these relations. Phillip Naylor shows that the use of top-down reconciliatory gestures has had limited effects in the aftermath of brutal French colonization of Algeria and severe conflicts during the 1950s and 1960s. He argues that resource allocation and reasons became more important than reconciliation. However, he does point particularly to history and memory politics as significant aspects of improving relations and overcoming the past.

Introduction 9

Finally, Emilia Heo gives an on-the-ground example of how youth involvement might play out in college class rooms in overcoming a hostile past, understanding "the other side" and exchange in Korean-Japanese relations. She bases her discussion on experiences with teaching reconciliation to Korean and Japanese students.

In the foreword to *Reconciliation after Violent Conflict: A Handbook*, Archbishop Desmond Tutu wrote, "There is no handy roadmap for reconciliation. There is no short cut or simple prescription for healing the wounds and divisions of a society in the aftermath of sustained violence" (Tutu 2003, 3). Other authors have argued that after the 1990s we have entered into an era of "new wars", in which the logic of binary, state-dominated relationships between armed combatants and their funding sources have broken down and disintegrated or become globalized. Hence, traditional methods of security and, consequently, peace building have become outdated (Kaldor 1999, 2013). What good can the application of reconciliation measures possibly do in an era of extreme politics, ongoing severe conflicts, large-scale human rights crises and deteriorating political relationships on multiple continents? Perhaps a more important question, and one that our participants show in their wide-ranging and interdisciplinary contributions, would be as follows: if we acknowledge that every post-conflict relationship has its own unique flavour and inherent logic based on distinct and diverse histories, cultures, nature of the armed violence involved, and religious and philosophical traditions, how do we strive to find customized solution to long-term peace? In answering this question, first, sharing better understandings of available resources across borders and, second, acknowledging that those resources must function in the distinct historical and cultural environment where they are applied if they are to become useful and successful, would be a good beginning. The contributions in this volume strive to accomplish precisely such a conversation.

Notes

1 Unless otherwise stated, all citations from non-English sources, including this one, are the authors' translation.
2 As one of our contributors, Emilia Heo, shared during our second conference, her experience of organizing meetings for Korean and Japanese college students: "there is just *something* between them . . . It is unnatural. It is not like the encounter of any two groups of foreign students."
3 The term "intellectual resources" (*sixiang ziyuan*) for coming to terms with the past, or "past-resources" in short, is adapted from Liu and Lin's book, in which the authors assert that the negligence of appropriate resources within and without classical Chinese tradition has led to the "lack of depth" in Chinese literature when it comes to dissecting human evil and conducting deep repentance (2002, 145–156).
4 William Long and Peter Brecke use two models of reconciliation: a signalling model applying to the formal and public gesture of reconciliation and a forgiveness model based on the idea of Truth and Reconciliation Commissions in which deeper societal processes take place that reshape social relationships.

References

Assmann, Aleida and Ute Frevert. 1999. *Geschichtsvergessenheit. Geschichtsversessenheit. Vom Umgang mit deutschen Vergangenheiten nach 1945.* Stuttgart: Deutsche Verlags-Anstalt.

Bar-Siman-Tov, Yaacov. 2004. "Introduction." In *From Conflict Resolution to Reconciliation*, edited by Yaacov Bar-Siman-Tov, 3–9. New York: Oxford University Press.

Baum, Gregory. 1997. "The Role of the Churches in Polish-German Reconciliation." In *The Reconciliation of Peoples: Challenges to the Churches*, edited by Harold Wells and Gregory Baum 129–143. New York: Orbis.

Brandt, Willy. 1961. *Deutschland, Israel und die Juden. Rede des Regierenden Bürgermeisters von Berlin vor dem Herzl-Institut in New York am 19. März 1961* [Germany, Israel and the Jews]. Berlin: Landeszentrale für politische Bildungsarbeit.

Chung, C.K. Martin. 2015. "Repentance: The Jewish Solution to the German Problem." *Jahrbuch des Simon-Dubnow-Instituts* 14: 129–155.

Dahl, Elizabeth. 2008. "Is Japan Facing Its Past? The Case of Japan and Its Neighbors." In *The Age of Apology: Facing Up to the Past*, edited by Mark Gibney, Rhoda E. Howard-Hassmann, Jean-Marc Coicaud and Niklaus Steiner, 241–255. Philadelphia, PA: University of Pennsylvania Press.

Daly, Erin and Jeremy Sarkin. 2007. *Reconciliation in Divided Societies: Finding Common Ground.* Philadelphia, PA: University of Pennsylvania Press.

Galtung, Johan. 2001. "After Violence, Reconstruction, Reconciliation, and Resolution." In *Reconciliation, Justice, and Coexistence*, edited by Mohammed Abu-Nimer, 3–23. Lanham: Lexington Books.

Hansen, Sven. 2011. "Geschichte der Anderen. Chinas Blick auf deutsche Vergangenheitsbewältigung." http://www.boell.de/en/node/275908. Accessed 15 Oct. 2014.

He, Yinan. 2009. *The Search for Reconciliation: Sino-Japanese and German-Polish Relations since World War II.* New York: Cambridge University Press.

Hirsch, Alexander Keller, ed. 2012. *Theorizing Post-Conflict Reconciliation: Agonism, Restitution and Repair.* New York: Routledge.

Iwabuchi, Tatsuji. 1997. *Die Vergangenheitsbewältigung und die japanische Literatur* [Japanese Literature and Coming to Terms with the Past]. Tokyo: Deutsche Gesellschaft für Natur- und Völkerkunde Ostasiens.

Kaldor, Mary. 1999. *New and Old Wars: Organized Violence in a Global Era.* Stanford, CA: Stanford University Press.

———. 2013. "In Defence of New Wars." *Stability: International Journal in Defence of Security and Development* 2: 4, p. Art. 4.

Lederach, John Paul. 1997. *Building Peace: Sustainable Reconciliation in Divided Societies.* Washington, DC: US Institute of Peace Press.

Liu, Zaifu and Gang Lin. 2002. 罪與文學: 關於文學懺悔意識與靈魂維度的考察 [Confession and Chinese Literature]. Hong Kong: Oxford University Press.

Llewellyn, Jennifer J. and Daniel Philpott, eds. 2014. *Restorative Justice, Reconciliation, and Peacebuilding.* Oxford, New York: Oxford University Press.

Long, William J. and Peter Brecke. 2003. *War and Reconciliation.* Cambridge, MA: MIT Press.

Rigby, Andrew. 2001. *Justice and Reconciliation: After the Violence.* Boulder, CO: Lynne Rienner Publishers.

Introduction 11

Rothfield, Philipa, Cleo Fleming and Paul A. Komesaroff, eds. 2008. *Pathways to Reconciliation: Between Theory and Practice.* Aldershot, Burlington: Ashgate.

Schneider, Christoph. 2006. *Der Warschauer Kniefall.* Konstanz: UVK.

———. 2008. "Der Kniefall von Warschau. Spontane Geste – bewusste Inszenierung?" In *Das Jahrhundert der Bilder: 1949 bis heute,* edited by Gerhard Paul, 410–417. Göttingen: Vandenhoeck & Ruprecht.

Skaar, Elin, Siri Gloppen and Astri Suhrke. 2005. *Roads to Reconciliation.* Lanham: Lexington Books.

Togo, Kazuhiko, ed. 2013. *Japan and Reconciliation in Post-War Asia: The Murayama Statement and Its Implications.* New York: Palgrave Macmillan.

"Truth and Reconciliation Commission of South Africa Report. Volume 1." 1998. http://www.justice.gov.za/trc/report/finalreport/Volume%201.pdf. Accessed 15 Dec. 2015.

Tutu, Desmond. 1999. *No Future without Forgiveness.* New York: Doubleday.

———. 2003. "Introduction." In *Reconciliation after Violent Conflict: A Handbook,* 10–18. Stockholm: International Institute for Democracy and Electoral Assistance.

Young, James E. 1998. "Die menschenmögliche Lösung der unlösbaren Aufgabe." *Der Tagesspiegel,* 25 Aug.

Part I

Reconciliation resources and obstacles

1 South Africa's reconciliation process

Tools, resources and obstacles in the journey to deal with its atrocious past

Jeremy Sarkin[1]

The process to achieve reconciliation in South Africa is viewed, by many, as being successful (Daly and Sarkin 2007, 6). That perception is more commonly held outside the country and was a view that was particularly true of the process in the years immediately after the country's transition to democracy. Regardless, the process is viewed as a significant learning tool for other states embarking on reconciliation journeys (Gibson 2006). There is no doubt much to be learned from the process (pros and cons) about what was done, why it was done, by whom it was done and the manner in which it occurred (Sarkin 2015a). However, it is vital to recognize that each country has to formulate a reconciliation process that is specific to its own context (Daly and Sarkin 2004, 666). This is not to suggest that countries undergoing similar experiences cannot learn from South African reconciliation practices but to emphasize that different contexts require different reconciliation designs and implementation. As such, the design of each process should be formulated through meaningful national dialogue, which cuts across all social cleavages. This South Africa did remarkably well, in that the transition, and particularly the process of dealing with the past, and promoting reconciliation, was the subject of meaningful, open and wide-ranging negotiations (Sarkin 2008b, 93). This ensured that no part of the reconciliation process was undermined through reasons of social exclusion. The narratives expressed during the years of the transition in all quarters, be they political, social, economic, religious, human rights and so forth all stressed the positive reasons for moving from a divided past to an inclusive future. Memory and narratives thus were critical to the transition and dealing with the past. A master narrative used by the political leadership was that South Africa, and its transitional process, was unique and that the initiatives were South African with no external strings or involvement. This was not, however, totally the case as the international community played at least some role, such as ensuring the Inkatha Freedom Party's participation in the 1994 elections. South Africa's transition was also effected by the fall of communism at the end of the 1980s. Those events together with other external issues, such as the independence of Namibia, sanctions, the sports boycott and so forth all had a role in putting pressure on the Apartheid regime to agree to the transitional process.

16 *Jeremy Sarkin*

The process of having an interim Constitution, followed by an election followed by the drafting of the final Constitution, helped to bring many into the process, even those who were sceptical about what the future would hold. The process of inclusion and grand narrative was followed though by establishing a Truth and Reconciliation Commission (TRC), which was to benefit victims in various ways, including by allowing them to tell their stories. Story telling was seen to be an important part of the process, because stories or narratives are seen to be key to transmitting what occurred, while at the same time helping to unlock the trauma that was suffered. The process of discussion and dialogue were key hallmarks of the whole transitional process that aided the reconciliation process specifically. The master narratives across the political, social, economic and other sectors were all designed to ensure a smoother transition that might not have occurred otherwise. As this chapter notes, the transition was not peaceful, but it may, in the absence of the processes that occurred, have seen far more violence. Many more people may have succumbed without the processes that occurred. The processes garnered tremendous public attention, with broad interest and involvement being significant. The constitutional process itself proclaimed that two million people participated, which helped to further legitimize the process and bring people together.

Significantly, the South African experience indicates that processes in which people are meaningfully engaged and that deal with the aspirations and historical legacies of all groups in a society have greater potential for positive impact (Stein 2008, 462). It is imperative to remember, however, that reconciliation processes are never ending (Du Toit and Doxtader 2010, ix), and without continual fuel, nurturing and open mindedness, they can regress at any point. Gains made can easily be undone if the process is impaired and detrimental words and events are not immediately addressed. Thus, Nelson Mandela averted a major catastrophe after the assassination of ANC leader Chris Hani in the run up to the 1994 elections by using calming words. Spoilers, defined as those who can derail, negatively effect, or try and affect a political process, can undermine and, in fact, hinder reconciliation processes. In South Africa there were potential spoilers but they were brought into the process in various ways. Thus, just a week before the 1994 elections, the Inkatha Freedom Party (IFP) was given political assurances that saw it participate in the voting. The IFP was allowed to govern the KwaZulu-Natal province after the elections, despite allegations of voting irregularities. The IFP was also incorporated into the Government of National Unity and the leader of the party given a cabinet post. All of these were done to ensure the IFP's cooperation with the new government. Assurances were also given to right-wing parties, as well as to the security forces, that could have ensured that the outcome of the election was not adhered to. These were political moves to prevent the possibility of steps being taken to undermine the fledgling democracy, but the decisions had dramatic reconciliatory effects not only on those factions but also on the nation as a whole.

This chapter focuses on the objective lessons that can be gleaned from South Africa's process of dealing with its brutal past. It focuses on the resources that inspired and befitted the process. It spotlights the issues that furthered the process, including the institutions, people, methods and events that allowed the process to unfold in such a positive way, at least in the years shortly after the transition. It also examines the nation-building process that benefited the reconciliation process but notes that a democratic culture existed in civil society even before the transition. This aided the process as it assisted with the inculcation of a national democratic order and promoted nation building. The process of nation building, therefore, had a very positive role in supporting the reconciliation process. The role of groups and individuals are examined to see the parts that they can play. Various sporting events also played a role in the process. These processes are examined to understand what contributed positively and negatively to the reconciliation process. The process is also reviewed, to allow others to learn what can and should be done, with the understanding that each country is different, and that reconciliation processes cannot simply be replicated. Each country needs to embark upon its process, but lessons and mistakes from elsewhere can be useful.

South Africa's reconciliation journey

For most it was unimaginable that the seemingly hopeless situation that existed at the beginning of 1990 in South Africa, characterized as it was by international ostracism and the use of force by the state and by liberation movements alike, would result in a peaceful transition to democracy in 1994. Notably, while political violence killed nearly 20,000 people in the four years leading to the transition (Sarkin 1998, 628), there were very few prosecutions and even fewer convictions (Sarkin 2015b). Political groupings were alienated from each other and were the cause of much violence. In this regard, the nation-building processes, discussed later, had important positive effects for reconciliation. Also important for reducing tensions and violence were institutions such as the Goldstone Commission, which investigated political violence, as well as the peace structures, which helped to mediate and play roles promoting peace and non-violence in communities. These had a significant bearing on the reconciliation process as well.

Reconciliation processes do not start and end at a particular point. They continue and need to be maintained and built on. It is always necessary to be ready to change course if the circumstances demand it and remain open to new techniques and points of view. Since not all political leaders will necessarily be on board with reconciliation processes, it is necessary to allow persons from all sectors, including religious leaders, to step in and play a part. In South Africa, all types of people were given the opportunity to be involved in the process. This was enhanced by the fact that the process was inclusive, transparent and open, in determining, for example who was chosen to be part a TRC Commissioner. The openness of the process contributed in no small measure to its success.

While South Africa is a heterogeneous country, much of the conflict occurred in the black communities between warring political factions and thus the conflict was much more about politics than about race. While race and class were clear

18   *Jeremy Sarkin*

polarizing issues, opposition groups were composed across these cleavages. This helped the process of reconciliation. The makeup and vibrancy of South Africa's society before the transition, and in particular its civil society, is, therefore, a key issue to understanding how and why the process unfolded, and the positive way in which the political and reconciliation processes occurred. Even before the transition, much of civil society was integrated, was non-racial and had ideas and processes to move the country forward. Much groundwork was done before the transition, by various grassroots organizations, communities and individuals. Thus, it is important to recognize the foundational efforts made by various anti-Apartheid organizations and individuals. While the TRC was created to promote the goals of "national unity and reconciliation," (The Promotion of Reconciliation Act, section 3(1)) groups and individuals did much reconciliation work outside that institution.

South Africa has always had an extremely vibrant and robust civil society (Backer 2003). Groupings included the religious groups, sporting communities, political groups, and civil society organizations. The UDF and a range of organizations like the Black Sash and the Detainees Parents Support Committee promoted non-racialism and, therefore, reconciliation. Numerous organizations were involved in multiple ways, and work was done in schools, universities, sports clubs, political organizations, art and recreation activities, and so forth (Buikema 2012, 292).

While reconciliation is often viewed as a societal or individual issue, there are many layers at which reconciliation can and does occur. It can occur at a personal level, between individuals, between groups and even between nations or other international actors (Kaminer 2008, 1589). The extent to which reconciliation can occur differs from society to society and nation to nation. It can occur individually for a person or in confluence with others. It can be a result of collective action or because symbolic gestures have been embraced. It can be brought about by a transition, by people coming together to vote or when the national team of a country wins that event. In these senses reconciliation can be short and fleeting or long-term and ongoing.

Reconciliation can be promoted by words being stated, or by actions, oral or written. It can be through a planned step or on impulse through an unplanned presence at an event that commemorates the other side's fallen heroes. It could be through an agreement or take the form of a simple handshake or some other act, which indicates acceptance or tolerance of the other. Sometimes it is the payment of reparations that is needed to begin the journey. Moreover, reconciliation can be boosted at the political level through diplomatic encounters, speeches from the political leadership and government gestures.

The role of individuals is essential to reconciliation processes. Individuals have the ability to promote or undermine reconciliation at all levels. Individuals played an important part in South Africa (Bargal and Sivan 2004). The role of individual leaders was crucial (Du Toit 2003, 141). The role of Nelson Mandela was important. He mastered the art of both verbal and non-verbal forms of reconciliation.

South Africa's reconciliation process 19

Mandela may have made the strongest impression when he wore a rugby jersey with the number of the captain of the South African team at the 1995 Rugby World Cup (Carlin 2007), hosted and won by South Africa (Hoglund and Sundberg 2008). This event was the first major international event held in South Africa in the post-Apartheid era and has been labelled a hallmark event in the politics of reconciliation and identity formation in the new South Africa. But Mandela drove reconciliation with others as co-drivers, including Archbishop Tutu and others as well. Even before them, there were many other significant individuals, including Chief Albert Luthuli, who was awarded the Nobel Peace Prize in 1961. Others included Helen Susman, Frank Chikane, Beyers Naude, Allan Boesack, Cyril Ramaphosa, Helen Joseph, Oscar Mpetha, Albertina Sisulu, Chief Albert Luthuli, O. R. Tambo, to name a few.

While leadership is important, it is not the ultimate reason for a successful reconciliation process since leadership itself occurs within a context. South Africa benefited from good leaders, because there was a space and opportunity for such leadership. Mandela, for example was chosen as the face of the opposition to Apartheid, since he was in prison, and out of the public eye, and an ideal symbol for the movement. He became the ultimate leader because there was a need for such leadership.

Symbolism was also important to the reconciliation process. To achieve or promote reconciliation, a simple handshake between former enemies or a visit is perhaps the best-known symbol of reconciliation. For example Mandela's visit to the widow of former Prime Minister Hendrik Verwoerd, the man who designed the Apartheid system, was seen to boost to race relations in the country. However, symbolism alone is not enough, and a range of other bilateral acts aided in promoting the reconciliation process, including the signing of various peace accords adopted before 1994. These agreements were vital in demonstrating the willingness of the leaders to work with each other. It is important to understand that the transition and process of political accommodation and reconciliation in South Africa began before 1994.

In the South African context, clear markers were a critical part of the transition that aided the reconciliation process. For example to make peace and national unity a reality, and to encourage the reconstruction of society, both the Preamble to the Promotion of National Unity and the Promotion of Truth and Reconciliation Act, and the Post-amble to the Interim Constitution overtly recognized the need for reconciliation between the people of South Africa (Doxtder and Salazar 2007). The "National Unity and Reconciliation provision" in the Constitution (see further Gross 2004, 47) states that there shall be "understanding instead of vengeance, reparation instead of retaliation, ubuntu instead of victimisation" (Heribert 1999) emphasizing the goal of national unity and asserting that national reconciliation is an essential pre-requisite (Gready 2010). Thus, much was done to promote reconciliation in spaces outside what was considered the reconciliation process. Thus, reconciliation and nation building were cooperative aspects of the process to move the country forward.

20 *Jeremy Sarkin*

South Africa's nation building and reconciliation process

Nation building concerns the constructing or reconstructing of a national identity. It is not about having a single national level identity but about assimilating, to some degree, and accommodating multiple identities at the national level. When disparate identities within one country begin to recognize their identity as part of the national identity, the state is more politically stable and viable in the long run.

In South Africa before 1994, groups, especially minority ones be they religious, racial, cultural, linguistic, often felt connected to the group rather than the nation. South Africa's nation-building process has inculcated a national identity without removing the other identities that exist. These other identities are now seen to form part of one nation.

While the TRC had the specific task of dealing with reconciliation, it is important to note that the process of reconciliation is deeply linked to the nation-building process. Nation building and achieving reconciliation is not an event but an ongoing process. While reconciliation is especially difficult and heavily dependent on the context of that particular place, it is also very sensitive. One event, at any time, can easily affect it. It just takes one negative statement by an elder, or a bomb. Reconciliation is a long-term goal, which requires deliberate, measured programmes and processes. This is very true of South Africa, where in recent years reconciliation has not been nurtured and has, in fact, regressed over time.

In the years immediately after the transition, South Africa carried out various nation-building measures. These included the design and process of drafting a new constitution and the implementation of new public holidays, including an aptly named Day of Reconciliation. These had very positive impacts on reconciliation as well as they promoted the idea of reconciliation (Wilson 1996) and made them seem part of the transformation and democratization process.

Various national sporting events, such as the 1995 Rugby World Cup (Hoglund and Sundberg 2008) and the Soccer World Cup of 2010 (Ndlovu-Gatsheni 2011) that were held in South Africa, also assisted the process. In this regard at the 2000 Laureus sports awards, Nelson Mandela said:

> Sport has the power to change the world. It has the power to inspire, it has the power to unite people . . . It speaks to youth in a language they understand. Sport can create hope . . . It laughs in the face of all types of discrimination.
>
> (Moses 2014)

Sport can "bridge social, religious, racial & gender divides, hence contributing to lasting peace" (Beutler 2008, 365).

The reconciliation process was also aided by the nation-building process and the processes to draft a new constitution. While a constitution's role is dependent on the manner in which it is drafted as the process of drafting influences its reception in society, a constitution is also significant in that it can influence and mould a politics of memory. This was the case in South Africa. Moreover, while a constitution provides a road map for the future of the society as it contains the values and principles to be adopted by the state and its mechanisms of operation, it itself is dependent on other forces and institutions in society that can enable its role in shaping society. In South Africa, the constitutional texts, and the tools of interpretation that are used, reflect the memories and legacies of South Africa, making the Constitution a living monument as well as a memorial of the past atrocities. Its design is also a product of the memories and historical experiences of the drafters and those who participated in the drafting process. Given our history, therefore, the South African Constitution was developed with an extra focus on the notions of inclusion, accountability and oversight. Human rights are also key features of the document on the basis of the nation's history of disregard for such values in the past. All of this is set up to ensure that past atrocities do not recur in the future, this is not a negation of the past, but an act to guarantee that the past is not repeated. These are important as they assist in promoting reconciliation.

The 1996 Constitution established many new and important rights for its citizens that demonstrate a recognition and cognizance of the past violence and the hope to overcome possibilities of such violence recurring and, instead, seeks to unite the people of South Africa by giving all citizens an equal place in the democracy. The Constitution also strives to be a living document that ensures a mechanism to transform South African society. South Africa's history and socioeconomic makeup is woven throughout the Constitution and is very cognizant of the Apartheid philosophy and its effects and seeks to promote equality for all. Its features include a bicameral legislature which is based upon the principle of the sovereignty of the Constitution; a justiciable Bill of Rights; an independent judiciary, including a Constitutional Court; an electoral system based on proportional representation; and structures which ensure government at national, provincial and local levels. Additionally, all these various state institutions, including a Public Protector, Human Rights Commission, Commission for the Promotion and Protection of the Rights of Cultural, Religious and Linguistic Communities, Commission for Gender Equality and an Electoral Commission, support a constitutional democracy and also seek to promote the ideals of the Constitution. The incorporation of these institutions gave impetus to reconciliation in that many saw these as a means to further deal with the problems of the past and find ways to overcoming the difficulties the country faced.

There were various elements of these processes that assisted in promoting reconciliation. The reconciliation process thus benefited from the political and constitutional negotiation process and the focus on the protection of the rights of various groupings. It was seen that there was a need to ensure protection for minorities in the bill of rights, otherwise unrestrained majoritarianism could permanently and significantly harm such groups and possibly the reconciliation process. The process was assisted, therefore, by protecting the rights of a range of groups, including religious, cultural and linguistic communities (On the issues concerning one religious minority, see Maharaj 2013). This allowed the various communities to see the process of protecting minority rights as an extension of

22 Jeremy Sarkin

their own identities, because the process was itself an extension of state, and thus allowed them to make a connection between their identity and the new inclusive South African identity that the state was trying to create, hence cooperation ensues.

In the past, even though South Africa had a multilingual population, it had only two official languages – English and Afrikaans. The Constitution now provides for 11 languages and notes that "conditions shall be created for their development and for the promotion of their equal use and enjoyment". In addition, provision was also made for the development of an independent Pan South African Language Board to develop South African languages as well as:

> all languages commonly used by communities in South Africa, including German, Greek, Gujarati, Hindi, Portuguese, Tamil, Telugu and Urdu; and Arabic, Hebrew, Sanskrit and other languages used for religious purposes in South Africa.
>
> (The Constitution of the Republic of South Africa 1996, sec. 6 (5)(b))

The promotion of language was also a reconciliatory tool and allowed all linguistic groups to feel included and specifically recognized.

The South African truth and reconciliation commission

The political negotiations of the early 1990s identified a truth and reconciliation process with a commission as an ideal means to aid people in coming to terms with the violent past. It was felt that ignoring historical truths leads to collective amnesia and is corrosive to the body politic; a process of public truth telling, or story telling, would be critical to the healing process. This was important as noted by Ben Okri (1997) who stated that when "we have made an experience or a chaos into a story we have transformed it, made sense of it, transmuted experience, domesticated the chaos" (113).

Truth telling can reverse disempowerment because in the telling it becomes the survivor's own story, which the person tells in their own words, in their own way. The process was also important to ensure collective and public acknowledgement of the horror of past human rights abuses. Without it, anger, resentment and revenge would have persisted at very high levels and it would have been impossible for South Africans to establish the rule of law and a culture of human rights. Thus, reconciliation and nation building were often coherent partners.

The fact that the hearings were broadcast on all media platforms assisted the narrative of the process. It helped to inform the broad citizenry about the events and activities of the transition but also about the past.

Openness and transparency were promoted by having a public and accessible parliamentary process that saw all political parties and civil society actors participate in the process, helped legitimize the design of the TRC. Acceptability and legitimacy of the process was a hallmark of it and led to acceptance and cooperation, even by those who were not really in favour of it. All sectors of the society accepted it and saw it as independent of the government. These perceptions were aided by forming a well-balanced commission that had highly respected commissioners who were appointed independently and openly. Those individuals were seen to be representative of a variety of ethnic and political backgrounds and constituencies.

Most of those who opposed the process eventually came round and supported it, even though amnesty was to be given. It was supported partly because the TRC was tasked with developing a complete picture of the causes, nature and extent of the gross human rights violations for the period 1 March 1960 to 6 December 1993, and despite that fact that it was to grant amnesty to perpetrators of political crimes. While there was antagonism towards such an idea by many, at least initially, it was realized that more was to be gained by such a process. This was the case, because it was believed that without giving amnesty for truth, less truth would be forthcoming. Amnesty became more palatable when it was realized that it would not be the blanket amnesty variety of other countries and would be given only if the various criteria were met, including if the truth about what had occurred was told (Sarkin 2008b, 97). The amnesty process was seen to be a pragmatic response to the past when it was realized that, because of the lack of resources and lack of evidence, few prosecutions were possible. The package was accepted because the TRC was also tasked with establishing the fate and/ or whereabouts of victims. It also had to restore the dignity of survivors of gross abuse by giving them an opportunity to relate their accounts of the violations they had suffered and then had to recommend reparation measures. The TRC also had to compile a comprehensive report detailing the activities and findings of the commission that included recommendations for preventing future human rights violations. Thus, amnesty was seen to be just a small part of the process all of which would assist in dealing with the past in the best way possible and assist the nation-building and reconciliation process.

Thus, the TRC allowed South Africans to deal with gross violations of the past three and a half decades, recovering a buried history, albeit a limited one. It provided victims across the political spectrum with a legitimate forum to relate their stories of suffering and reclaim their human dignity. Perpetrators were also given a forum to expiate their guilt. This did not mean that there were those who were willing to accept the TRC process and particular its amnesty provisions. Perpetrators were mostly unwilling participants. Many came forward not out of commitment to the process but for fear of others incriminating them.

The role of the courts was also important in the process. This was particularly so because of the new legitimate Constitutional Court, with many more women and black judges than were on the other courts. This transformation was an important aspect of the transition, in that it was recognized that there was the need for independent, impartial, non-racial adjudication without discrimination of any type. Without the independence of the judicial branch of government, the rule of law and the protection of fundamental rights would have been jeopardized. Therefore, South Africa opted for an independent selection process for judges as well as giving judges security of tenure and legitimacy.

24 Jeremy Sarkin

One of the first cases heard by the new Constitutional Court challenged the constitutionality of the legislation establishing the Truth and Reconciliation Commission It was argued, together with the denial of the right to claim civil compensation from the state, that perpetrators who were granted amnesty could not be exempt from criminal and civil liability as this violated the constitutional right to have justiciable disputes settled by a court of law or another independent and impartial forum. In the spirit of reconciliation and to promote the transitional process the Constitutional Court found the amnesty provisions to be constitutionally valid. It noted that the granting of amnesty in respect of criminal prosecutions was central to the process of reconciliation and transition to democracy. On civil liability, the court emphasized that amnesty did not necessarily refer to the narrow context of criminal prosecution and ruled that wrongdoers would be discouraged from revealing the truth, which was central to the reconciliation process, if there was a threat of potentially substantial civil damages claims. The court also dismissed the applicants' assertion that the state was obliged, under international law, to prosecute persons responsible for committing gross human rights violations finding that South Africa was not bound by the international instruments relied on by the applicants. With regard to the issue of state immunity from civil claims arising from wrongs committed by the states employees, the court conceded to the argument that wrongdoers would not be discouraged from coming forward if their own liberty or property was not threatened by their revelations; however, it stressed that Parliament had legitimately exercised the choice to divert limited state resources to reconstruction and development. In addition, Parliament had provided for a reparations process in the Act, which would take into account the claims of each victim. This ruling was extremely important to the reconciliation process and put to an end the disagreements, at that time, about the TRC process.

Often the events that assisted the reconciliation process and should have been planned by the TRC occurred by accident (Pankhurst 1999). Statements of victims resonated in the general community and assisted reconciliation (Backer 2007). At the same time, there were instances in which statements by commissioners or political parties hindered reconciliation. These actions were perceived as antagonism (see further Ross 2003). Noteworthy, however, were the "magic moments" in the TRC process, when perpetrator and victim came together in the spirit of reconciliation and remorse was expressed and forgiveness offered. These statements tended to reverberate through the various communities and had spillover effects. Though these moments were few and far between, through a little planning they could have occurred more often and could have had wider effect.

While the Human Rights Violations Committee's hearings were more conducive to the attaining of reconciliation, the amnesty hearings were not suited to promote reconciliation. This was because of the nature of the proceedings, the type of persons conducting such proceedings and last, the type of persons who constituted the main players at those hearings – the perpetrators. The pain that emerged during the process was not helpful in the immediate aftermath of the hearing, as victims often had hardened attitudes that softened over time. There were instances of victims being magnanimous during the process despite the agony they had to endure in hearing about what happened to them or their loved ones.

While the TRC was set up to facilitate national unity and reconciliation, by the end of the process many were forced to question the extent to which the TRC actively attempted to play its part in this regard. More active steps could have been taken to promote reconciliation by word and deed rather than to wait for it to be a supposedly natural outcome of the process.

While it is most often assumed that the role of the TRC is essential in promoting reconciliation, it is most often the State that is the most important role-player. While the government as whole, as well as individual members, played an important role in the reconciliation process, they were not always as forthcoming when it came to helping the TRC in fulfilling its reconciliation mandate. At times, the government and the various political parties even wilfully undermined the process by attacking the TRC, other political parties and individual leaders. Their motives and objectives were questioned as was as their patriotism and commitment to the process.

Conclusion

South Africa's reconciliation process contains many lessons for other places. The process indicates that much is needed for reconciliation to happen. Specific types of resources can benefit such processes. However, it is not simply a question of a country having these resources or not. Some of these resources can be created and found. Some can be nurtured. Training can bring out what is needed in some instances, as can various types of support measures. The resources do not have to be costly. Symbolism and steps, which are often easy, are needed and can be effortlessly carried out.

History plays a fundamental role in both nation building and reconciliation. Reconciliation, therefore, has to be retrospective and prospective, as not only does it require coming to terms with the past, but also setting up systems that deal with the legacy of the past. Structural issues need to be addressed and constitutional reform needs to occur. All of these things need to happen so as to convince victims and others who fear the future that their concerns have been adequately addressed and that there now exist mechanisms in the legal framework that ensure that everyone will be able to influence the future. In other words, the reasons for prior conflict are removed and all feel included in the process and believe they can influence the process, at least to some degree.

It is certainly clear that when deciding on the mechanics and methodology of reconciliation programmes and policy, it is imperative to recognize that each country has its own distinct set of political, social, cultural, ethnic and linguistic issues. These issues bear on the types of processes that may be successful. Since no two countries are the same in their conflict, there can be no universal model that all countries can adopt when pursuing reconciliation. However, it is also important to learn from the practices of countries that have already been through these

26 Jeremy Sarkin

programmes and processes, to adopt the best and most useful practices when creating specific reconciliation programmes.

South Africa's transition also reflects that reconciliation and nation building are two sides of the same coin. A people who have lived in a conflict situation, who are enraged at each other, can only think about reconciliation and become a part of the process if the process is made a part of the social fabric of that society. This can be done through a diverse range of cultural initiatives including by the building of, and encouraging participation in, associations that are committed to reparation of relationships, educational projects and youth exchange programmes. While such projects can be organized and initiated by the government, their success is dependent on the reaction and engagement of the many players who form part of the reconciliation process.

Critically, the constitutional process in South Africa as a crucial component in the nation-building process had major spillovers for reconciliation. The fact that many participated in nation building, in a variety of ways, enhanced the opportunities for reconciliation. This allowed the reconciliation process to benefit from what occurred during the events to build a nation and the greater magnanimous attitude that it inspired in many people in the country.

While government plays a major role in the reconciliation process, it is not the only important player. Thus, the role of groups and individuals are vital. Individual leaders can play a dynamic role, as is seen in the case of South Africa. While it is commonly believed that the reconciliation process in South Africa was the work of the TRC, large parts of the reconciliation process occurred outside of that institution. Institutions and institution-building processes, including the design and implementation of bodies such as the SA Human Rights Commission, the PAN South African Language board, the Commission on Gender Equality and others all played a part in boosting reconciliation. The effect of reforming and building new courts was also important as was the role played by other institutions in promoting reconciliation, although in a more indirect way.

Note

1 BA LLB (Natal) LLM (Harvard) LLD (UWC) Attorney South Africa, Attorney New York USA; Professor of Law, University of South Africa; Distinguished Visiting Professor of Law and member of CEDIS, Nova University, Lisbon Portugal; former Chair-Rapporteur, UN Working Group on Enforced or Involuntary Disappearances. E-mail: JSarkin@post.harvard.edu.

Bibliography

Asefa, H. 1993. *Peace and Reconciliation a as a Paradigm*. Nairobi: Nairobi Peace Institute.

Backer, David. 2003. "Civil Society and Transitional Justice: Possibilities, Patterns and Prospects." *Journal of Human Rights* 2(3): 297–313.

———. 2007. "Victims' Responses to Truth Commissions: Evidence from South Africa." In *Security, Reconstruction, and Reconciliation: When the Wars End*, edited by M. Ndulo, 165–196. London: University College London.

Bargal, David and Emmanuel Sivan. 2004. "Leadership and Reconciliation." In *From Conflict Resolution to Reconciliation*, edited by Yakoov Bar-Siman-Tov, 125–148. Oxford: Oxford University Press.

Beutler, Ingrid. 2008. "Sport Serving Development and Peace: Achieving the Goals of the United Nations through Sport." *Sport in Society* 11(4): 359–369.

Buikema, Rosemarie. 2012. "Performing Dialogical Truth and Transitional Justice: The Role of Art in the Becoming Post-Apartheid of South Africa." *Memory Studies* 5(3): 282–292.

Carlin, John. 2007. "How Nelson Mandela Won the Rugby World Cup." *The Telegraph*, 19 Oct. http://www.telegraph.co.uk/news/features/3634426/How-Nelson-Mandela-won-the-rugby-World-Cup.html. Accessed 21 Sep. 2015.

The Constitution of the Republic of South Africa, 1996 (South Africa).

Daly, Erin and Jeremy Sarkin. 2004. "Too Many Questions, Too Few Answers: Reconciliation in Transitional Societies." *Columbia Human Rights Law Review* 35(3): 661–728, 666.

———. 2007. *Reconciliation in Divided Societies: Finding Common Ground*. Philadelphia, PA: Pennsylvania University Press.

Doxtader, Erik and Philippe-Joseph Salazar. 2007. *Truth and Reconciliation in South Africa: The Fundamental Documents*. Cape Town: Institute for Justice and Reconciliation.

Du Toit, Fanie, ed. 2003. *Learning to Live Together: Practices of Social Reconciliation*. Cape Town: Institute for Justice and Reconciliation.

Du Toit, Fanie and Erik Doxtader, eds. 2010. *In the Balance: South Africans Debate Reconciliation*. Sunnyside: Jacana Media.

Gibson, James L. 2006. "The Contributions of Truth to Reconciliation Lessons from South Africa." *Journal of Conflict Resolution* 50(3): 409–432.

Gready, Paul. 2010. *The Era of Transitional Justice: The Aftermath of the Truth and Reconciliation Commission in South Africa and Beyond*. London: Taylor & Francis.

Gross, Aeyal M. 2004. "The Constitution, Reconciliation, and Transitional Justice: Lessons from South Africa and Israel." *Stanford Journal of International Law* 40: 47.

Heribert, Adam. 1999. "The Presence of the Past: South Africa's Truth Commission as a Model?" In *Religion and Politics in South Africa*, edited by Abdulkader Tayob and Wolfram Weisse, 139–158. Munster: Waxmann Verlag.

Höglund, Kristine and Ralph Sundberg. 2008. "Reconciliation through Sports? The Case of South Africa." *Third World Quarterly* 29(4): 805–818.

Interim Constitution of the Republic of South Africa Act No. 200 of 1993.

Kaminer, Debra, Anna Grimsrud, Landon Myer, Dan J. Stein and David R. Williams. 2008. "Risk for Post-Traumatic Stress Disorder Associated with Different Forms of Interpersonal Violence in South Africa." *Social Science & Medicine* 67(10): 1589–1595.

Kappler, Stefanie. 2013. "Peacebuilding and Lines of Friction between Imagined Communities in Bosnia-Herzegovina and South Africa." *Peacebuilding* 1(3): 349–364.

Lederach, John Paul. 2001. "Civil Society and Reconciliation." In *Turbulent Peace: The Challenges of Managing International Conflict*, edited by Chester A. Crocker, Fen O. Hampson and Pamela Aall, 841–854. Washington, DC: USIP.

Maharaj, Brij. 2013. "Challenges Facing Hindus and Hinduism in Post-Apartheid South Africa." *Journal of Sociology and Social Anthropology* 4(1–2): 93–103.

28 *Jeremy Sarkin*

Moses, Edwin. 2014. "Sport for Good: Nelson Mandela's Vision, One Community at a Time." *Huffington Post*, 26 Jun. http://www.huffingtonpost.com/edwin-moses/sport-for-good-nelson-man_b_5534794.html. Accessed 11 Sep. 2015.

Ndlovu-Gatsheni, Sabelo J. 2011. "The World Cup, Vuvuzelas, Flag-Waving Patriots and the Burden of Building South Africa." *Third World Quarterly* 32(2): 279–293.

Okri, Ben. 1997. "The Joys of Storytelling." In *A Way of Being Free*, 29–48. London: Phoenix.

Pankhurst, Donna. 1999. "Issues of Justice and Reconciliation in Complex Political Emergencies: Conceptualising Reconciliation, Justice and Peace." *Third World Quarterly* 20(1): 239–255.

Peterson, Bhekizizwe. 2012. "Dignity, Memory, Truth and the Future under Siege: Reconciliation and Nation-Building in Post-Apartheid South Africa." In *The New Violent Cartography: Geo-Analysis after the Aesthetic Turn*, edited by Sam Okoth Opondo and Michael J. Shapiro, 216–235. New York: Routledge.

The Promotion of National Unity and Reconciliation Act, No. 34 of 1995 (South Africa).

Ross, Fiona C. 2003. "On Having Voice and Being Heard Some after-Effects of Testifying before the South African Truth and Reconciliation Commission." *Anthropological Theory* 3(3): 325–341.

Sarkin, Jeremy. 1998. "The Development of a Human Rights Culture in South Africa." *Human Rights Quarterly* 20(3): 628–655.

———. 2008a. "Achieving Reconciliation in Divided Societies: Comparing the Approaches in Timor-Leste, South Africa and Rwanda." *Yale Journal of International Affairs* 3(2): 11–28.

———. 2008b. "An Evaluation of the South African Amnesty Process." In *Truth and Reconciliation: Did the TRC Deliver*, edited by Audrey Chapman and Hugo van der Merwe, 93–115. Philadelphia, PA: University of Pennsylvania Press.

———. 2015a. "Dealing with Enforced Disappearances in South Africa (With a Focus on the Nokuthula Simelane case) and around the World: The Need to Ensure Progress on the Rights to Truth, Justice and Reparations" *Speculum Juris* (1): 21–48.

———. 2015b. "Understanding the Journey to Reconciliation in Transitional Societies: Using the Metaphor of a Motor Vehicle Road Trip to Understand South Africa's Path (Process) to Political Reconciliation." *International Journal of African Renaissance Studies* 10(2): 87–103.

Stein, Dan J., Soraya Seedat, Debra Kaminer, Hashim Moomal, Allen Herman, John Sonnega and David R. Williams. 2008. "The Impact of the Truth and Reconciliation Commission on Psychological Distress and Forgiveness in South Africa." *Social Psychiatry and Psychiatric Epidemiology* 43(6): 462–468.

Wilson, Richard A. 1996. "The Sizwe Will Not Go Away: The Truth and Reconciliation Commission, Human Rights and Nation-Building in South Africa." *African Studies* 55(2): 1–20.

2 Amity symbolism as a resource for conflict resolution

The case of Franco-German relations

Mathias Delori

Introduction

On September 4, 2013, French President François Hollande and German President Joachim Gauck visited Oradour-sur-Glane, a French martyr village of the Second World War whose population was massacred by an SS division during the Liberation. During the ceremony, the two heads of state stood together in silent commemoration, holding each other's hand. By so doing, they reproduced a symbolic gesture which had resonated strongly in 1984, that of President François Mitterrand and German Chancellor Helmut Kohl holding hands in front the memorial to the battle of Verdun. These elements illustrate a more general fact: over the last couple of decades, Franco-German relations have been maintained within an idealistic atmosphere which celebrates "reconciliation" and "friendship" between the two countries. These celebrations take the form of grandiloquent speeches, spectacular political gestures, and commemoration rituals which are intended to give a particular meaning to Franco-German cooperation.

This chapter analyzes forms, the historical importance, and the logic of those symbolic practices. I try to understand whether they have had an impact on Franco-German political relations, and what this tells us, more generally speaking, about how symbolic resources can be used in post-war conflicts.

The text proceeds as follows. The first section presents into more details the semiotic (the form) and the semantic (the content) elements of this "amity symbolism". It revolves around three intermingled ideas: the narrative of Franco-German reconciliation, the image of the Franco-German "couple" or "Tandem", and the prophecy of the fraternization of young people. I will show that the habit of displaying such fictional elements emerged in the 1960s and has never been put into question ever since.

Second, I will show that specialists diverge when assessing the political signification of those practices. On the one hand, realist scholars analyze the latter as mere communicational actions, arguing that they reflect the need to give a moral veneer to decisions mainly driven by material interests. On the other hand, some journalists and historians have argued that these idealistic references to Franco-German "friendship" or "reconciliation" reflects the actors' genuine moral

30   *Mathias Delori*

motivations. In the following, I will put forward a "middle-range" argument. I will show that this political symbolism did not revolutionize the course of history but, nevertheless, modified the "common sense" – to speak like Gramsci – of Franco-German relations.

Finally, I will review the factors which have contributed to these ambivalent but nevertheless remarkable effects. My general argument is that this transnational political symbolism amounts to an embryo of national political symbolism (Anderson 1991). More precisely, it has drawn upon three symbolic resources: a well-instituted imaginary, the ambiguities of natural language, and the logic of ritualization. All these resources contributed to naturalize the narratives, images, and allegories displayed by the actors of the Franco-German theatre.

A set of practices which emerged in the early 1960s

It is important to have in mind the general chronology of Franco-German rapprochement in order to understand the political significance of Franco-German amity symbolism. In the following, I will follow the mainstream periodization of Franco-German post-war relations by distinguishing three timespans: the conflictual aftermath of the war (1945–1950), the pragmatic rapprochement (in the 1950s), and the emergence of Franco-German amity symbolism (in the early 1960s).

From 1945 to 1949, Germany had stopped to exist as a sovereign state. The German "territories" were officially ruled by the Allied Control Council, an institution bringing together representatives of the four occupying powers: the United States, the United Kingdom, France, and the Soviet Union. In practice, however, the allies conducted separate occupation policies. This holds true, in particular, for France. From 1945 to 1949, France implemented a materialistic security policy towards Germany. This policy consisted in exploiting German economic resources (in particular, the coal and steel production), trying to annex some border territories (like the Sarre region), and blocking the reconstitution of a (West) German democratic state. It is important to note that France pursued this material security policy until the very end of the occupation statute. Indeed, France did not follow the Anglo-Saxons when they revised their policy towards Germany. In 1947, for instance, France refused to join what appeared as a prelude to the creation of a West German state, namely the merging of the British and American zones. Until 1949, the French seemed obsessed by one single question: how to deprive the Germans from the material capability to invade France again?[1]

Most specialists agree that Franco-German political rapprochement started in the early 1950s in the context of European integration. In this respect, May 9, 1950, constitutes, undoubtedly, a key date. At that time, French Foreign Minister Robert Schuman proposed to eliminate "the age-old opposition of France and Germany" by creating a "supranational community" in charge of organizing the production of coal and steel. This proposal resonated with German Chancellor Adenauer's policy of *Westintegration*. Consequently, the West German

Franco-German relations 31

government accepted without any hesitation. Hence, the French government put an end to the state of war with Germany (July 26, 1951), and both governments started cooperating within the framework of the European Coal and Steel Community. The prospect of German rearmament thwarted the process during about four years (1950–1954). However, the Paris agreements of October 1954 solved all the remaining concrete war legacies: the French opposition to the rearmament of West Germany, the dispute concerning the Sarre region, and the disagreements concerning cultural cooperation. Consequently, European integration restarted after the signing of the treaties of Rome in 1957.

At that time – that is during the 1950s – French and German official representatives conceived of Franco-German cooperation on a very pragmatic basis. They cooperated within the European framework but hardly talked about Franco-German "reconciliation" as a goal per se. In the few cases when they did, their discourse appeared abnormal and inaudible. A good illustration of this is Chancellor Adenauer's proposal of March 1950 to create a "Franco-German union" with one single Franco-German parliament. Contrary to R. Schuman's declaration of May 9, 1950, Chancellor Adenauer's ode to Franco-German reconciliation went completely unnoticed.[2] Another example is, precisely, Schuman's declaration of May 9, 1950. The word "reconciliation" does not appear in the text. The idea is present – notably when Schuman talks about eliminating the "age-old opposition between France and Germany". Yet it is always framed as a means towards a greater end: the creation of a "unified Europe".

The rapprochement initiated by de Gaulle and Adenauer in the early 1960s constituted an important turn in this respect. It gave birth to a new social practice: the habit of commenting on Franco-German cooperation through grandiloquent political speeches and symbolic gestures (Buffet and Hauser 1998, 201; Rosoux 2002; Nourry 2005). One can mention, among other examples:

- The "ceremony of Reims" on July 8, 1962, when de Gaulle and Chancellor Adenauer participated in a mass together in the cathedral of Reims (about 30 years after the destruction of the cathedral by the German artillery).
- de Gaulle's speech to the German youth in Ludwigsburg, Germany, on September 9, 1962.
- The "hug" between de Gaulle and Adenauer after the signing of the Elysée treaty on January 22, 1963.

Parallel to this, the Elysée treaty foresaw the creation of a "Franco-German fund" in order to encourage youth meetings. Although this project entailed a strong educational component, it was also all the more symbolic. Until then, the most striking images concerning the "meeting" of French and German young people were those of their mutual assassination within the trenches of the First World War (Audouin-Rouzeau 2004; Audouin-Rouzeau 2008) and of their unfortunate fraternization in German and French military structures: the German Waffen SS from 1941 to 1945 and the French Légion Etrangère from 1945 to 1962.[3] In

32   *Mathias Delori*

this context, the youth exchange policy instituted in 1963 sent a completely different message. French and German young people were asked to meet in a pacific context on a massive basis (300,000 participants each year).

The symbolic dimension of this youth exchange policy emerges from the public statements of the time. A senior official in charge of this policy declared repeatedly, for instance, that this massive youth exchange policy aimed at "realizing the largest migration of peoples ever organized in human history in peace time and with pacific intentions".[4] The French minister of youth went a step further by declaring, in 1970, that "French and German young people want to go beyond reconciliation. They want the fusion of both nations."[5]

All this illustrates that the early 1960s constituted a turning point for the story under investigation here. It is important to note, in this respect, that this political symbolism has never been put into question ever since. Since the early 1960s, it has been revolving around three main tropes: the narrative of Franco-German reconciliation, the image of the Franco-German "couple" or "Tandem", and the prophecy of the fraternizing of young people.

In 2003, for instance, the French and German governments decided to celebrate the fortieth anniversary of the Elysée treaty. They did so by bringing together all French and German members of parliament in the palace of Versailles. Like the aforementioned ceremony of Reims of 1962, this one worked up with the memories of the war (here the memory of the treaty sanctioning Germany after the First World War) in order to legitimize rapprochement. Six months later, a Franco-German "youth parliament" sat under the cupola of the German Bundestag in the presence of French President Chirac and German Chancellor Schröder. With historical hindsight, the semantic continuity appears all the more striking.

Beyond the realist and idealist readings of Franco-German reconciliation symbolism

The question of the actual political significance of those symbolic practices has led to stimulating debates within scholarship. Two opposite assessments have emerged in this respect.

The first may be called "realist" in the sense of the realist theory of international relations (Gilpin 1996). Realists have pointed out the gap between this idealism and the reality of Franco-German relations. This idea emerges, for instance, from G. Ziebura's seminal book entitled "Die deutsch-französischen Beziehungen seit 1945. Mythen und Realitäten" (Franco-German relations since 1945. Myths and realities) (Ziebura 1970). As the title suggests, the book opposes "myths" and "realities" and argues that political leaders resort to the former in order to hide some cynical calculations. This view has led to a voluminous literature which argues that de Gaulle and Adenauer were mainly concerned by power and security interests and that they invented the story of Franco-German reconciliation, the image of the Franco-German "couple", and the "demagogy" of the fraternizing of young people in order to legitimize their controversial strategic alliance. As a matter of fact, some recent findings fuel this interpretation. For instance, Nassima Bougherara has shown that the Soviet Union and the United States suspected that the Elysée treaty entailed secret clauses concerning military nuclear cooperation. Consequently, they firmly criticized the treaty. In this context, it seems reasonable to hypothesize that de Gaulle and Adenauer resorted to reconciliation symbols in order to "counter" the mainstream characterization of the Elysée treaty as a war alliance.

A revised version of this realist reading of Franco-German reconciliation symbolism states that de Gaulle and Adenauer invented this set of myths, narratives, and allegories for instrumental reasons and that the latter became constitutive elements of French and German identities afterwards. John Baylis observed such a mechanism in the context of the Anglo-American special relationship. Quoting H. Morgenthau, he noted that, more often than not, "the Government fashions an imaginary world that pleases it, and then comes to believe in the reality of that world and acts as though it were real."[6] Rosoux has convincingly developed this argument concerning Franco-German reconciliation symbolism (Rosoux 2002).

Finally, some other realist thinkers have argued that this political symbolism has had no effect on what really matters (to them), namely defence and security cooperation. Buffet made a strong statement in this respect in his book on "myths and international relations":

> If the test of mutual confidence and even of the willingness to organize a common defense is applied, it becomes apparent that the relationship glories in symbolism: while the hard facts of operational and doctrinal nuclear concertation are worked out with Britain or even the US, Franco-German defense relations revolve around symbolic parades and the creation of goodwill-furthering joint brigades which are operationally useless, and stripped even of their symbolism with the abandonment of conscription in France.
>
> (Buffet and Hauser 1998, 203)

On the other extremity of the theoretical spectrum, some authors have taken a more idealist perspective, that is a perspective which highlights the importance of the moral motivations of this symbolism's main narrators. Thus, an important literature insists on the (alleged) personal friendship between de Gaulle and Adenauer and their "genuine" will to associate the French and German peoples to their personal rapprochement. This literature usually argues that de Gaulle and Adenauer inherited from an important cultural legacy: the efforts of those private actors who reinitiated after 1945 the cultural dialogue between France and Germany (Defrance and Pfeil 2005).

Given its idealistic tropism, this literature insists on the idea that Franco-German reconciliation symbolism changed the course of history in a substantial way. Several authors have made this assessment concerning the youth exchange programme. According to Ménudier, this programme constitutes an "exemplary contribution to the unity of Europe" (Ménudier 1988, 1). Defrance made a similar point when arguing that it is the "fleuron" of all Franco-German reconciliation policies (Defrance and Pfeil 2007, 101).

34 *Mathias Delori*

This literature is often depicted as "hagiographic" as it insists heavily on the heroic dimension of the reconciliation process (Deloye 2006). It is interesting in the sense that it helps to overcome a limitation of the realist literature: namely, the notion that states would be the only actors of international relations and that they would only pursue interests defined in terms of national security and power. However, as noted by Lefranc, this literature suffers an epistemological bias: it does not take any distance vis-à-vis the witnesses' testimonies. Yet witnesses of reconciliation processes are not neutral. Rather, they have a strong tendency to "enchant" the reconciliation processes they participated in. Consequently, it is important to deconstruct the witness's discourse or, to put it differently, framing this discourse as what it is: a constitutive element of the object under investigation (Lefranc 2006, 8). In the following, I will follow Lefranc's piece of advice and analyze this political symbolism as what it is: namely, a set of symbolic and ritual practices whose effectiveness has to be studied empirically.

Although covariation does not mean causality, one can observe that two changes occurred along with the institutionalization of the reconciliation symbolism of Franco-German relations. The first concerns public opinions. Although this change is difficult to assess, it is clear that Franco-German amity symbolism consolidated the pacifying process which started in the early 1950s in the context of European integration. Indeed, quantitative studies reveal that the level of mutual trust increased in the 1960s. Before that time, the French and German public opinions ranked the other country among the countries they trusted the least. From the early 1960s on, mutual representations "normalized". Concretely, French and German respondents started to rank the other country between the fifth and tenth position of the countries they trust the most, a level specialists consider as "normal" if one takes into account the structural determinants of mutual trust: the size of the country, its geographical proximity, its GDP, and so forth (Rabier and Inglehart 1984).

Besides, several qualitative enquiries have shown that the image of the other country changed during the 1960s. Admittedly, French and German people have kept representing each other in a stereotypical way. However, positive stereotypes have taken the upper hand over negative ones (Demorgon 2002). For instance, many French people seem to consider that German people are "organization prone". Yet this cliché no longer has the negative connotations it used to have. On the contrary, it is often coined on a positive way in order to highlight that French people could probably learn from this alleged German talent for organization (Jeanneney 2000). This illustrates a more general trend: positive stereotypes have taken the upper hand on negative ones.

The reason for this effect on mutual representations has been given by Rosoux in her seminal study of the uses of the past in Franco-German relations. Rosoux showed that French and German political leaders invented various stories in order to legitimize rapprochement. She mentioned, among others, the story presenting the First World War as a "shared martyrdom" (ceremony of Verdun in 1984), that which frames the different Franco-German wars as a set of "European civil wars" (speech of French President Valéry Giscard-d'Estaing of May 7, 1975), that which depicts reconciliation as a return to the original (mythical) union of Charlemagne's empire (de Gaulle's speech of May 26, 1966, in Verdun), and so forth. All those stories, Rosoux argued, contributed to "work up with the past" in Ricoeur's sense. They appeased the memory of the conflictual past and naturalized Franco-German rapprochement.

The second measurable effect concerns the common understanding of the role of Franco-German bilateral cooperation within the European framework. Before the early 1960s, cooperation between France and Germany had rather been understood as a fortunate consequence of European integration (see earlier). Franco-German amity symbolism told a different story. Through the notion of reconciliation, bilateral cooperation between France and Germany stopped being understood as an instrument for a greater good. Rather, it became a "greatness" in Boltanski and Thévenot's sense (Boltanski and Thévenot 1991), that is something one can aim at per se.

Although trivial at first sight, this move from the "realm of technology" to the "realm of morality" (Latour and Venn 2002) is important. Indeed, it initiated a change within the European integration dynamic by legitimizing what specialists of the field call the Franco-German special partnership, a key idea proven several times in European integration history. To cite only a few examples, this Franco-German "special relationship" contributed to the following:

- Outlining the Common Agricultural Policy in the 1960s (Pinder 1998).
- Initiating the institutional reform that led to the direct election of European Parliament in 1979 (Cole 2001).
- Setting up the monetary union in the early 1990s (Nourry 2005) and so forth.

It emerges from what precedes that the institutionalization of Franco-German amity symbolism went along with some changes in mutual representations, and thus both at the level of public opinions and the political elite. Self-reflective social scientists often insist on the notion that covariation does not mean causality. In this very case, the fact that representations and policy practices changed when this political imaginary institutionalized does not imply an effect of the latter on the former. Although it is true that social scientists do not have access to causes, they put forward hypotheses based on observations. I turn to this question in the next section by investigating the mechanisms which (probably) explain the power of Franco-German amity symbolism.

The symbolic ressources used by French and German reconciliation entrepreneurs

The general argument put forward here is that Franco-German amity symbolism turned into a meaningful political allegory because it met with the grammar of (national) political symbolism. Three mechanisms are worth being mentioned in this respect.

36   *Mathias Delori*

Relying on some well-institutionalized tropes

Students of domestic political symbolism have demonstrated that the latter does not come out of the blue. In order to find some resonances among its audience, the latter has to rely on some shared images and narratives. This is the reason why political symbolisms often develop in an incremental way. In his famous book on this issue, Pierre Nora argued, for instance, that the French national novel needed more than one century before finding an institutionalized shape (Nora 1997).

This general observation sheds some light on the (relative) power of Franco-German amity symbolism. A good example is the ceremony of Verdun 1984, when French President Mitterrand and German Chancellor Kohl took each other's hands in front of the ossuary of Douaumont. A couple of hours before the famous photograph, both political leaders accompanied a group of 2,000 French and German young people on the former battlefield. Together, they planted seventy "peace trees" in order to commemorate the seventieth anniversary of the start of the First World War.

This theatre play was the exact reproduction of another play acted 60 years before. In 1926, French pacifist militant Marc Sangnier invited thousands of French and German young people in his park of Bierville, near Paris. Some French official representatives – including the Council vice-president of France and the crown prince of Saxony – attended the ceremony. Everybody then drove to a battlefield of the First World War nearby Reims in order to plant one "reconciliation tree" commemorating the end of the "Great War".

Mitterrand and Kohl probably did not have this example in mind when they organized and played the political liturgy of Verdun in 1984. However, the resonances between the symbolic elements displayed in both cases – the reconciliation narrative, the sites of memory of the First World War, the presence of young people and official representatives, the peace/reconciliation trees, and so forth – is not a pure coincidence. All these tropes had been stated (to reference Foucault) in different contexts during the entire twentieth century. In 1984, it was a well-constituted political imaginary.

Playing with ambiguous symbols

Students of national political symbolisms have documented that the best symbols are those which legitimize a given political order or policy whilst leaving some space for varying interpretations. The reason for this is functional. On the one hand, the symbols need to transform social representations in a particular way (by fashioning a national novel, for instance). On the other hand, the new idea is unlikely to be heard if it completely disrupts or contradicts former narratives. Ambiguity serves this purpose of working on meaning without explicitly contradicting existing narratives and memories.

According to Agulhon, this logic played a central role in the success of the "Marianne allegory" under the French Third republic. The later was declared

Franco-German relations   37

in 1871 in the context of the defeat against Prussia. At that time, important segments of the French public opinion seemed nostalgic of the old regimes, in particular the Bourbon or Orleanic monarchies and the Napoleonic empires. In this context, the republicans tried to find some myths and allegories likely to rally the sceptics to their cause. Agulhon convincingly shows that Marianne became a powerful symbol because of its "constructive" ambiguity. On the one hand, it was explicitly republican and echoed some popular "left-wing" images like in Delacroix's famous painting "*La liberté guidant le peuple*". On the other hand, it clearly echoed the image of Virgin Mary and some other catholic and monarchist symbols like Joan of Arc (Agulhon 1989).

In the case of Franco-German relations, this logic explains the success of the myth of Charlemagne. This myth states, basically, that France and Germany used to constitute one single country under the reign of Charlemagne, and that this state of being, namely the "union of both countries", constitutes the natural norm of Franco-German relations. A good illustration of this narrative is de Gaulle's speech of Verdun 1966, when he stated that the Elysée treaty signed three years before "re-establishes a natural bond, a natural bond that had been unfortunately broken when Charlemagne's Empire burst 1123 years ago" (Rosoux 2002, 66).

Now, this story did not come to de Gaulle's mind in 1966. The myth of the Franco-German Carolingian union is a very old social construct. Not to mention its very old occurrences (Durand-Le Guern and Ribémont 2009), the Nazis popularized this myth during the Second World War when they grouped all the French voluntary combatants within the SS division "Charlemagne". This popular image reemerged, in a pacific and democratic way, after the creation of the "Charlemagne prize" in 1949.

From then on, Charlemagne started working as an ambiguous and, therefore, powerful symbol of reconciliation. In the post-war context, the myth told a story which resonated with the memories of several social groups: those who conceived of Franco-German rapprochement as a continuation of the pacific rapprochement of the 1920s, those who wanted to continue Pétain and Hitler's collaboration policy, those who assumed that France and Germany were starting a new episode of their common history, and so forth.

Ritualizing the myth

Franco-German amity symbolism displays one third and last characteristic: its extreme degree of ritualization. Sociologists and anthropologists define rites as embodied symbolic practices which are repeated over time in order to state what a given society holds to be sacred. Those body choreographies displaying the Franco-German couple obviously fall into this category. This ritualization dynamic also emerges from the fact that French and German political leaders have adopted the habit of celebrating the reconciliation itself (instead of working with the conflictual past as they used to do until the 1980s). Whereas the first anniversaries of the Elysée treaty had gone largely unnoticed, the thirtieth, fortieth, and fiftieth anniversaries led to some important ceremonies. In

38 *Mathias Delori*

September 2012, François Hollande and Angela Merkel even commemorated nothing less than the "Speech to German Youth" given by Charles de Gaulle 50 years before!

At first sight, the ritualization of this symbolism suggests that current political leaders lack imagination. I have personally made such a comment in a previous publication (Delori 2007). However, a closer investigation may lead to a different assessment. Indeed, anthropologists and sociologists teach us that political rites – like those displayed at a domestic level – have ambivalent effects. On the one hand, they are noticeably powerless when it comes with giving content to public policies or providing an accurate image of a given community. On the other hand, political rites succeed in shaping a powerful sense of belonging (Durkheim 1912). Several reasons have been put forward in order to explain this ambivalent performance.[7] Whatever the explanation, this ambivalent performance is noticeable in the case of Franco-German relations. On the one hand, French and German people know little about the actual cultures and societies of France and Germany. On the other hand, they show strong attachment to the general principle of Franco-German cooperation (see earlier).

Conclusion

This chapter analyzed the origins, consistency, and political signification of Franco-German amity symbolism. I have showed, first, that it emerged in the early 1960s and has never been put into question ever since. Second, I have pleaded for a normalization of the study of this set of symbolic practices, that is for a perspective which would overcome the shortcomings of the realist and idealist literatures. My central argument is that this symbolism did not revolutionize but nevertheless modified the "common sense" of Franco-German relations in two ways. The reason for this ambivalent performance lies in the allegorical character of this symbolism. It did not provide a clear "policy frame" to French and German political leaders, that is a detailed political programme to be applied like a road map. Yet this set of ideas constituted more than a simple diplomatic veneer. It took the form of an embryo of political symbolism. As such, it instituted a sense of belonging and the notion that the bilateral relation between France and Germany can be a motor of European integration.

Notes

1   This picture suffers only one apparent exception: the cultural domain. Throughout this period, the Direction de l'Education Publique of the French occupation administration – the administrative department in charge of cultural issues – implemented a policy which appears, with historical hindsight, as more constructive. It is important to note, however, that this policy did not pursue a different goal. See: Mombert, Monique. 1995. *Sous le signe de la rééducation: jeunesse et livre en Zone Française d'Occupation: 1945–1949.* Strasbourg: Presses universitaires de Strasbourg.
2   Beuve-Méry, Hubert. 1950. "La proposition de M. Adenauer pour une union franco-allemande éveille jusqu'ici peu d'écho, 10 mars 1950." *Le Monde, 1593: 3.*

3 During the Second World War, thousands of French young people enlisted in the so-called "Charlemagne" Waffen SS division. From 1945 to 1962, thousands of young German people enrolled in the French *Légion Etrangère*. They constituted the most important military units during the Indochina and Algerian wars. See: Bene, Christian. 2012. *La collaboration militaire française dans la Seconde Guerre mondiale*. Paris, Éditions codex; Michels, Eckard. 2012. "Deutsche in der Fremdenlegion (1945–1962): Mythen und Realitäten". In *Mythes et tabous dans les relations franco-allemandes. Mythen und Tabus der deutsch-französischen Beziehungen im 20. Jahrhundert*, edited by U. Pfeil. Paris, Berne, Berlin, Peter Lang: 127–140.
4 Rovan, Joseph. 1972. "Les relations franco-allemandes dans le domaine de la jeunesse et de la culture populaire (1945–1971)." *Revue d'Allemagne et des pays de langue allemande* 4: 675–704.
5 Comiti, Joseph. 1970. "Les jeunes de France et d'Allemagne veulent aboutir à la fusion des deux pays." *La nouvelle république de Centre-Ouest*.
6 Baylis, John. 1984. *Anglo-American Defense Relations, 1939–1984: The Special Relationship*. London: Macmillan.
7 The most important one deals with the functional "polysemy" of political rites. The fact that they do not have any clear meaning is both an asset and a weakness. It is an asset when it comes to generating a sense of community belonging. It is a weakness in the sense that it cannot provide any clear representation of the signified.

Quoted references

Agulhon, Maurice. 1989. *Marianne au pouvoir. L'imagerie et la symbolique républicaines de 1880 à 1914*. Paris: Flammarion.
Anderson, Benedict R. O'G. 1991. *Imagined Communities*. London: Verso.
Audouin-Rouzeau, Stéphane. 2004. *La guerre des enfants: 1914–1918*. Paris: A. Colin.
———. 2008. *Combattre, Une anthropologie historique de la guerre moderne (XIXe-XXIe siècle)*. Paris: Seuil.
Baylis, John. 1984. *Anglo-American Defense Relations, 1939–1984: The Special Relationship*. London: Macmillan.
Bene, Christian. 2012. *La collaboration militaire française dans la Seconde Guerre mondiale*. Paris, Éditions codex.
Beuve-Méry, Hubert. 1950. "La proposition de M. Adenauer pour une union franco-allemande éveille jusqu'ici peu d'écho, 10 mars 1950." *Le Monde*, 1593: 3.
Boltanski, Luc and Laurent Thévenot. 1991. *De la justification: les économies de la grandeur*. Paris: Gallimard.
Buffet, Cyril and Béatrice Hauser. 1998. *Haunted by History: Myths in International Relations*. Oxford: Bergham Books.
Cole, Alaistir. 2001. *Franco-German Relations*. Harlow: Longman.
Comiti, Joseph. 1970. "Les jeunes de France et d'Allemagne veulent aboutir à la fusion des deux pays." *La nouvelle république de Centre-Ouest*.
Defrance, Corine and Ulrich Pfeil. 2005. "Le traité de l'Elysée et les relations franco-allemandes." In *Le traité de l'Elysée et les relations franco-allemandes. 1945–1963–2003*, edited by Corine Defrance and Ulrich Pfeil, 7–41. Paris: CNRS éditions.
———. 2007. "Au service du rapprochement franco-allemand. Dialogue d'historiens de part et d'autre du Rhin." In *L'Europe et ses passés douloureux*, edited by Georges Mink and Laure Neumayer, 91–103. Paris: La Découverte.
Delori, Mathias. 2007. "La symbolique franco-allemande en panne d'idées ? Pour un retour critique sur le grand récit de la réconciliation." *Les Cahiers d'Histoire. Revue d'Histoire Critique* 100: 11–21.

40 *Mathias Delori*

———. 2016. *La réconciliation franco-allemande par la jeunesse. La généalogie, l'événement, l'histoire (1871–2015).* Paris, Berlin, Bruxelles: Peter Lang.

Deloye, Yves. 2006. "Introduction: éléments pour une approche socio-historique de la construction européenne." *Politique Européenne* 18: 5–15.

Demorgon, Jacques. 2002. "Evolution, Evaluation des échanges franco-allemands." *Allemagne, d'Aujourd'hui* 162: 191–204.

Durand-Le Guern, Isabelle and Bernard Ribémont. 2009. *Charlemagne: empereur et mythe d'Occident.* Paris: Klincksieck.

Durkheim, Emile. 1912. Les formes élémentaires de la vie religieuse.

Gilpin, Robert. 1996. "The Richness of the Tradition of Political Realism." In *Neorealism and Its Critiques,* edited by R. O Keohane, 301–321. New York: Columbia University Press.

Jeanneney, Jean Noël. 2000. *Une idée fausse est un fait vrai: les stéréotypes nationaux en Europe.* Paris: O. Jacob.

Krotz, Ulrich and Joachim Schild. 2013. *Shaping Europe. France, Germany, and Embedded Bilateralism from the Elysée treaty to Twenty-First Century Politics.* Oxford: Oxford University Press.

Latour, Bruno and Couze Venn. 2002. "Morality and Technology: The Ends of the Means." *Theory, Culture and Society* 19(5/6): 247–260.

Lefranc, Sandrine. 2006. "Introduction. Créer du lien social." In *Après le conflit, la réconciliation ? Actes révisés des journées d'études organisées les 12 et 13 décembre 2005 par l'Institut des sciences sociales du politique, l'Université de Paris X et ENS Cachan,* edited by Sandrine Lefranc, 7–26. Paris: M. Houdiard.

Ménudier, Henry. 1988. *L'Office franco-allemand pour la Jeunesse. Une contribution exemplaire à l'unité de l'Europe.* Paris: Armand Colin.

Michels, Eckard. 2012. "Deutsche in der Fremdenlegion (1945–1962): Mythen und Realitäten". In *Mythes et tabous dans les relations franco-allemandes. Mythen und Tabus der deutsch-französischen Beziehungen im 20. Jahrhundert,* edited by U. Pfeil. Paris, Berne, Berlin, Peter Lang: 127–140.

Mombert, Monique. 1995. *Sous le signe de la rééducation: jeunesse et livre en Zone Française d'Occupation: 1945–1949.* Strasbourg: Presses universitaires de Strasbourg.

Nora, Pierre. 1997. *Les lieux de mémoire.* Paris: Gallimard.

Nourry, Christelle. 2005. *Le couple franco-allemand. Un symbole européen.* Bruxelles: Bruylant.

Pinder, John. 1998. *The Building of the European Union.* Oxford: Oxford University Press.

Rabier, Jacques René and Ronald Inglehart. 1984. "La confiance entre les peuples: déterminants et conséquences." *Revue francaise de science politique* 34(1): 5–47.

Rosoux, Valérie. 2002. *Les usages de la mémoire dans les relations internationales: le recours au passé dans la politique étrangère de la France à l'égard de l'Allemagne et de l'Algérie de 1962 à nos jours.* Bruxelles: Edition Bruylant.

Rovan, Joseph. 1972. "Les relations franco-allemandes dans le domaine de la jeunesse et de la culture populaire (1945–1971)." *Revue d'Allemagne et des pays de langue allemande* 4: 675–704.

Ziebura, Gilbert. 1970. *Die deutsch-französischen Beziehungen seit 1945. Mythen und Realitäten.* Pfullingen: G. Neske.

3 Forget and forgive?

Central European memory cultures, models of reconciliation and Polish-German relations

Annika Frieberg
San Diego State University

In December 1970, in Warsaw, Poland, Willy Brandt fell to his knees in front of the memorial commemorating the 1943 Warsaw Ghetto Uprising. He apologized wordlessly for German crimes committed against the Polish nation in the context of the German occupation of Poland 1939 to 1945 and the Holocaust. Was his apology effective? In international relations, philosophy, and peace research, a multitude of work on the dynamics of reconciliation, including truth and reconciliation processes and apology in foreign relations has appeared since the 1990s (Schneider 2006, 2012). The supporters of apology and truth telling defend the processes' transformative effects on post-war and post-genocidal societies. Meanwhile, critics have pointed to the necessity for gestures of regret to be accompanied by real change, including sincerity, majority support in the apologizing population, and reparations (Govier and Verwoerd 2005; Barkan and Karn 2006; Corntassel and Holder 2008). Scholars have argued for the victims' prerogative to determine when and whether they are ready to extend forgiveness to those issuing apologies. They also claim the victims' right to demand justice above regret, for example in the form of international tribunals. Much of the scholarship on reconciliation processes and apologies mention Polish-German relations as a positive model for peace processes. Here, I bridge comparative international conversations on peace processes with historic and specific research on Polish-German relations from a Central European borderland perspective before, during, and after the Second World War. The entwined and complex nature of Central European national histories decisively influenced how participants engaged with reconciliation. It must be taken into consideration in the development of theory and models of reconciliation.

Polish-German relations reached their low point during and immediately after the Second World War. However, the two peoples' coexistence and territorial conflict dated much further back. The earliest German-speaking settlers arrived in the eastern Polish territories in the Middle Ages. Further migrations took place in the seventeenth, eighteenth, and nineteenth centuries, particularly as Poland was partitioned by the Russian, Prussian, and Habsburg imperial neighbours in 1773, 1793, and finally erased fully from the map of Europe in 1795. Imperial

42 Annika Frieberg

shifts and German settlements in Polish territories created a complex multiethnic situation. In the 1920s, when Poland once more had sovereignty, ethnic Catholic Poles constituted 19 of 27 million inhabitants. The German minority was 1 million, or roughly 3.7% of the population. The western territories had higher ethnic German concentrations (Kamusella 2009; Chu 2012, 21). Other minorities within the borders of interwar Poland included Yiddish, Ukrainian, Lithuanian, and Russian speakers. Catholicism dominated the country's religious life but Poland also had Judaic, Orthodox Christian, Uniate, Protestant, and Muslim minorities. Also Galicia, the southern formerly Habsburg part of the country, was a truly mixed religious, ethnic, and cultural landscape where the boundaries between German, Jewish, Austrian, or Polish national belonging often blurred (Judson 2006; Frieberg 2010). The redrawing of borders based on the 1919 Versailles Treaty was frequently founded in regional plebiscites and sharpened the divisions between ethnic populations in this area (Blanke 1993; Blanke 2001). The territorial conflict worsened and the governments in Weimar Germany and Poland became increasingly invested in the fate of their minorities according to the dynamics that Rogers Brubaker once coined "external homeland nationalisms" (Brubaker 1996).

In this context of competitive yet entangled nation building and nationalizing, the Third Reich occupied Poland in September 1939. The Soviet Union and Germany once more partitioned Poland between them. Nazi Germany imposed one of the harshest occupation regimes in Europe. The occupying Germans envisioned clearing the new eastern territories entirely of Poles in order to create *Lebensraum*. Poles would be permitted to exist as a slave people within the borders of a smaller land area of the so-called General Government. To this end, the Germans transferred 2.8 million Poles to the Reich to contribute to the war effort as forced labour. A total of almost 6 million Polish citizens, including 3 million Jews, died. Meanwhile, the London-based Polish government in exile, from 1942 lobbied and planned for the removal of Poland's ethnic German population as a security measure in case of an allied victory. The expulsion of Germans from Poland took place in a two-stage process between 1944 and 1948 and involved, with the support and assistance of the victorious Allied Powers, the relocation of several million Germans out of Poland (Ther and Siljak 2001; Thum 2003; Glassheim 2010).[1] Such is the longue durée perspective and background of the need for reconciliation between Poles and Germans in the post-war era.

As a consequence of the growing attention to history written about and applied to the nineteenth and early twentieth century multicultural empires, borderlands, and areas in Europe where borders have been redrawn multiple times during the eighteenth century and forward, scholars furthered new theories by which to understand Central European history. In the 1990s, Polish-German relations were still a state-centered venture, intent on stabilizing and reaffirming the boundaries and demography of post-war Europe. In the 1990s after the final Border and Friendship Treaties between the reunited Federal Republic of Germany and Poland, a body of research emerged on Polish-German relations in the twentieth century. Such research traced the positive relations from a political and cultural perspective, presenting a path, and a model, for reconciliation (Jacobsen, Tomala and Kunesch-Jörres 1992; Wolff-Powęska 1993; Pięciak 1996; Tomala 1997; Bingen 1998; Ruchniewicz 2005; Böll, Wysocki and Ziemer 2009). Scholars debated which individuals, political leaders, and institutions within Poland and West Germany that could be credited with the positive changes. The Polish-German work and emerging scholarly community was conceived as an integral aspect of promoting stronger European relations but was also part of Polish and especially German domestic debates between conservatives and Social Democrats about preferable foreign policy alternatives. In the early 2000s, in addition, Poland was building support, sponsored by Germany, for its entrance into the European Union which became a reality in 2004.

However, scholarship also considered Polish-German relations based on the 1980s and 1990s nationalism research as initiated by scholars such as Hans Kohn (1961), Anthony D. Smith (1979), Ernest Gellner (1983), Eric Hobsbawm (1990), and Benedict Anderson (1991). These founding fathers of nationalism studies identified nations as culturally constructed units emerging with industrialization and modernity in Europe. They disagreed, however, to which extent top-down construction of nationalism interacted with the grassroots utilization of it, and also on whether nationalism and nation building was inherently destructive. In the 1990s, in an effort to explain the "return" of nationalism after the fall of communism in Eastern Europe, a large number of scholars utilized such studies to better understand the potentially destructive tendencies of post-war nation building as evidenced not only during the 1930s and 1940s European fascist era, but also during the 1990s Yugoslav Wars. Kohn, Anderson, and Gellner all discussed the emergence of nationalism in Central Europe extensively. Later scholarship followed suit, for example Jeremy King in *Budweisers into Czechs* (2002), which was a micro-history of the nationalizing of the population in Budweis/Budějovice, or Gregor Thum in his definite history of the polonization of Breslau/Wrocław in Silesia (Thum 2003). Thum as well as Timothy Snyder in his *The Reconstruction of Nations* on the history of Poland, Lithuania, Ukraine, and Belarus, showed that the nationalization process in Central Europe continued well after 1945 into the first decades of the Cold War (Snyder 2003).

In the 1990s, Polish-German studies were also complicated by the reintroduction of transnational studies into the field of history. Transnational studies is often defined as the flow of peoples, ideas, and contacts across borders or, alternatively, transnational relations as "regular interactions across national boundaries when at least one actor is a non-state agent or does not operate on behalf of a national government or an intergovernmental organization" (Risse-Kappen 1995, 459). Transnationalism was originally used in economic theory in the 1970s to analyze economic flows across borders. In the 1980s and 1990s it was co-opted by a multiplicity of fields, prominently international relations, to serve as a tool for the study of migration and the growing importance of non-state actors and non-governmental organizations in world politics. In Central European history, it offset the bounded and nation-centred nature of traditional Cold War studies

44 Annika Frieberg

and recognized the fluid and changing character of multiethnic populations in borderlands transformed through multiple state-formations and – upheavals.[2]

Transnational studies inspired a new understanding of German history. They indicated the fragmented and unstable nature of the modern German state and acknowledged the state's federal past, the late unification in the 1870s, the frequent discontinuity of German states in the nineteenth and twentieth centuries, and the east-west division of the state for the duration of the Cold War. Konrad Jarausch and Michael Geyer discussed this fragmentation in a seminal essay collection, *Shattered Past: Reconstructing German Histories* (2003), arguing that the "shattered" nature of German history required a recasting of its master narrative into multiple narratives. Others pointed out that the spread of German minority populations in Europe necessitated a more open-ended discussion of German national identities and pasts (Brubaker 1996; Wolff 2002). Based on such arguments, it is also necessary to consider reconciliation as diverse and pluralistic processes rather than based on top-down, centralized, and bilateral relations.

Other methodological approaches to French-German and Polish-German relations included entangled history and *histoire croisée*. Arguing that scholarship must escape the normative paradigm of the nation-state, comparativists extended their studies to find cross-border patterns and trends in intersocietal relations. In the German context, the Bielefeld school of history became particularly prominent in launching comparative studies.[3] Critics of comparative history argued that such studies nevertheless collapsed back into nation-centred frameworks. Instead, they proposed ventures of transfer histories emphasizing the cultural and political transfers and shared elements across borders as an antidote. A third approach was that of French sociologists Michael Werner's and Bénédicte Zimmerman's *histoire croisée*. It validated simultaneous and multiple approaches, including comparison and transfer, to transnational history. They also proposed that one's own personal perspective and bias must be inserted into the writing of entangled histories (Werner and Zimmerman 2006; Ther 2009).

Translated into concrete research approaches to Central Europe, these methodologies encouraged studies wherein multiple regional and national identities competed and overlapped in populations, especially during the 1930s and 1940s, an era of displacement and multiple ethnic cleansings. German historian Philipp Ther particularly recommended such studies of East Central European borderlands (Ther 2003). Today, there is a solid body of work on such loose regional identities, and their competition with overlapping national identities in Silesia, Masuria, Galicia, and in the Polish eastern territories, the *Kresy* (Kamusella 2009; Kasianov and Ther 2009; Chu 2012; Polak-Springer 2012; Kamusella et al., 2016). In these regions, language and nationalizing policies were imposed on local populations. Local populations, in turn, reacted sometimes with resistance but more often with pragmatism, basing national choices and decisions on concrete and practical considerations.

An important body of work also addressed the notion of "national indifference" in the borderlands. Historian James Bjork argued that the German and Polish nationalizing projects in Upper Silesia alienated the local population because of

Polish-German relations 45

their contradictory messages and that such populations instead turned to a bilingual Catholicism as a steadier and more constant identity choice (Bjork 2008). Tara Zahra approached the question of national belonging and national indifference through two studies of Central European orphans before, during, and after the Second World War. Given the enormous national and personal losses, these children were often claimed by rebuilding nations after the war. However, in the interaction between adopted children and their new families or in the personal preferences of teenagers who would rather stay where they had spent the war than "return" to native countries they barely remembered, national indifference took on new, practical meanings (Zahra 2008, 2011).

These plural and fluid models also have an impact on conflict and conflict resolution. I will focus on two common models of reconciliation to illustrate the challenges which incorporating borderland studies with conflict resolution. I will also show how, despite these difficulties, mixed spaces and borderland backgrounds often functioned as assets in Polish-German relations. One should remember that Polish-German relations were never a simple dyadic relationship. It is, in fact, a fallacy to discuss "Polish-German relations" assuming that they could be cleanly separated out from Polish-Jewish or Polish-Israeli, Polish-Russian, or Polish-Ukrainian relations. On closer investigation, they also fall apart into Polish-West German and Polish-East German relations. However, the participants themselves often spoke of "Polish-German relations" as though they were inseparable. In 1968, the Bensberger Memorandum, signed by 128 West German Catholics, assured its readers that German Catholics would "support with all their powers, that the German people respect the Polish people's national right to existence" (*Ein Memorandum Deutscher Katholiken Zu Den Polnisch-Deutschen Fragen* 1968). By separating out the German people from the state, they circumvented the problem of the German state's division and generalized their statement to all Germans. However, Catholics from the German Democratic Republic were in no way involved in the development of the document.[4] This tendency points to a larger problem of models. Models of conflict resolution tend to insufficiently incorporate multiple and varying modes of state- and national belonging as well as modern-day multi-group conflicts (He 2009). The relationship of the Poles to their post-war state differed in profound ways from the relationships of the Germans to theirs. Poles, after over 100 years of partitions and under top-down, widely unpopular communist rule, imagined their nation as spiritually separate from their state. This is evident in the Polish bishops' letter of reconciliation to the German bishops and in the bishops' and Cardinals' statements. Meanwhile, their German counterparts were more inclined to conflate the state and the nation despite Germany's post-war division.[5]

Social scientists William J. Long and Peter Brecke developed two larger reconciliation models in their study *War and Reconciliation: Reason and Emotion in Conflict Resolution*. They called them the signalling model and the forgiveness model. The application of these models to Polish-German relations clarifies some of the challenges which plurality, shifting demography, and borderland identities present to conflict resolution models and theory (Long and Brecke 2003).

46 Annika Frieberg

A signalling model, as described by Long and Brecke, is a moment when a leading representative of the state or nation makes a significant, costly, and irreversible gesture (Long and Brecke 2003, 3). The gesture carries cultural significance to recipients of it. The researchers mention Brandt's kneefall as such a gesture. The problem with the signalling model becomes apparent if an ethnically diverse or divided population does not identify fully with the leading representative issuing the apology. In the Federal Republic, according to polls undertaken by the Spiegel on December 14, 1970, *after* the gesture, 30%–40% of West Germans supported Brandt's initiative ("Spiegel-Umfrage: Durfte Brandt knien?" 1970).

The recipients' understanding of the apology matters equally, of course (Howard-Hassmann and Lombardo 2008).[6] In Poland, in 1970, the kneefall took place in front of the Warsaw Ghetto Monument. To the part of the Polish population subscribing to the ethnic Polish nationalism that was widespread mid-century and also in the aftermath of the anti-Zionist purges in 1968, Brandt's kneefall could be interpreted as directed to Poland's Jewish population, not ethnic Poles. While it was widely recognized in international and West German media, the kneefall was never transmitted through East German communist media nor were East Germans made part of the gesture (Wolffsohn and Brechenmacher 2005; Schneider 2006).[7] Finally, the gesture also took place within a communist commemorative and state framework. The German state representatives who travelled to Warsaw directed their dialogue and the bilateral agreements primarily at Polish communist moderate elites. Did the Polish larger population identify sufficiently with their state to recognize the West German diplomatic performance towards it, also after the overturning of the communist state? The initially weak connection between the apology and the Polish people required elites, media, and scholarship to emphasize and reinforce the importance of it in the 1970s as well as the 1990s. Fortunately, Brandt's kneefall, precisely because of its impulsive and non-verbal nature, was particularly well suited as a universal invitation for all Germans to partake in remorse (Münkel 2004).[8] Brandt modelled an individual expression of responsibility, remorse, and recognition vis-à-vis the neighbour. In this way, Germans could also retroactively identify with the gesture and with this particular representation of their nation while Poles could, if they chose, feel embraced by it.

Long and Brecke also introduced the so-called forgiveness model to theorize the process of reconciliation, more common in the aftermath of an internal conflict such as civil war, genocide, or ethnic cleansing. A prime example of a forgiveness model was the post-Apartheid Truth and Reconciliation Commission headed by Archbishop Desmond Tutu in South Africa (Freeman and Hayner 2003; Skaar, Gloppen and Suhrke 2005; Breed 2006; Chapman and van der Merwe 2008).[9] Interestingly, elements of a forgiveness model were used in Jewish-Polish, or German-Polish or Polish-Ukrainian relations, serving as evidence to the entangled histories of these nations, and the civil war–like elements of the Second World War in Eastern Europe (Mazower 1999, 212; Judt 2005, 32).[10] At the time of the war's outbreak, Polish, German, and Jewish populations had lived side-by-side in imperial and contested areas with shifting borders for

Polish-German relations 47

hundreds of years. After 1945, both nations were reconceived in public space as emerging through a "Stunde Null" as demographically coherent, stable, and homogeneous units. If truth telling and open dialogue were necessary aspects of a peace process, in this case they also had to be balanced with the creation and conceptual stabilizing of newly "imagined" national communities (Suhrke 2005; Anderson, 2006).[11]

Polish-German post-war relations raise questions about the value and importance of truth telling in reconciliation. Given the fragmented demographic and geographic situation, truth telling became a problematic prospect for post-war dialogue and reconstruction. The stabilization of homogeneous nations in the aftermath of drastic changes to demographic profiles and borders in the immediate post-war perspective required highly selective interpretations of the past and national memories. Premature or misplaced truths in this complex post-war reality threatened to undermine the establishment of dialogue. In the 1965 Polish Bishops' Letter of Reconciliation to the German bishops, the concluding phrase that resonated around the world was "We forgive and ask for forgiveness" (*Materialien Und Dokumente Zur Botschaft Der Polnischen Bischöfe* 1966)[12] One of the central figures to Polish-German non-state relations in these early days, Józefa Hennelowa, stated later that when she and other young church-loyal Catholics heard about the letter they understood why the bishops asked them to forgive but not why they were asking the Germans for forgiveness.

> We knew that it was our duty as Christians to forgive, also when this is difficult but we could not understand why the bishops had stated that "We ask for forgiveness." Back then, this was an absolute black hole in which we could not find ourselves again.
>
> (Hennelowa and Graczyk 2006, 202)[13]

The truth was, ultimately, that Poles had committed crimes against Germans during and immediately after the war. However, one might argue that this truth threatened to hamper the initiation of dialogue as mediated by the churches. Consequently, when the Polish Cardinal, Stefan Wyszyński, led thousands of Poles that had gathered on the holy site of Jaśna Góra the following spring of 1966 in chanting "We forgive! We forgive!" as a defiant gesture towards the state and a way to shore up Polish support for the bishops' initiative, he and the crowds omitted the phrase "We ask for forgiveness" (Heller 1992, 171).[14] The public discourse between Poles and Germans was primarily concerned with creating mutually acceptable memories of the past as a foundation for dialogue. The high numbers of displaced populations in Poland, East Germany, and West Germany and their truths were obstacles to building such consensuses. In multiethnic societies where atrocities have occurred and resource-competition is ongoing, the question is whether truth telling is desirable or possible as a path to peace.

On the other hand, the displaced and multilingual populations sometimes also functioned as resources in the establishment of early relations. Several of the Polish activists had existing French or German pre-war networks in place that they

48 Annika Frieberg

could utilize to build and expand connections with the other society. Bishop Kominek, the initiator of the 1965 bishops' letter, had long-standing German conversation partners that he had met in the 1920s and that he consulted with in drafting the letter of 1965 (Hanich, Komin and Kominek, 2012).[15] Another example was that of Klaus Otto Skibowski, an advisor to German Chancellor Konrad Adenauer, who organized initial visits of Polish Catholic intellectuals to West Germany in the 1950s and later played a role in the German-Masurian relations. Skibowski networked with Poles despite the hostile political climate and his own politically founded hesitations about the recognition of post-war Polish-German border based on the previously existing contacts between his family and prominent Polish Catholics.[16]

In addition, the bilinguality of borderland elites played a role in building dialogue and in finding common ground. Kominek as well as Stomma were fluent in German. In Stomma's case, his fluency came from childhood experiences under German First World War occupation and Kominek grew up in Silesia and went to German-language schools (Pailer 1995).[17] On the other hand, Bensberger Circle member Winfried Lipscher came from a German-speaking family but attended lyceum and became fluent in Polish before leaving for West Germany with his family in 1958 (Pfluger and Lipscher 1993). Finally, one might argue that the reason for the high number of participants in cross-border relations with a borderlands background can be a consequence of the borderlanders' alternative approaches to self-victimizing national myths and memories. Several of the Polish key figures in early Polish-German relations came from Lithuania and the intellectual circles in Vilnius (in Polish: Wilno). The German occupation in Vilnius had been less harsh than in the General Government during the war. Given this fact and Lithuania's geographic location near the Russian border, the Wilno-Poles tended to consider Russia the more troubling enemy and maintained a somewhat less antagonistic stance towards the Germans (Jarocki 1990, 28, 30; Hennelowa 2001; Snyder 2003, 54).

In the Cold War era, Polish-German relations seemed an extremely successful instance of conflict resolution. However, it also presented unique and specific challenges because of the disconnectedness between states and societies, unstable national boundaries and borders, multiple state upheavals, and disjointedness. A successful reconciliation process requires us to pay full attention to the involved countries' layered and multiethnic past. Polish-German peace building in particular must be understood in the context of post-war efforts to stabilize and reconstruct national units in Europe. Particularly, apologies might be less fruitful in multiethnic or borderland contexts because of the difficulties involved in representing, as well as satisfying, multilayered populations. It is also important to consider the temporality of such gestures. If they are directed to representatives of a time-bound or unstable state, will they remain landmarks of peace after that state disintegrates or that leadership is replaced? On the other hand, as Brandt's 1970 gesture shows, an apology might gain additional traction several decades later, in a new political context. Media plays a crucial role in translating the gesture to greater applicability in broader societal layers. As for truth telling,

Polish-German relations 49

another key aspect of reconciliation, Polish-German relations indicate that there are tangible limits to such practices. Truth telling can equally hamper as further the initiation of contacts and dialogue. It can certainly be detrimental to (re)constructing nationally unified communities after the end of federal state solutions or empires. Polish-German relations suggest that consensus building and the identification of mutually acceptable truths played a more important role in early post-war reconciliation. Unfortunately, consensus building often comes at the cost of minority rights, memories, and representation. Polish-German relations were neither a fully dualistic nor a single, central development. Diverse, non-state, drawn-out, local, and individual processes contributed to the establishment of improved relations and dialogue between those societies. In such developments, bilingual populations with transnational networks and loosened or alternative national identities can also become great resources to reconciliation.

Notes

1 Much research emerged on the expulsions of Germans from Eastern Europe in the early 2000s. See, for example Ther and Siljak (2001). See also research by Thum (2003) Glassheim (2010) on ethnic cleansing and the transformation of the borderlands.or

2 For example Pieter Judson (2006) described the emergence of recruiting nationalist organizations in the Habsburg imperial borderlands in the late nineteenth and early twentieth centuries.

3 This term refers to a group of historians, including Hans-Ulrich Wehler, Jürgen Kocka, and Reinhard Koselleck, based at the University of Bielefeld, and promoting social and political history. The Bielefeld School has existed since the 1970s.

4 I base this assertion on the study of correspondences surrounding the Bensberger Memorandum and Circle as preserved in the Friedrich-Eberth-Stiftung in Bonn.

5 German post-war reconciliatory intellectuals, elites, and journalists were more inclined to assume a natural symbiosis between state and nation, a symbiosis which they they applied to analysis of Poland. The fact that the German nation was, in fact, divided into two states, they considered an unnatural and problematic state.

6 As a series of European powers apologized in the 1990s for colonial abuse in Africa, Rhoda E. Howard-Hassman and Anthony Lombardo (2008) researched the reception of such apologies among African elites. These recipient elites emphasized the need for reparations, particularly considering the continued economic inequality between the apologizing western powers and the African recipients of apologies.

7 See, for example Schneider, Christoph. 2006. *Das Warschauer Kniefall.* Konstanz: UKV Verlagsgesellschaft GmbH or Wolffsohn, Tomas and Michael Brechenmacher. 2005. *Denkmalssturz? Brandts Kniefall.* Munich: Olzog Verlag GmbH, 26.

8 For the performative aspects of Brandt's politics, see Münkel, Daniela. 2004. "Als 'deutscher Kennedy' zum Sieg? Willy Brandt, die USA und die Medien." *Zeithistorische forschungen* 1: 172–194.

9 Gloppen, Siri. 2005. "Roads to Reconciliation: A Conceptual Framework." In *Roads to Reconciliation,* edited by Elin Skaar, Siri Gloppen and Astri Suhrke, 27–37. Lanham, Boulder, New York, Toronto, Oxford: Lexington Books; Freeman, Mark and Priscilla B. Hayner. 2003. "Truth-Telling." In *Reconciliation after Violent Conflict: A Handbook,* edited by David Bloomfield, Teresa Barnes and Luc Haynes, 122–139. Halmstad: Bulls Tryckeri AB; Breed, Ananda. 2006.

50 *Annika Frieberg*

"Performing Reconciliation in Rwanda." *Peace Studies* 18(4), Oct–Dec: 507–513; *Truth and Reconciliation in South Africa: Did the TRC Deliver?* edited by Audrey R. Chapman and Hugo van der Merwe. Philadelphia: University of Philadelphia Press.

10 See Judt, Tony. 2002. *Post-War: A History of Europe since 1945.* New York: Penguin, 32 or Mazower, Mark. 2002. *Dark Continent: Europe's Twentieth Century,* 2nd ed. New York: Vintage Books, 212.

11 For the concept of the imagined national community see Anderson, Benedict. 2006. *Imagined Communities: Reflection on the Origins and Spread of Nationalism,* rev. ed. London, New York: Verso, for imagined communities in reconciliation Skaar, Elin, Siri Gloppen and Astri Suhrke, "Introduction." In *Roads to Reconciliation,* edited by Elin Skaar, Siri Gloppen and Astri Suhrke, 4. Lanham, Boulder, New York, Toronto, Oxford: Lexington Books, 2005.

12 "Die Botschaft der polnischen Bischöfe an die deutschen Bischöfe, Rom, 18. November 1965," *Bonn-Warschau* 139.

13 Hennelowa, Józefa, "Gespräch mit Józefa Hennelowa." In *Wir vergeben und bitten um Vergebung' Der Briefwechsel der polnischen und deutschen Bischöfe von 1965 und seine Wirkung,* edited by Basil Kerski, Thomas Zycia and Robert Żurek, 202. Osnabrück: Fibre. Hennelowa is referring to meetings in the Catholic milieu with Wojtyła and his young mentees that he had gathered around himself in Krakow as Archbishop.

14 Heller, Edith and Gabriele Lesser. 1992. *Macht, Kirche, Politik.* Köln: Treffpunkt-Verlag, 171.

15 See Hanich, Andrzej and Bolesław Kominek. 2012. *Ksiądz infułat Bolesław Kominek.* Opole: Nakład Wyczerpany.

16 Skibowski, Klaus Otto. 2005. Interview by Annika Frieberg, Bonn, 3 Feb.

17 Pailer, Wolfgang. 1995. *Stanisław Stomma.* Bonn: Bouvier, 26.

References

Anderson, Benedict R. O'G. 1991. *Imagined Communities.* London: Verso.

Anderson, Benedict. 2006. *Imagined Communities: Reflection on the Origins and Spread of Nationalism,* rev. ed. London, New York: Verso.

Barkan, Elazar and Alexander Karn. 2006. *Taking Wrongs Seriously.* Stanford, CA: Stanford University Press.

Bingen, Dieter. 1998. *Polen-Politik der Bonner Republik von Adenauer bis Kohl, 1945–1990.* Baden-Baden: Nomos Verlagsgesellschaft.

Bjork, James E. 2008. *Neither German Nor Pole.* Ann Arbor, MI: University of Michigan Press.

Blanke, Richard. 1993. *Orphans of Versailles.* Lexington: University Press of Kentucky.

———. 2001. *Polish-Speaking Germans?* Köln: Böhlau.

Böll, Friedhelm, Klaus Ziemer and Wiesław Wysocki. 2009. *Versöhnung Und Politik: Polnisch-Deutsche Versöhnungsinitiativen Der 1960Er-Jahre Und Die Entspannungspolitik,* 1st ed. Bonn: Dietz.

Breed, Ananda. 2006. "Performing Reconciliation in Rwanda." *Peace Studies* Oct-Dec. 2006: 507–513.

Brubaker, Rogers. 1996. *Nationalism Reframed.* Cambridge, England: Cambridge University Press.

Chu, Winson. 2012. *The German Minority in Interwar Poland.* Cambridge: Cambridge University Press.

Corntassel, Jeff J. and Cindy L. Holder. 2008. "Who's Sorry Now? Government Apologies, Truth Commissions and Indigenous Self-determination in Australia, Canada, Guatemala and Peru." *Human Rights Revue* 9(4): 465–489.

Ein Memorandum Deutscher Katholiken Zu Den Polnisch-Deutschen Fragen. 1968. Mainz: Matthias-Grünewald-Verlag.

Frieberg, Annika. 2010. "Transnational Spaces in National Places: Early Activists in Polish–West German Relations." *Nationalities Papers* 38(2): 213–226. doi:10.1080/00905990903517843.

Gellner, Ernest. 1983. *Nations and Nationalism.* Ithaca, NY: Cornell University Press.

Glassheim, Eagle. 2010. Zbigniew Bochniarz and Gary B. Cohen, Eds. "The Environment and Sustainable Development in the New Central Europe. New York: Berghahn Books, 2006, 260, Illus., Maps, Tables." *Austrian History Yearbook* 41: 284. doi:10.1017/s0067237809990415.

Govier, Trudy and Wilhelm Verwoer. 2005. "Forgiveness: The Victim's Prerogative." *South African Journal of Philosophy*, 21(1): 97–111.

Hanich, Andrzej, Bolesław Kominek and Bolesław Kominek. 2012. *Ksiądz Infułat Bolesław Kominek.* Opole: Państwowy Instytut Naukowy - Instytut Śląski w Opolu.

Hayner, Priscilla and Mark Freeman. 2003. "Truth-Telling." In *Reconciliation after Violent Conflict: A Handbook*, 1st ed., edited by David Bloomfield, Teresa Barnes and Luc Huyse, 122–139. Halmstad: Bulls Tryckeri AB.

He, Yinan. 2009. *The Search for Reconciliation.* Cambridge: Cambridge University Press.

Heller, Edith and Gabriele Lesser. 1992. *Macht, Kirche, Politik.* Köln: Treffpunkt-Verlag.

Hennelowa, Józefa. 2006. "Gespräch mit Józefa Hennelowa." In *Wir Vergeben Und Bitten Um Vergebung*, edited by Basil Kerski, Thomas Kycia and Robert Zurek, 197–210. Osnabrück: Fibre.

Hennelowa, Józefa and Roman Graczyk. 2001. *Bo Jestem Z Wilna –.* Kraków: Społeczny Instytut Wydawniczy ZNAK.

Hobsbawm, E.J. 1990. *Nations and Nationalism Since 1780.* Cambridge, England: Cambridge University Press.

Howard-Hassman, Rhoda and Anthony Lombardo. 2008. "Words Require Actions: African Elite Opinion about Apologies from the 'West.'" In *The Age of Apology. Facing Up to the Past*, 1st ed., edited by Mark Gibney, Rhoda Howard-Hassman, Jean-Marc Coicaud and Niklaus Steiner, 216–228. Philadelphia, PA: University of Philadelphia Press.

Jacobsen, Hans Adolf, Mieczysław Tomala and Dagmar Kunesch-Jörres. 1992. *Bonn-Warschau 1945–1991.* Köln: Verlag Wissenschaft und Politik.

Jarausch, Konrad Hugo and Michael Geyer. 2003. *Shattered Past.* Princeton, NJ: Princeton University Press.

Jarocki, Robert. 1990. *Czterdzieści pięć lat w opozycji* (o ludziach "Tygodnika Powszechnego"), Kraków: Wydawnictwo Literackie.

Judson, Pieter M. 2006. *Guardians of the Nation.* Cambridge, MA: Harvard University Press.

Judt, Tony. 2005. *Postwar.* New York: Penguin Press.

Kamusella, Tomasz. 2009. *The Politics of Language and Nationalism in Modern Central Europe.* Basingstoke, England: Palgrave Macmillan.

Kamusella, Tomasz et al., eds. 2016. *Creating Nationality in Central Europe, 1880–1950: Modernity, Violence and (Be)Longing in Upper Silesia.* London: Routledge, 2016.

52 *Annika Frieberg*

Kasianov, Georgij Vladimirovič and Philipp Ther. 2009. *A L onal History*. Budapest: Central European University Press.

King, Jeremy. 2002. *Budweisers into Czechs and Germans*. Princeton, NJ: Princeton University Press.

Kohn, Hans. 1961. *The Age of Nationalism*. New York: Harper.

Long, William J. and Peter Brecke. 2003. *War and Reconciliation*. Cambridge, MA: MIT Press.

Materialien Und Dokumente Zur Botschaft Der Polnischen Bischöfe. 1966. Warszawa : Polnische Berichte.

Mazower, Mark. 1999. *Dark Continent*. New York: A.A. Knopf.

Münkel, Daniela. 2004. "Als "Deutscher Kennedy" Zum Sieg? Willy Brandt, Die USA Und Die Medien." *Zeithistorische Forschungen* 1: 172–194.

Pailer, Wolfgang. 1995. *Stanisław Stomma*. Bonn: Bouvier.

Pięciak Wojciech. 1996. *Polacy i Niemcy pół wieku później – księga pamiątkowa dla Mieczysława Pszona*, ed. Wojciech Pięciak. Krakow: Wydawnictwo Znak.

Pflüger, Friedbert and Winfried Lipscher. 1993. *Feinde Werden Freunde*. Bonn: Bouvier.

Polak-Springer, Peter. 2012. "Landscapes of Revanchism: Building and the Contestation of Space in an Industrial Polish-German Borderland, 1922–1945." *Central European History* 45(3): 485–522. doi:10.1017/s0008938912000362.

Risse-Kappen, Thomas. 1995. *Bringing Transnational Relations Back In: Non-State Actors, Domestic Structures and International Institutions*. Cambridge: Cambridge University Press.

Ruchniewicz, Krzysztof. 2005. *Zögernde Annäherung*. Dresden: Thelem.

Schneider, Christoph. 2006. *Der Warschauer Kniefall. Ritual, Ereignis und Erzählung*. Konstanz: UVK Verlagsgesellschaft.

Skaar, Elin, Siri Gloppen and Astri Suhrke. 2005. *Roads to Reconciliation*. Lanham: Lexington Books.

Smith, Anthony D. 1979. *Theories of Nationalism*. New York: Harper & Row.

Snyder, Timothy. 2003. *The Reconstruction of Nations: Poland, Ukraine, Lithuania, Belarus, 1569-1999*. New Haven, NJ: Yale University Press.

Ther, Philipp. 2003. "Beyond the Nation: The Relational Basis of a Comparative History of Germany and Europe." *Central European History* 36(1): 45–73. doi:10.1163/156916103770892168.

———. 2009. "Comparisons, Cultural Transfers, and the Study of Networks. Toward a Transnational History of Europe." In *Comparative and Transnational History. Central European Approaches and New Perspectives*, 1st ed., edited by Heinz-Gerhard Haupt and Jürgen Kocka, 204–226. New York: Berghahn.

Ther, Philipp and Ana Siljak. 2001. *Redrawing Nations*. Lanham, MD: Rowman & Littlefield.

Thum, Gregor. 2003. *Die fremde Stadt Breslau 1945*. Berlin: Verlag Wolf Jobst Siedler GmbH.

Tomala, Mieczysław. 1997. *Patrząc na Niemcy. Od wrogości do porozumienia*. Warsaw: Polska Fundacja Spraw Międzynarodowych.

Tomala, Mieczysław. 2005. *Polityka I Dyplomacja Polska Wobec Niemiec*. Warszawa: Dom Wydawniczy "Elipsa."

Van der Merwe, Hugo and Audrey R. Chapman. 2008. *Truth and Reconciliation in South Africa*. Philadelphia, PA: University of Pennsylvania Press.

Werner, Michael and Benedicte Zimmermann. 2006. "Beyond Comparison: Histoire Croisee and the Challenge of Reflexivity." *History and Theory* 45(1): 30–50. doi:10.1111/j.1468–2303.2006.00347.x.

Wolff, Stefan. 2002. "From Colonists to Emigrants: Explaining the 'Return-Migration' of Ethnic Germans from Central and Eastern Europe." In *Coming Home to Germany. The Integration of Ethnic Germans from Central and Eastern Europe in the Federal Republic*, 1st ed., edited by David Rock and Stefan Wolff, 1–18. New York: Berghahn.

Wolff-Powęska, Anna. 1993. *Polacy Wobec Niemców*. Poznań: Instytut Zachodni.

Wolffsohn, Tomas and Michael Brechenmacher. 2005. *Denkmalssturz? Brandts Kniefall*. Munich: Olzog.

Zahra, Tara. 2008. *Kidnapped Souls*. Ithaca, NY: Cornell University Press.

———. 2011. *The Lost Children*. Cambridge, MA: Harvard University Press.

4 Apology and confession

Comparing Sino-Japanese and German-Jewish intellectual resources for reconciliation

C. K. Martin Chung

> But we have sinned . . . this is the most essential part of confession.
> – (Maimonides 1994, 425)[1]

One of the more common Chinese terms used for "reconciliation" is *hejie*. "He" can signify peace and harmony. "Jie", on the other hand, conjures up images of untying (*jiekai*) and understanding (*lijie*). To untie "knots in the heart" (*xinjie*) is, therefore, one way of conceptualizing reconciliation in Chinese culture. Under this conceptualization, there are different knots to be untied in the Sino-Japanese relationship: the 300,000 number of casualties in the Nanjing Massacre; the missing word of *shazai* 謝罪 in the litany of Japanese official statements of apology; not the least the symbolic meaning of the Senkaku/Diaoyu Islands. Yang Daqing has already elaborated on the pitfalls of the "number issue" in Nanjing-related debates (2012, 186–189), the de-deification of which is essential to the untying of that particular knot. He Yinan, on the other hand, has challenged the entanglement of "national mythmaking" in both China and Japan by using the German-Polish experience (2009). This chapter is dedicated to the untying of another knot, the knot of *shazai*, in light of comparative research.

For some Japanese it is puzzling why after successive official apologies Japan is still being accused by some Chinese and Koreans for "not having apologized". One Chinese argument by the former premier Zhu Rongji for the non-recognition of the Murayama apology (and subsequent sound-alikes) is that it was not specifically addressing the Chinese people as such (Yang 2013, 32). From the Korean side, on the other hand, one criticism is that the word shazai has been missing (Yamazaki 2006, 48, 55, 162).[2] Lately, Japanese prime minister Shinzo Abe lamented that Japanese born after the war should not be made to bear the "fate of shazai" (sankei.com 2015).[3] A few days later, a state media in China explicitly requested that emperor Akihito should learn from Willy Brandt to do xiezui on behalf of his father, the deceased wartime emperor Hirohito (posthumously Showa) (xinhuanet.com 2015). The "knot" in this case thus takes the form of disagreement on what constitutes a proper apology, and whether and how it should be expressed.

Sino-Japanese and German-Jewish resources 55

Shazai, sajoei in Korean or xiezui in Mandarin is, in fact, a Chinese concept. It is of ancient origins, as we'll see later, but is still applied at present in Chinese discourse on Sino-Japanese relations. Azuma Shiro is upheld by Zhu Chengshan, curator of the Memorial Hall of the Victims in Nanjing Massacre, for example as a xiezui-model (Zhu 2002). Xiezui is also used by others to label Germany in comparison with "revisionist" Japan, as can be seen lately in the exponential growth of the term in the website of the foreign ministry of the People's Republic of China (PRC), wherein Chinese ambassadors and consuls-general around the world praised Germany's "xiezui" and blamed Japan's alleged lack of such.[4]

Though state apologies have been a subject of scholarly interest (Lübbe 2001; Dudden 2008; Lind 2008), none as far as the present author can gather has delved into the origins and connotations of Chinese xiezui and their implications for the present "apology diplomacy" or "apology politics" in East Asia. This study aims to fill this gap by tracing the intellectual roots of xiezui in classical Chinese writings, especially in *Shiji*, or the *Records of the Grand Historian*. This will establish xiezui as a distinct system of post-wrongdoing expression centred on the idea of hierarchical trespasses. This is why it is a great mistake, I argue, to prescribe xiezui as a solution to the present-day problem of reconciliation in the region, for it confuses power-hierarchical concerns with moral ones. The chapter ends by highlighting the Jewish idea of "confession" as an alternative response to past wrongdoing. The aim is to examine traditional narratives of apology (or confession) as intellectual resources for political reconciliation, while at the same time calling attention to the peculiar obstacles they sometimes present.

Xiezui as a system of post-wrongdoing expression

A simple search in the database of Chinese classics shows that xiezui is no contemporary construct. It appears about a dozen times just in *Shiji*, the first of the Twenty-Four Histories, alone – this is not counting incidences in which the shortened form "xie" is used. If related or interchangeable concepts such as *qingzui* and *xieguo* are added, the incidence count jumps to over twenty. Considering the length of the *Records* (some half a million characters in 130 books), this constitutes in no way "widespread" usage. There are also other classics in which the incidence counts of xiezui are higher. But given the unparalleled moral and epistemological weight enjoyed by Shiji when it comes to Chinese historiography and historical thinking (Wang and Iggers 2002, 9), this study concentrates on these known incidences in the *Records*, traditionally ascribed to the grand historian Sima Qian.[5] The objective is to explore xiezui as an existent system of apology involving not just individuals by also "states" at this early stage (Shiji was written around 100 BCE).[6] With this we can then contrast not only other systems of post-wrongdoing expression but also its own contemporary applications, which include government statements as well as popular entertainment, such as the 2010 film, *Confucius* (produced in the Mainland and starring Chow Yun-fat from Hong Kong), in which one of the more memorable scenes of state

56   C. K. Martin Chung

apology took the form of returning conquered territories from the State of Qi to the State of Lu. The latent suggestion for interstate relations at present cannot be more apparent.

To begin with the obvious, xiezui, or literally, "thanking guilt/punishment", like any other concepts, does not "function" alone. It is used in conjunction with concepts such as *dezui*, or "acquiring guilt", *deguo*, or "acquiring mistake", *qingzui*, or "inviting guilt/punishment", and *xieguo*, or "thanking mistake". In theory, the apologizing party has by way of action or omission first acquired guilt vis-à-vis the apology-seeking party, who may or may not demand an account of guilt (*wenzui*). The offending party then invites punishment from the offended party and expresses gratitude for the lessened/limited punishment or outright pardon.

For example in the "Biographies of the Marquis of Wei Qi and the Marquis of Wu An", a man named Guan Fu acquired guilt towards (dezui) the Marquis of Wu An by way of expressing some disrespectful remarks during a drinking spree in the latter's wedding banquet. It gave rise to the need of apology (xiezui), which in this context was "ordered" by the Marquis but refused by his subject (107:20–21).[7] In due time, the Marquis of Wu An would also have to do xiezui for his own guilt. We'll come back to this story later.

When it comes to the actual acts of xiezui, a number of gestures and expressions are described in Shiji. In the previous example, the xiezui demanded was in the form of kowtow, or bowing down one's head, which is one of the most common gestures (60:30; 101:5). Other incidents of xiezui include baring one's body (79:20; 81:2, 8; 103:6; 118:2; 124:10), carrying thorns or one's own instrument of punishment (81:2, 8; 58:10), and crawling on all fours (79:20). There are other more sophisticated acts of xiezui, such as political realignment and returning previously won territories, which will be further analyzed later.

Going beyond these physical demonstrations of xiezui, there are several salient features of this system of apology. The first one concerns the question of what constitutes "guilt", or zui. From the cases in Shiji surveyed in this study, it seems that xiezui takes place primarily in the context of what one may call "hierarchical trespasses". One party trespasses against the other and thereby overstepping the power relations between the two, resulting in either the deprivation of honour or the failure to demonstrate loyalty as due the offended party. As explained in *Lunheng*, a Han Dynasty classic: "when an official has acquired guilt towards (*dezui*) the sovereign, when a son has trespassed against (*huoguo*) the father, he should reform himself and apologize (*xiezui*)" (Ming Yu 45:19).[8] Aside from the example of Guan Fu already cited, in the "Biographies of Knight Errants", xiezui was performed by an "arrogant man" who had not shown respect to Guo Jie, a chivalric figure, as others were used to do (124:10).[9] In the "House of the Three Kings", the prince of Yan apologized (*xieguo*) after his planned rebellion against the emperor, his brother, had been exposed (60:30).

Even in the "House of Confucius" where the famous "reconciliation meeting" (*haohui*) at Jiagu between the rulers of Lu and Qi was documented, apology (*xieguo*) in the form of returning invaded territories was occasioned not by

Sino-Japanese and German-Jewish resources 57

the recognition of the wrongful act committed (i.e. Qi's invasion of Lu lands), but by the Qi sovereign's self-professed acquisition of guilt towards (*dezui*) the sovereign of Lu, because the entertainment programmes run by Qi officials were deemed by Master Kong, who was serving Lu at that time, as "barbarous" and thus not appropriate for the occasion. The dwarf entertainer met, in fact, the fate of "separating the arms from the legs", or abdominal vivisection, at the behest of Confucius for punishment. The gesture of apology thus followed the advice of Qi's leading officials to their sovereign, who was troubled by the acquired guilt: "a gentleman who has committed a mistake (*guo*) apologizes (*xie*) by deeds whereas a petty man apologizes for his mistake with words" (47:17). Hence as a gentleman who had embarrassed himself by allowing unbecoming entertainment to be performed, the ruler of Qi apologized to his counterpart in Lu by the concrete deed of returning conquered lands.

There are some exceptions to hierarchical trespasses, which we'll look at later. But in connection with this conception of guilt, another characteristic of xiezui will be examined in the meantime, which concerns the identities of the apology-giving and apology-seeking parties. Given the preoccupation with hierarchy in xiezui as a system of apology, it should come as no surprise that in most cases the offended party were imperial entities if not the emperor himself. In such a relational context, the damage of the "wrongful" act in question was considered solely in between the hierarchy-trespasser and the trespassed. Aside from the relevant examples already cited, one can add the illustrative instance of xiezui in the "House of Prince Xiao of Liang". After committing the politically motivated murder of a group of officials, Prince Xiao did xiezui first to his queen mother with the help of the princess, and then to his emperor brother with the help of the queen, by carrying his own instrument of punishment (58:9–10). The trespasser was "reconciled" on the spot with the queen and the emperor, with no word on or for the murdered victims.

In some cases, xiezui took place in situations where there was no moral content whatsoever; it appeared merely as expression of power politics. For example in the "House of Lu Zhougong", xiezui was, in fact, a political act of bowing down to a foreign power to the disadvantage of one's own political opponent at home. Ji Pingzi from the State of Lu apologized (*xiezui*) to the king of Jin in an effort to prevent the latter from welcoming and hence siding with his political contender and exile, Lu Zhaogong (33:64). Similarly, in the "Treatise on the Eastern Yue", xiezui was nothing but political kowtow by Min Yue to the emperor of Han, recognizing the power of the latter and reaffirming the political allegiance of the former (114:4). The primary concern of xiezui for hierarchical trespasses in view of power relations is particularly visible in examples where questions of right or wrong are sidelined by realities of might. For example in another more memorable scene of Shiji, the "Feast of Hong Gate", or popularly known as *hong men yan*, in the "Annals of Xiang Yu", Liu Bang, who would eventually rise to found the Han Dynasty, "apologized" (xie) to Xiang Yu, for nothing other than the "wrongdoing" of having conquered the Qin capital of Xianyang ahead of the more senior-ranking and powerful Xiang Yu. This is in spite of the fact that King

58   *C. K. Martin Chung*

Huai (II) of Chu, whom both Liu and Xiang were serving, had promised the city as a reward to whoever conquered it first (7:18). The resulting apology took the form of a symbolically poignant seating arrangement in a "feast", through which the relative superiority and inferiority of Xiang and Liu were re-instituted, hence the honor-redistributive function of xiezui. According to Yu Ying-shih, who considered this act of xiezui on the part of Liu Bang as a brilliant stratagem:

> Xiang Yu agreed at the end to be seated at the west facing east, and Liu Bang to be seated at the south facing north, this shows that he had already considered Liu as his underling and officially accepted Liu's expression of servitude. By the time when both host and guest were seated, Xiang had already given up the thought of killing Liu.
>
> (1982, 194)

The third characteristic of this system of apology concerns the consequences of xiezui. From the cases examined in this study, there is no one single prevalent outcome of xiezui: in some cases the wished-for pardon was granted; others resulted in some form of shaming (possibly as an honor-redistributive device); while still others were directly associated with death as the proper form of xiezui. It seems that in all these instances, the main idea is to redistribute honour and to expressly recognize the prevalent hierarchy violated by the apologizing party. Hence the focus on the "lowering" of trespasser rather than on examining the wrongful act itself.

For success cases of reconciliation, aside from the example of Prince Xiao cited earlier ("reconciled just like before", 58:10), perhaps the most memorable one was Lian Po's xiezui to Lin Xiang Ru. True to form, the event began with a (perceived) hierarchical trespass, in which Lian Po, a war hero, felt that the recent promotion of Lin Xiang Ru to a higher rank, who was but a "mere worker with mouth and tongue . . . from lowly origins", was a great injustice suffered. He decided to insult the literati whenever they met. Lin, however, avoided such encounter, even faking illness and going into hiding. His followers were indignant that their master proved such a coward; they threatened to call it quits. Lin explained that he was not afraid of Lian – for he had just proven his courage even before the much more fearful king of Qin, for which he had earned his promotion to begin with. Lin avoided collision with the general because of his concern for the country – as the two top officials of the State of Zhao, their feud would have meant a golden opportunity for Qin to invade their state. "I've been avoiding him," Lin explained, "for I prioritize the nation's concerns over private vengeance" (81:8). Upon learning this, Lian Po bared his body and carried thorns, accompanied by friends to Lin's house to apologize (*xiezui*)[10] to him. "Being a shallow person, I did not know your magnanimity is of such depth!" The two reportedly became companions of life and death.[11]

Xiezui, however, was not always successful. As the following example shows, it can also mean abject humiliation. In the State of Wei there was a poor but brilliant political adviser named Fan Sui. He was wrongly accused of treason by his superior, Xu Jia, suffered torture and was thrown into the lavatory where people urinated on him as precautionary humiliation for others (79:2). Fan Sui somehow managed to survive his ordeal, escaped to the State of Qin under a pseudonym, and eventually became the chief councillor there. Then came a time when Wei felt threatened by the military expansion of Qin, thereupon sending Xu Jia there to gather information. Knowing this, Fan Sui put on ragged clothes and walked to meet his former superior. The two met, with Fan Sui pretending to be just a lowly worker, offering to help Xu Jia, who was eager to meet the famed chief councillor of Qin. Xu eventually learned that Fan was, in fact, *the* powerful councillor he had endeared to meet. Thereupon the Wei official bared his body, crawled on his knees, bowed his head, and apologized (*xiezui*) to Fan Sui:

> I never imagined you could rise up to such a high-level position on your own, I dare not read the books of the world anymore, dare not engage myself again with world affairs, my punishment is the boiling death (*tang huo zhi zui*), please exile me to barbarous lands, my life and death are in your hands.
>
> (79:20)

The Qin councillor "forgave" him,[12] but made him swallow a feast of humiliation: all the emissaries were invited to a sumptuous banquet "sitting above", while Xu was fed horse fodder by two criminals "sitting below" (79:21). This abject shaming was, of course, not directed only at Xu as a person, but at the entire State of Wei, for Fan demanded that Xu convey the message to the King of Wei: "bring me the head of Wei Qi [culprit of Fan's torture and humiliation] or else I'm going to massacre Daliang [capital of Wei]" (79:21).

Fan Sui was described by the Grand Historian as someone who "would reward even the favor of a meal, and avenge even an unfriendly glare" (79:22). Yet his granting his former enemy to do xiezui through shaming could seem "merciful" in comparison with some other cases where it was associated with death. The political xiezui by Min Yue to the Han emperor mentioned earlier was, in fact, consummated by presenting the head of the king ("We'll kill our king to apologize [xie] to the Son of Heaven") as proof of renewed allegiance (114:4). In another instance, a collective xiezui was executed as a form of substitutive punishment. In the "Biographies of Huai Nan and Heng Shan", Emperor Wen of Han blamed himself for not having listened to his adviser, Yuan Ang, on how to properly punish his rebellious brother, King of Huai Nan, resulting in the unintended death of the latter and thereby earning the emperor the notorious "name of killing one's own brother". Yuan counselled the emperor to "loosen oneself up" (*zi kuan*) by "merely" beheading those officials who had recommended the punishment of Huai Nan, as a means to "apologize to the world" (*yi xie tian xia*) (118:10). Emperor Wen accepted the counsel, ordered the execution, and had their corpses exposed to the public (*qi shi*).[13]

In the one instance of xiezui in Shiji in which the moral rather than power-hierarchical character of the "guilt" in question is beyond doubt, the expression

60   C. K. Martin Chung

was accompanied by a brooding guilt that finds no way out other than death. The face-deprived Marquis of Wu An (see earlier) ordered the arrest of the disrespectful and xiezui-refusing Guan Fu as well as his family and relatives, to be punished with "beheading and exposure". Guan Fu's ally, the Marquis of Wei Qi, came head to head with Wu An in front of the emperor in order to save his friend's life. Eventually both Wei Qi and Guan Fu were executed. The victor, however, did not enjoy the deaths of those who had "acquired guilt" towards him but, instead, suffered from what one may call "severe pangs of conscience". In the spring following Wei Qi's execution, "the Marquis of Wu An fell ill and unceasingly cried out his apology (*xiezui*)" (107:25). A witch-doctor was called in to look at him, who reported of seeing the ghosts of Wei Qi and Guan Fu besieging the Marquis, wanting to kill him. The guilt-stricken man eventually died.

From xiezui-system to "xiezui-model"

These examples in Shiji, as the paradigmatic text of Chinese historical understanding, suggest that xiezui as a system of apology is primarily about hierarchical trespasses in a bilateral relationship, with the function of redistributing honour, resulting in, at times, the pardoning of the hierarchy-trespasser (with no or lessened punishment), while at other times associated with shaming and death. While it is to be explored whether such a system of apology was "effective" in generating reconciliation in ancient China, our study, which is primarily concerned with the problem of applying xiezui in the East Asian context at present, must now turn to the problem of applicability. Is xiezui applicable in the present context? Can it address the present-day need for a moral response after state-sanctioned crimes against civilians? Can it still be a common reference point for post-atrocity relations in East Asia?

Chinese observers have long perceived in Willy Brandt's *Kniefall* in Warsaw *the* model xiezui in contemporary history, which Japanese leaders should purportedly learn from if not outright imitate. Aside from the numerous albeit casual remarks already cited earlier, there are also book-length treatments of the topic. The People's Liberation Army Press, for example published a book in 2000 advertising Brandt's gesture as testament to Germany's xiezui to the Polish people, in contrast to "Japan's revisionism" (Peng 2001, 137, 208). On the other hand, even when Taiwanese scholars express reservation about Beijing's demand for Japanese xiezui, it tends to differ only in terms of *who* should receive the apology (i.e. the Republic of China instead of the People's Republic), instead of questioning the applicability of the ancient concept itself (Chen 2015). In other words, it seems that from across the political and intellectual spectrum in the Chinese-speaking world, the unspoken consensus is that xiezui is an appropriate category with which contemporary political apologies are to be perceived and evaluated.

Yet this external view of Brandt's Kniefall as xiezui is a gross misreading of the gesture, neglecting the internal understanding of it. Consequently the prescription of this so-called xiezui-model is based on a flawed interpretation. In fact, within German-Jewish discourse, the act was first and foremost perceived

Sino-Japanese and German-Jewish resources 61

as *confession* (*Bekenntnis* in German) – that is a religious act derived from Judaism through Christianity – before the murdered victims, the murdered Jews and Poles in the Nazi era, not the amalgamated "Polish people" as such, much less the communist state itself.[14] As a contemporary *Der Spiegel* reporter described the scene:

> This unreligious man, who was not co-responsible for the [Nazi] crimes, who was not even there . . . now kneels down at the former Warsaw Ghetto – he kneels not for his own sake. . . . He confesses (*bekennt*) to a guilt that he himself does not have to bear, and asks for forgiveness, which he himself does not require. He kneels there for Germany.
>
> (Schreiber 1970)

This representation borrowed heavily from religious symbols surrounding the idea of confession as atonement sacrifice (Psalm 51:19). For in the Book of Isaiah, one finds almost an identical description: the sin-offering, who has done no injustice, bears "our" crime, guilt, and sin, willingly and silently (53:5–12).[15]

Eugen Kogon, son of Jewish parents, resister of the Third Reich and survivor of Buchenwald, took Brandt's confession as indicator of Germany's by then still limited but nonetheless existent "alert consciousness of history and of humanity". For the survivor, "it is appropriate to bring the question [about meaning of the past] above and beyond politics – whose ability to answer such question is limited by its principle of expediency – into the heart of religion," (Kogon 1979, 11) thus affirming the religiously informed interpretation of past atrocities and post-atrocity relations between the victims and the perpetrators (Schneider 2006). On a wider perspective, the German elite expressions of remorse from Theodor Heuss's in 1949 to Willy Brandt's in 1970 to Richard von Weizsäcker's in 1985 have been "heard" as confessions rather than apologies. As a president of the Central Council of Jews in Germany evaluated these expressions in 1986:

> Needless to say, all federal presidents since Theodor Heuss have deplored the mass murder and confronted with the inherited guilt. Without such confessions (*Bekenntnisse*) and without the political decisions of all federal chancellors, dialogue with the Jews and stable relations with Israel would be unthinkable.
>
> (Nachmann 1986, 15)

Though initially garnering slightly more negative than positive evaluation at home, Brandt's confession gradually became cherished by the wider German populace (Der Spiegel 1970; Schneider 2006). It would be unthinkable, indeed, how such communication would have taken place at all if the gesture were to be interpreted under the framework of xiezui – that is as political kowtow by the democratically elected West German chancellor to the then communist regime in Poland, conceding subservience and allegiance. The pre-existence of a confession-informed paradigm pre-empted such a possible interpretation. It was among the

62 C. K. Martin Chung

reasons why – alongside the inconvenient fact that the location was a Jewish, not a Polish memorial site – Brandt's Kniefall was not widely publicized in communist Poland (Tessmer 2000, 17, 138).[16]

Sure enough, even as xiezui has been misapplied to interpret Brandt's gesture, its proponents may still argue for its present relevance, either in its traditional form as a system to address hierarchical trespasses, or in a redefined, modernized form. Both strategies have inherent problems. Regarding the first, opposition has long been heard in Japan against the "bow-and-scrape shazai diplomacy" vis-à-vis the PRC (Liu Jiangyong 2005). Unless reconciliation also entails the restoration of a tributary, hierarchical relationship, the insistence on xiezui in its traditional sense does seem incompatible with the modern understanding of "normal" interstate relations based on the equality of status. A more fundamental problem of this approach, however, is to let hierarchical concerns take precedence over moral ones, as if the whole problem of atrocities committed by the imperialists and militarists around the time of World War II is not that they violated the dignity of individual human victims but the long-standing hierarchical order of a smaller, lowlier Japan vis-à-vis a greater, higher China.[17]

On the other hand, while it is both possible and perhaps even desirable to redefine xiezui away from its traditional sense in order to render it compatible with a vision of reconciliation in which equality of status is envisaged, none as far as the present author can gather has explicitly attempted this redefinition, thus leaving its present-day usage ensnared in its old connotations. Furthermore, given the intellectual burden of this concept, that is its distinct hierarchical conceptualization (see Ming Yu 45:19 earlier), one wonders whether it is worth the effort to redefine it at all instead of adopting alternative concept(s) compatible with reconciliation as "restoration of right relationship" after wrongful acts (Philpott 2012, 5).

There is, however, a third strategy for xiezui-proponents who see or believe they see in Brandt's Kniefall a model apology. It involves the willingness to give up xiezui as prescription on the one hand, and to learn from (instead of making use of) Brandt's act of Bekenntnis as an example of confession, which functions as an alternative system of post-wrongdoing expression, on the other.

Confession as an alternative system of post-wrongdoing expression

Maimonides wrote in his *Doctrine of Repentance* that "the most essential element of confession", which "the entire Israel has long adopted", is the phrase: "but we have sinned" (1994, 425). Indeed, confession in the Bible is first and foremost a community expression towards their God. "We have sinned, and have committed iniquity, and have done wickedly, and have rebelled, even by departing from thy precepts and from thy judgments" (Daniel 9:5).[18] Human conflicts are not perceived as purely between individuals and groups (hence bilateral, or two-dimensional) but always in view of the divine dimension: when individuals or nations commit "iniquity" and "wickedness" against one another, it is

Sino-Japanese and German-Jewish resources 63

simultaneously "rebellion" against and "departure" from God. This three-dimensionality has several important implications for "confession" vis-à-vis "apology" in terms of the content of guilt, audienceship, and goal.

In terms of content, it is not the trespassing of the prevalent social hierarchical order or social power relations that constitutes "guilt", but the turning away from God and his laws, and the turning to the evil deeds of the nations. In the Book of Nehemiah, the collective confession of the Israelites spoke about "their sins" and the "wrongdoings of their fathers" (9:2), which included their pride and stubbornness (9:16, 29), disobedience and murder of the prophets (9:26), committing "evil" and "wickedness" (9:28, 33). In fact, successive traumas of being subjugated by foreigners – what would have been perceived as *dezui* or *yuan* against oneself in the two-dimensional hierarchical paradigm – were presented in this confession as the just divine punishment for one's own (fathers') sins and wrongdoings (9:33).

In terms of audienceship, the actorness of God was emphasized even in situations where apparently "only" human atrocities were involved. When David confessed his guilt of having orchestrated the murder of Uriah the Hittite to cover up his affair with the victim's wife, Bathsheba, he said: "I have sinned against the Lord" (2 Samuel 12:13). And when Joseph's brothers confessed their guilt of having sold him to slavery and begged him to "forgive your brothers" – after Joseph had concealed his true identity in a similar way to Fan Sui's hiding his powerful status from Xu Jia – the victim declined to assume that he had such power, and asked his brothers instead: "am I in the place of God?" (Genesis 50:19). Even in the perhaps most xiezui-like scenario where Jacob/Israel bowed down seven times before his brother Esau, from whom he had "cheated" his birthright as the first born, it was in no way to be construed as political kowtow – for the two did not form a political union[19] as Esau proposed, but parted ways, hence reconciliation without integration or subjugation (Genesis 33:3, 12–17). Seeking the face of the victim was likened to seeking the face of God (33:10), hence the double-audience of confession.

The chief goal of confession is education, not redistributing honour, that is learning from the kind of sin/guilt/wrongdoing committed in order not to commit the same (again).[20] As Rabbeinu Yonah emphasized in his fourteenth principle of repentance about confession: "articulate your sins, as well as the sins of your ancestors. Because you'll suffer the consequences of their sins if you follow in their ways" (Yonah 1999, 57). The demand for confession is not an occasion for shaming the confessor to redistribute honour. As Maimonides explicitly warned in the context of explicating repentance, it is a sin to "exploit the shame of the neighbor to one's own advantage", and a "great sin" it is, "to speak to the repentant: remember your former actions [. . .] in order to shame him" (Maimonides 1994, 445, 485). The repentant actually enjoys even a "higher rank" than those who are immaculate (1994, 481). The listeners to a public confession are called to be witnesses, not judges or pardon-givers on behalf of the victims (1994, 427–429). This is especially the case when the true victims have passed away (1994, 423–429).

64   *C. K. Martin Chung*

Even the true victims who are still alive, whom the confessor must seek to "compensate, placate and ask for forgiveness", and for whom the perpetrator's confession presents an opportunity for curative mourning,[21] should not be "hard-hearted and implacable", or risking bearing the guilt of the repentant (Maimonides 1994, 425–427). An illustrative biblical example would be the servant of the prophet Elisha, Gehazi, who "abused" the repentant Naaman for personal gains and ended up suffering his leprosy (2 Kings 5).

Finally, the concept of confession – as part of the process of repentance – is associated with life, not death: "I do not want the death of anyone, word of Yahweh, but that you repent and live" (Ezekiel 18:32). Confessing, or *bekennen* in German, can be used both in the admission of guilt (*etwas bekennen*) and in the affirmation of the new way of life (*sich zu etwas bekennen*). In other words, the "negative" exposure of one's own guilt is often accompanied by the "positive" vision of how repentance, or "turning", as *tshuvah* in Hebrew literally means, can be achieved, which involves both human and divine participation (Chung 2015).

Conclusion: limitations of xiezui and the potentials of co-confession

Reflecting on the term "political reconciliation", one can come to two opposing directions: political reconciliation as "reconciling" with the prevalent power-political status, or as the introjection of "reconciliation" in its moral and theological sense into politics. If the first is meant, then xiezui as a system of apology seems to be particularly well suited for Sino-Japanese "reconciliation", that is the lowlier, perpetual Japan has acquired guilt towards (*dezui*) the superior, perpetual China in the past, who has now risen back to its former glory to demand an account (*wenzui*), and xiezui as political kowtow is the expected expression. The claims of victims as commoners and subjects remain peripheral to – or instrumentalizable for – "higher" politics.

If the second is meant, however, that is political reconciliation is about (re-) establishing rightful rather than merely hierarchical relationships in post-atrocity collective settings, then xiezui appears to have only very limited utility at best, and a fundamental redefinition of the concept is required. At the very least, it has to explicitly reject the power-hierarchical elements in xiezui and reorient it towards the human dignity of the individual victims who have personally suffered under state-sanctioned crimes. In this and in this sense alone can xiezui have a meaningful contribution towards political reconciliation: as the symbolic act of a state bowing down before the individual victim, admitting past wrongdoing against while pledging present and future allegiance to human dignity at the same time. Such xiezui would be a constitutional act akin to the first article of the German Basic Law, which is itself a Bekenntnis.[22]

Finally, concerning the utility of apology from individual Japanese citizens today to the victims of their forefathers, I would like to borrow an insight from Takahashi Tetsuya's conception of post-war responsibility as "response-possibility". The philosopher remarks on the Women's International War Crimes Tribunal on Japan's Military Sexual Slavery held in Tokyo in 2000: "the fact that women are

Sino-Japanese and German-Jewish resources   65

the ones spearheading this [trial] should force us men to reflect deeply" (2005, 24). This is an ingenious way to reframe the problem of coming to terms with the "ianfu" past, for now not only Japanese men can or should respond to it, but other men – Chinese and Korean included – too.

Indeed, the desecration of female dignity by men is confined neither to Japan nor to the past. In 2003, for instance, a group of Japanese men were reported to have engaged in an orgy tour in a hotel in Zhuhai, China. The Chinese press was all the rage as it happened in early September, that is around the anniversary of the 9.18 incident (Xin Kuai Bao 2003). I visited the hotel once and a local resident reminded me about the incident and said, "It's the shame of Zhuhai." By that shame he probably meant that the Zhuhai hotel should not have served the Japanese customers as it would incur still more national shame – on top of that deprived honour in the so-called "century of humiliation" in the past. Such is the logic of xiezui. With Takahashi's response-possibility as men vis-à-vis the abused women, however, which I think is conducive to the Jewish praxis of co-confessing, a Chinese man should have asked instead: "who are engaging in orgy tours there in the other 364 days?" Or: "who have actively constructed or tacitly approved a socio-economic and legal system in which such desecration by men is still possible?"

The late distinguished Japanese Germanist Iwabuchi Tatsuji once remarked that ordinary Japanese citizens' confrontation with their own war guilt was only "half-hearted" in comparison with the Germans because "in Japan we do not have the corresponding expressions of *mitmachen* [acting in complicity] or *Mitläufer* [unengaged accomplice]" (1997, 13). I suspect that the lack of a self-inclusive concept of co-confession, or *mitbekennen*, is a shared deficiency in East Asia.[23]

Notes

1 Unless otherwise stated, all quotations from non-English sources are my own translation.
2 It is, therefore, interesting to note that in the latest (28 December 2015) Japanese-Korean joint announcement on the issue of "comfort women", whereas shazai is not the term used for apology in the Japanese version, in the Korean one, however, *sajoei* 사죄 appears as an expression of the Japanese prime minister Shinzo Abe to the female victims (mofa.go.jp 2015).
3 Shazai is the term used in the Japanese original, with the official English translation using "[being] predestined to apologize" (japan.kantei.go.jp 2015). Interestingly, whereas the official Chinese translation follows the English one and speaks of *daoqian de suming*, Chinese media tend to refer back to the Japanese original and speak of *xiezui suming* (Embassy of Japan in China 2015; people.com 2015).
4 See the numerous essays by Chinese ambassadors from Cameroon to Yemen available on the ministry's website (www.fmprc.gov.cn).
5 A word of caution: xiezui in Shiji was used in my view primarily as descriptor of historical events; hence one would be erroneous to assert that Sima Qian was intentionally promoting a particular concept of apology.
6 Though it would be interesting to trace the changes and modifications in meaning of the term across time, in view of scope we shall leave it to subsequent research.

66 C. K. Martin Chung

7 For ease of access, quotations from Shiji in this study are marked first by the number of the particular book (107 in this case) and then by the number of the particular paragraph(s) (20–21 according to ctext.org) from which they are drawn. For the translation of Shiji I rely on the vernacularized version (Sima Qian 1985) with consultation of the classical text of the *Zhonghua Shuju* 1959 edition.

8 In the context, the author of Lunheng was explicating the justifications for the traditional rain sacrifice. It is clear that xiezui is conceived as the externally visible and communicable sign of "change" (whether it be of governments or individuals) to appease the anger of the offended party (whether it be the father, the sovereign or heaven) whereas internal reform remains invisible. See Wang (1962, 336–338).

9 Guo Jie practiced benevolence towards this arrogant man and finally impressed him to do xiezui.

10 Xiezui was used in the classical text of Shiji. In popular memory, however, this event is called *fujing qingzui*, or apologizing by carrying thorns.

11 Whether this case qualifies as a "moral" example of xiezui is open to debate. On the one hand, one could argue that hierarchical (internal) and survival (external) concerns rather than the (in)appropriateness of the act of insult dominated the narrative all throughout. On the other hand, one could counter that Lian's xiezui arose from the realization of the moral superiority of his opponent, at which stage the hierarchical and survival concerns no longer mattered.

12 For Xu Jia had taken pity on him when his identity was still concealed.

13 By an ironic stroke of fate, Yuan Ang would, in due time, fall victim to murder, and his murderer would be pardoned by another emperor after doing xiezui. Yuan was among the victims of the purge by the prince of Xiao mentioned earlier.

14 See the contention of this point in Herzinger (2010).

15 It was no coincidence that when Brandt was named the Person of the Year in 1971 by *TIME* Magazine, the cover of the issue was an artwork showing the new "iron chancellor" not kneeling in Warsaw but nailed on the cross.

16 Also based on a conversation the author had with Adam Krzemiński, a veteran journalist of the Polish weekly *Polityka*, in Tokyo on 18 June 2015.

17 It is true that one may still argue that hierarchical concerns are themselves matters of morality in traditional China, that is one cannot draw too sharp a line between the two. The application of relativist critique here, however, is self-defeating for the Chinese proponents of xiezui, for then there is no point asking the Japanese elites to learn from the German examples of apology, or any other, at all.

18 Cf. Nehemiah 9:33; 1 Samuel 12:10.

19 "Esau" and "Israel" are also names of collectives: the Edomites and the Israelites respectively.

20 See 2 Kings 22:13 and Nehemiah 1:6–7. The repentant is also tasked to teach others not to commit the same sin as oneself had done, hence public confession's added social educational function (Yonah 1999, 313–314).

21 See Joseph's weeping upon his brother's private and public confessions (Genesis 43:30; 45:2).

22 Paragraph 2 of Article 1 of the German Basic Law reads: "The German people therefore acknowledge (*bekennt sich zu*) inviolable and inalienable human rights as the basis of every community, of peace and of justice in the world." Official English print version of Oct. 2010.

23 There is a veritable "local resource" in Han-Buddhist rituals: the practice of "co-repentance for former sins" (*gongchan xianzui*) (*Liang Huang Chan* 1986, 366). The extraction and application of this resource for the purpose of political reconciliation in the region, however, is yet to be done.

References

Chen, Edward. 2015. "北京要求日皇明仁為二戰謝罪的政治目的" [The Political Aim of Beijing's Request for Apology from Akihito]. *Ming Pao*, 4 Sep.

Chung, C.K. Martin. 2015. "Repentance: The Jewish Solution to the German Problem." *Jahrbuch des Simon-Dubnow-Instituts* 14: 129–155.

Der Spiegel. 1970. "Kniefall angemessen oder übertrieben?" *Der Spiegel* 51, p. 27.

Dudden, Alexis. 2008. *Troubled Apologies among Japan, Korea, and the United States.* New York: Columbia University Press.

Embassy of Japan in China. 2015. "安倍晉三內閣總理大臣談話 (2015年8月14日)" [Speech of Abe Shinzo 2015.8.14]. http://www.cn.emb-japan.go.jp/bilateral/bunken_2015danwa.htm. Accessed 2 Nov. 2015.

He, Yinan. 2009. *The Search for Reconciliation: Sino-Japanese and German-Polish Relations since World War II.* New York: Cambridge University Press.

Herzinger, Richard. 2010. "Willy Brandts Kniefall ist zur Ikone geworden." *Die Welt*, 4 Dec.

Iwabuchi, Tatsuji. 1997. *Die Vergangenheitsbewältigung und die japanische Literatur.* Tokyo: Deutsche Gesellschaft für Natur- und Völkerkunde Ostasiens.

japan.kantei.go.jp. 2015. "Statement by Prime Minister Shinzo Abe, August 14, 2015." http://japan.kantei.go.jp/97_abe/statement/201508/0814statement.html.

Kogon, Eugen. 1979. "Einführung in die deutsche Ausgabe." In *Gott nach Auschwitz. Dimensionen des Massenmords am jüdischen Volk*, edited by Eugen Kogon and Johann Baptist Metz. Freiburg/Basel/Wien: Herder, pp. 7–12.

Liang Huang Chan. 1986. 金山御製梁皇寶懺 [Jinshan Yuzhi Liang Huang Bao Chan; a.k.a. *Liang Huang Chan*]. Taipei: Baima Jingshe Yinjinghui.

Lind, Jennifer. 2008. *Sorry States: Apologies in International Politics.* Ithaca/London: Cornell University Press.

Liu, Jiangyong. 2005. "论正确认识中日之间的历史问题" [On the Correct Understanding of Sino-Japanese Historical Problem]. http://www.china-un.org/chn/zt/fa60/t219658.htm. Accessed 31 May 2014.

Lübbe, Hermann. 2001. *'Ich entschuldige mich'. Das neue politische Bußritual.* Berlin: Siedler.

Maimonides, Moses. 1994. "Die Lehre von der Buße." In *Mischne Tora – Das Buch der Erkenntnis*, edited by Eveline Goodman-Thau and Christoph Schulte, 408–509. Berlin: Akademie Verlag.

mofa.go.jp. 2015. "Announcement by Foreign Ministers of Japan and the Republic of Korea at the Joint Press Occasion, 28 December 2015." Accessed 19 Apr. 2016. http://www.mofa.go.jp/a_o/na/kr/page4e_000364.html.

Nachmann, Werner. 1986. "Es begann mit den Juden . . . – über jüdischen Geist in Europa und Deutschland heute." In *Eine Rede und ihre Wirkung. Die Rede des Bundespräsidenten Richard von Weizsäcker vom 8. Mai 1985*, edited by Ulrich Gill and Winfried Steffani. Berlin: Rainer Röll, p. 13–21.

Peng, Yulong. 2001. 謝罪與翻案 [Offering an Apology vs. Reversing the Verdict]. Beijing: People's Liberation Army Press.

people.com. 2015. "安倍回避直接道歉: 戰后出生的不應背負謝罪宿命" [Abe Avoids Direct Apology]. http://bj.people.com.cn/n/2015/0815/c233087–25988885.html. Accessed 3 Nov. 2015.

Philpott, Daniel. 2012. *Just and Unjust Peace: An Ethic of Political Reconciliation.* New York: Oxford University Press.

sankei.com. 2015. "'戦後７０年談話' 首相談話全文" [70 Years after the War]. http://www.sankei.com/politics/print/150814/plt1508140016-c.html. Accessed 2 Nov. 2015.

Schneider, Christoph. 2006. *Der Warschauer Kniefall. Ritual, Ereignis und Erzählung.* Konstanz: UVK Verlagsgesellschaft.

Schreiber, Hermann. 1970. "Ein Stück Heimkehr." *Der Spiegel* 51, p. 29–30.

Sima Qian. 1959. 史記 [Shiji]. Beijing: Zhonghua Shuju.

———. 1985. 白話史記 [Vernacular Shiji]. Taipei: Linking.

Takahashi, Tetsuya. 2005. 戦後責任論 [On Postwar Responsibility]. Translated by XU Man. Beijing: Social Sciences Academic Press.

Tessmer, Carsten, ed. 2000. *Das Willy-Brandt-Bild in Deutschland und Polen.* Berlin: Bundeskanzler-Willy-Brandt-Stiftung.

Wang, Chung. 1962. *Lun-Heng.* Translated by Alfred Forke. New York: Paragon Book Gallery.

Wang, Q. Edward and Georg G. Iggers, eds. 2002. *Turning Points in Historiography: A Cross-Cultural Perspective.* New York: University of Rochester Press.

Xin Kuai Bao. 2003. "9–18 成群日本客珠海召妓" [Japanese orgy tour in Zhuhai]. *Xin Kuai Bao*, 26 Sep.

xinhuanet.com. 2015. "谁应为日本侵略战争罪行谢罪" [Who Should Apologize for Japanese War Crimes]. http://news.xinhuanet.com/mil/2015–08/25/c_1116366796.htm. Accessed 26 Oct. 2015.

Yamazaki, Jane W. 2006. *Japanese Apologies for World War II: A Rhetorical Study.* New York: Routledge.

Yang, Daqing. 2012. "The Nanjing Atrocity: Is Constructive Dialogue Possible?" In *Toward a History Beyond Borders*, edited by Daqing Yang, Jie Liu, Hiroshi Mitani and Andrew Gordon, 178–204. Cambridge/London: Harvard University Asia Center.

———. 2013. "Political Apology in Sino-Japanese Relations: The Murayama Statement and Its Receptions in China." In *Japan and Reconciliation in Post-War Asia: The Murayama Statement and Its Implications*, edited by Kazuhiko Togo, 23–45. New York: Palgrave Macmillan.

Yonah, Rabbeinu. 1999. *The Gates of Repentance.* Translation and Commentary by Yaakov Feldman. Northvale/Jerusalem: Jason Aronson Inc.

Yu, Ying-shih. 1982. 史學與傳統 [Historiography and Tradition]. Taipei: Reading Times.

Zhu, Chengshan. 2002. 東史郎謝罪 [Azuma Shiro Apologizes]. Shanghai: Cishu.

5 Ruist traditions of revenge and alternative resources for Ruist-inspired reconciliation

Lauren F. Pfister

Our purpose in writing on this theme is to highlight what has been often left unstated or even avoided in Ruist (*rújiā* 儒家 "Confucian") ethical reflections regarding vengeance and its justifications. Very few contemporary Ruist scholars, overseas sinologists and other scholars in the general realm of Chinese studies have mentioned, much less described and discussed, Ruist traditions related to the advocacy of family-based vengeance based upon principles of filial submission (*xiào*孝). Admittedly, it is much easier to avoid the problem, leaving it unaddressed as an authentic ancient Ruist tradition, because it has become anachronous in contemporary East Asian societies especially due to legal restrictions (Guō 2004). Nevertheless, as we will demonstrate, this response implies a selective reading of Ruist canonical literature which is not only difficult to justify but also further complicated by the fact that popular Chinese literature and mass media in contemporary Chinese cultural contexts are replete with illustrations of various kinds of revenge.

In order to address and resolve this specific Ruist ethical problem, we will first of all describe the nature of questions related to revenge as they appear in certain ancient Ruist scriptures as well as in popular Chinese culture. Following this, we will seek to argue for a more critically justified interpretation of these traditions. These arguments will move us towards offering a specific set of constructive responses from ethical resources found in the *Analects* or *Lúnyǔ*《論語》 and the teachings of the Míng dynasty Ruist, Liú Zōngzhōu 劉宗周.

Identifying the problem of vengefulness in Chinese cultural settings

As will be documented, vengefulness is not a new cultural phenomenon emerging only in recent years, but has a long set of traditions in Chinese literature which stretches back over nearly three millennia. Historical records include numerous examples of warriors and those in elite circles of society who were driven to pursue revenge against enemies who had killed or harmed their family members or comrades. Documented not only in classical literature in the Ruist traditions, examples were recorded also in various dynastic histories and often became themes for traditional literature, reflecting the aesthetic and ethical appeal of the

70   *Lauren Pfister*

most justified forms of blood revenge and also indicating the breadth of popular interest which these acts of vengeance received.

Ultimately, acts of revenge became a matter of immense cultural concern because of the relational chaos and social instability which was intensified by the perpetrators and continual cycles of vengeful retributions, so that vengeance in various forms was clearly considered a punishable offence supported by authorities for the sake of political stability by the time of the Táng dynasty (starting in the seventh century BCE) (Lǐ 2011). Even so, acts of revenge still continued to occur, partly because it involved a central ambivalence between values of moral cultivation and those associated with the maintenance of social order. This ambivalence has roots in different traditions honoured among Ruist scholars, some which justify vengeance as an act of filial and other family virtues, a search for "personal justice" when involved with enemies of one's main family members. In modern and contemporary cross-cultural ethical contexts, specifically in the context of Ruist-Christian dialogue, questions related to "blood revenge" have, at times, become a significant matter distinguishing certain accounts of classical Ruism from New Testament teachings.

Vengeful actions: their scope and justifications in traditional Chinese literary contexts

Chinese forms of revenge generally invoke principles which are known in many other cultures as well: if someone does an evil act which hurts or kills a relative or friend, vengeance requires a response. It may come in a "tit for tat" response in kind, or may seek some other kind of destructive action which will symbolize the degree of resentment and "satisfy" the perpetrator's sense of indignation at the previous injustice which had been done. As can be imagined, the second form of vengeance may easily justify worse kinds of harmful acts against either the perpetrator or those linked to that person, so that a series of violent acts may be produced that ultimately spiral into gross forms of social chaos for all those involved. What makes the theme of revenge particularly complex in the Chinese context is that it is not only portrayed as a matter of settling injustices experienced within human relationships, but also involves vengeful spirits of the dead who wreck havoc on perpetrators who have cruelly or unjustly destroyed the lives of the innocent or the righteous (Lǐ 2010).

The Chinese literary scholar, Wáng Lì 王立, has made the study of various kinds of vengeance in ancient and traditional literature one of his specializations, and so has demonstrated at great length the pervasiveness of themes (Wáng 1995, 1998). In his study referred to here as the *Grand Overview* (大观) of stories in ancient China, Wáng Lì identifies nine different categories of revenge acted out against enemies in response to their evil actions. Nevertheless, a closer review of these categories reveals that they are neither mutually exclusive nor emphatically involved with familial revenge. Surprisingly for those unaware of these literary traditions, the longest accounts of vengefulness are involved with angry spiritual beings, placed in two categories: spirits of the dead humans (鬼靈) and goblins or demons generated from the death or transformation of non-human sentient beings (精怪) (Wáng and Liú 1997).[1] Three other categories deal with what are regularly associated with forms of filial revenge, though the latter two may not necessarily fit into the technical category of vengeance motivated by filial piety (孝道) in ancient Chinese contexts because the actors are not sons within a patriarchal extended family structure. These three include blood revenge by filial sons (血亲复仇), revenge driven by embittered grief at the death of an assumedly beloved family member (喪悼復仇), and vengeful actions taken up by "faithful concubines" (忠妾復仇).[2] The remaining categories may not be exclusively independent of these stories of familial vengeance: they include those responding to violence (反暴) (Wáng and Liú 1997, 596–591), women in general (女性, and so also possibly including daughters and mothers in addition to wives and concubines) (592–722), and those who take up "righteous causes" because of their militant stance and high sense of honour, even though they may not be related by bloodline to those who have suffered from enemies (俠義復仇) (83–223).[3]

Our minor reflections on the volume of readings about themes of revenge are more fully elaborated and interpreted in essays which constitute the next long book produced by Wáng Lì on revenge, which we will refer to hear simply as *Main Themes* (主題) (Wáng 1998). From nearly the very beginning of the work, Wáng discusses revenge as a matter of "preserving dignity and realizing ethics" (尊嚴維護與倫理實現), but also indicates elsewhere that these attitudes were not free from misuse or excessive emotions (9–16, 28–35, 485–502). Notably, Wáng initiates his discussion of these main themes of revenge by referring not to filial sons and faithful spouses, but to "the culture of spirits" (鬼靈文化) and "warriors" (俠) (45–167). By this means one sense that he is seeking to elevate the basic ethical problem into what might be seen as a metaphysical plane involving the righteousness of ancestral spirits and heroic warriors who appeal to some universal law of justice in order to support their acts of vengeance. To indicate the importance of these interconnections between the spiritual and human realms, he also includes sections where spirits either prompt filial vengeance or perpetrate it themselves on the murderers, and may even prompt persons who are in mourning to act out of a sense of preserving personal or familial honour which has been wounded by such murderous acts (266–276, 377–403). In this regard, then, the supernatural realm becomes a further justification for citing ethical motives which have universal appeal when they are involved with blood revenge.

Subsequently Wáng Lì discusses the relationship between punitive law (*fǎ* 法) and revenge and comes to the conclusion that even though some ancient laws were ultimately developed to prohibit personal revenge, the conflict between ritual propriety (*lǐ* 禮) and the legal conditions was not able to be resolved with any finality, to the point that ritual propriety was honoured more than those punitive laws (168–181).[4] At this juncture it is also worthwhile to mention the thorough studies produced by another scholar from Táiwān, Lee Lung-hsien (Lǐ Lóngxiàn), who has made the problem of the development of legal restrictions to restrain the chaos created by moral vengefulness within traditional Chinese

72 *Lauren Pfister*

contexts a main topic of numerous studies (Lǐ 2008a, 2008b, 2011). Wáng's reference to propriety we will note again later, because it remains a major interpretive hurdle to overcome when any Ruist scholar seeks to argue that focusing on humane cultivation or *rén* is an adequate ethical justification for demobilizing these ancient Ruist traditions supporting acts of vengeance. Though Wáng and Lǐ both indicate that by the Táng dynasty laws were in place and were being used to prosecute those who continued to pursue personal vendettas, Wáng cites specific examples where judges in the latter-Hàn dynasty era even overturned those laws on the basis of the "justified" motivations of virtuous sons, daughters, and spouses (Wáng 1998, 171).

As we might expect, a full chapter does deal with filial sons who are considered ethically justified in pursuing blood revenge (235–298), as well as faithful lovers, mothers, and militant women who take up revenge for reasons related to their family's honour (299–376). Ethical conflicts faced by "faithful concubines" are discussed as well, since their justifications were often considered to be inadequate, and so if they were successful in realizing their vengeance, they would also commit suicide in order to avoid the criminal execution which they expected to receive (426–484).

Whether taken from the perspective of some form of familial honour (including a sense of personal duty) or from wider spheres embracing close friendships, vengeful human spirit and other spiritual reckonings by animals or their transformed demonic representatives, the aura surrounding the justifications for taking revenge suggest at the most basic level that these actions are taken to address a matter of justice which is required by some previously perpetrated evil deed. These justifications prompt some to pursue the target of their vengeance at great risk to themselves and sometimes also for others, but also raise questions about how and when satisfaction through revenge can be reached. Certainly, there is an immense amount of literature documenting these stories and their traditions. One would hope that there would be a sizeable amount of discussion among Ruist ethicists about these phenomena but, in fact, such studies are extremely rare. In fact, there is a "deeper" problem here, because there are also classical Ruist sources justifying certain kinds of vengeance.

Ruist justifications of filial vengeance: classical sources

If acts of revenge were justified on the basis of family honour, judges may rule against vengeful persons on the basis of current penal codes, but then honour their "moral" actions. Why was there such ambivalence over these matters, especially when most kinds of revenge could only cycle into greater harm and destruction for a wider range of persons?

One reason for this ambivalence is that the practice of familial vengeance was clearly advocated within canonical Ruist literature. For example a major teaching advocating "filial vengeance on the murder of one's elders", among other traditions, is recorded in *The Record of the Rites* (*Lǐjì* 《禮記》, *Tángōng* 檀弓) as a citation from Master Kǒng 孔夫子. Because this text is rarely referred to, the whole passage will be cited here. It will be repeated here in James Legge's English version (1986, 140).[5]

> Zǐxià 子夏 asked Master Kǒng [Confucius], 'How should (a son) conduct himself with reference to the man who has killed his father and mother?' (居父母之仇, 如之何) The Master said, 'He should sleep on straw, with his shield for a pillow; he should not take office; he must be determined not to live with the slayer under the same heaven (弗與共天下也). If he met him in the market-place or the court, he should not have to go back for his weapon, but (instantly) fight with him.'
>
> 'Allow me to ask,' said (the other), 'how one should do with reference to the man who has slain his brother?' 'He may take office,' was the reply, 'but not in the same state with the slayer; if he be sent on a mission by his ruler's order, though he may then meet with the man, he should not fight with him.'
>
> 'And how should one do,' continued Zǐxià, 'in the case of a man who has slain one of his paternal cousins?' Master Kǒng said, 'He should not take the lead (in the avenging). If he whom it chiefly concerns is able to do that, he should support him from behind, with his weapon in his hand.'

Ethically speaking, those philosophers and other intellectuals in Chinese cultural contexts who adamantly support the principled maintenance of all dimensions of filial piety by sons, since filial virtue (*xiào* 孝) is also claimed by Master Kǒng in the *Analects* (1:2) to be the very root of humane cultivation or *rén* 仁,[6] face a major interpretive challenge with relationship to this application of family values in the midst of traditional as well as contemporary society. Some foreign advocates of Ruist traditions have avoided the issue completely, realizing that the promotion of blood revenge was a matter that would cast a dark shadow over the positive family values and communitarian ethics often highlighted in modern Ruist accounts of virtue ethics.[7] In this light it is particularly significant that the Scottish missionary-sinologist, James Legge 理雅各 (1815–1897) explicitly mentioned the problem of "the duty of blood revenge", comparing it unfavourably to the cities of refuge found in the Hebrew scriptures of the Bible, which allowed "the manslayer to flee [there] from the duty of the avenger".[8] Reflecting on the situation of the Qīng dynasty in which he himself had been involved as a missionary for over thirty years, Legge in 1861 summarized the cultural problem drawn from this justification for vengeance in the following manner:

> Revenge is sweet to the Chinese. I have spoken of their readiness to submit to government, and wish to live in peace, yet they do not like to resign even to government the 'inquisition for blood'. Where the ruling authority is feeble, as it is at present, individuals and clans take the law into their own hands, and whole districts are kept in a state of constant feud and warfare.
>
> (Legge 1893, 111)

74 *Lauren Pfister*

We have already seen that these claims of Legge, in fact, part and parcel of specific Ruist canonical traditions and filled with numerous historical and fictional illustrations. A very basic problem related to Ruist family ethics is revealed here. In fact, Legge found "whole districts are kept in a state of constant feud and warfare" (Legge, 1893, 111). It is the social "constancy" of these cycles of vengeful actions which provokes immense social unrest and cultural instability.

From studies including those of Wáng Lì and Lǐ Lóngxiàn, there are numerous notable historical examples of various kinds of revenge recorded in canonical texts within the Ruist traditions, including the *Zuǒzhuàn*《左傳》(Wáng 1995, 1997; Wáng and Liú 1998; Lǐ 2005) and *Gōngyáng Zhuàn*《公羊傳》(Zāng 1996; Chén 1998; Lǐ 2005; Qiū and Wáng 2008) as well as Hàn dynasty historical texts (Liú 1994). Put into this light, we can understand more vividly why Ruist teachings may not address this problem, since the ambivalence created by the tension between classical virtues bound to family honour and legal restrictions that seek to restrain violence is made all the more prominent due to these classical justifications. This conflict of values was not merely an abstract matter. The social chaos caused by acts of revenge motivated by filial piety prompted later legal restrictions and harsh punishments to be established as early as the Táng dynasty. Still the tension between this particular kind of punitive judgement and the moral sensibilities rooted in family honour remained, with examples found even in the Qīng dynasty (Dalby and Wáng 2002, 2003).

Ambivalence in response to vengeful actions: a Ruist dilemma?

Yet even as we face this very significant ethical tension, there are still questions that can be raised regarding the legitimacy of those justifications which are placed in Master Kǒng's mouth. Surely, if Master Kǒng actually supported certain kinds of vengefulness on the basis of the virtue of filial piety, then a major dilemma would arise between moral values and legal norms. How would such a claim be denied? One way would be to challenge the historical authenticity of the statement made in the name of Master Kǒng within *The Record of the Rites* as quoted earlier. If it could be shown that there are good reasons to doubt that the historical Master Kǒng actually stated such things, one of the major justifications for the most stern form of revenge, the one tied to the fulfilment of filial virtue by concerned sons, might be countered by other means.

While moral positions drawn from the *Analects* may also suggest ethical principles which avoid advocating murderous vengeful actions, promoting instead more humane virtues including compassionate and other elements, a strong link remains in Master Kǒng's form of ethical cultivation between humane cultivation and propriety, and is strengthened even further in Master Mèng's 孟子 ("Mencius's") linking together of humane cultivation and rightness/righteous duty (*yì* 義), both of which are to be elaborated by propriety and wisdom.[9] Since both filial piety and ritual propriety are perceived as foundational and elaborative

Ruist traditions of revenge   75

virtues for any humanely cultivated Ruist scholar in these pre-imperial Ruist traditions, it is very difficult to avoid the practical implications promoting duties of vengeance in the teachings of *The Record of the Rites* unless one adopts a more self-conscious and critical reading of the Ruist canonical tradition. Even from the angle of the historical development of canonical standards in Ruist traditions, this issue is made more problematic precisely because the scriptures related to Ruist propriety, conditions for ritual orientation, and the details related to numerous rites were given canonical status a thousand years before the texts of the *Analects* and the *Mèngzǐ* were brought into the Ruist canon (Henderson 1991).

Approaches to Ruist ethical responses to overcome vengefulness: reconsidering teachings from *the analects*

As we have seen from the extended arguments earlier, a wide variety of forms of vengeance portrayed in ancient and popular literature is not all sanctioned by Ruist ethical principles but has been based on a principle: "if you hurt me or those for whom I care, I will hurt you or those for whom you care." This approach does not limit the vengeance to a more narrow focus, such as "an eye for an eye, a tooth for a tooth", seeking some kind of equivalence in the vengeful response, but responds to the situation in a manner that can be driven more by anger and intense hatred than by a careful reflection on the suitable degree of response. Does Master Kǒng offer such guidance?

With regard to a humanely cultivated person's attitudes when living among others outside of their family circle, Master Kǒng clearly explains that the value of humane cultivation 仁would regularly involve "not doing/giving to others what you do not want done to yourself" (己所不欲，勿施於人) (Analects 12:2, 15:24). In the light of the later historical traditions which portray Master Kǒng as advocating blood revenge against the murderer of one's closest kin in a patriarchal family setting, this ethical principle gives us reason to question the authenticity of that later tradition. Consider more carefully the immediate context of this statement in *Analects* 12:2. This ethical principle comes within a string of succinctly stated responses by Master Kǒng to Zhòng Gǒng仲弓, who was asking about the nature of the Master's most basic virtue, humane cultivation仁. In that context Zhòng Gǒng is encouraged to take on a dignified presence whenever he leaves the confines of his own home and especially among the common people who live in the same state. Then, after offering this famous ethical principle, the Master goes on to encourage him: if he does so, he will have no regrets either when travelling outside even within foreign states or when he stays at home. Certainly it is manifest that Master Kǒng seeks a collective harmony within the larger social and political realms of his day. This is made all the more emphatic, but without the same context, when this saying appears later on, and is described as a "lifelong standard for action" (可以終身行之者 Analects 15:24).

Even within the confines of an account of humane cultivation which is intimately connected to ritual propriety (as in the position advocated in *Analects* 12:1),

76　*Lauren Pfister*

one still should not pursue any action that one would not want done to oneself. Put more concretely, when would anyone ever *want* someone else to kill them, even if they had committed murder? Lacking both the natural desire towards self-preservation and the ethical problems associated with suicidal self-destructiveness, this particular kind of distorted desire would be denied justification because it would be considered ethically inconceivable.

For example acting with this kind of mutual concern does not depend on what others have done to me or those I care for, but is based on what I myself do not want to have happen to me, and so it shifts the focus of attention on my own sensitivities, my own dislikes, and not on what others have done to me. This provides an alternative approach to understanding how to respond to even murderous persons: it is not necessarily sanctioning aggressively vengeful actions which are based on a response to the evils of others but instead seeks to "overcome evil with cultivated humaneness" rather than to respond to evil with evil.[10] But the question still remains, what about those who had murdered one's parents, or paternal uncles, or paternal cousins? Here the question of litigation might be considered.[11] Though Master Kǒng would not prefer this to happen, there are times when, for the sake of collective reconciliation and social justice, that he could permit recourse to punitive laws. It is precisely in this way that later Ruists would employ punitive laws to stifle the social chaos caused by vengeful actions which tended to spiral into social unrest.

In this light, then, it is also significant to ask: is it every justifiable for a Ruist advocate to follow the principle of "loving your enemy" as found in the teachings of the Sermon of the Mount within the New Testament?[12] How should one handle even one's personal enemy in a manner which would not involve the worst aspects of personal vengeance and in order to avoid cycles of revenge which would extend to even inter-generational vengefulness? Here we need to note a significant set of emotional limits to Master Kǒng's responses to anger, one which appeared not to show a will to "overcome evil by generosity" (以德報怨), but instead sought to restrict the evil by "strictness" (以直報怨). Whether or not this would eliminate all forms of forgiveness is a matter which would need to be considered in other contexts, but there is no hint in the *Analects* that the form of cultivated humaneness which Master Kǒng advocated related to a divinely inspired form of forgiveness. His focus in this context was limited to human interactions. So when asked whether a person should respond to anger with virtue (*Analects* 14:34), the response came, "Respond to anger with strictness, but respond to virtue with virtue." Here it is important once more to see that vengeance is not countenanced, but a form of restraint and firmness. This does not appear to stretch to the point of requiring filial vengeance, even in spite of the historical examples of such actions in the literature of his age. In this sense, Master Kǒng as portrayed in the *Analects* was more restrained and concerned for social harmony than the image we have of him from *The Record of the Rites*. It is reasonable to expect that this is the more authentic position adopted by Master Kǒng, and so Ruist scholars should express critical caution in adopting and supporting any principle supporting vengeful actions.

More than a hundred years after Master Kǒng's death, the major Ruist disciple, Master Mèng ("Mencius") wrote out a far more explicit ethical reflection about reasons for rejecting vengefulness. In D. C. Lau's rendering of the passage (*The Mèngzǐ* 7B: 7),[13] this meditative counsel against taking revenge goes as follows:

> Only now do I realize how serious it is to kill a member of the family of another man. If you killed his father, he would kill your father; if you killed his elder brother, he would kill your elder brother. This being the case, though you may not have killed your father and brother with your own hands, it is but one step removed.

Hé Zuokāng makes the point by rendering in the last sentence in a more colloquial fashion: "So, although it was not you yourself who killed your father or elder brother, it is almost as if you had."[14] There seems every evidence, therefore, that the pre-Qín teachings of these two seminal Ruist master-teachers would not support a Ruist-inspired ethical form of familial vengeance.

Approaches to Ruist ethical responses to overcome vengefulness: reconsidering teachings from Liú Zōngzhōu

A further development of Ruist cultivation techniques moved towards a more radical self-critical understanding of the correction of one's faults in the teachings of Liú Zōngzhōu 劉宗周 (1578–1645), involving cultivation concerns which could also provide an internal moral hermeneutic that could be liberating in avoiding the pitfalls of the social chaos caused by familial vengeance. Liú's career and interpretive innovations related to the Ruist school founded by his predecessor, Wáng Yángmíng 王陽明 (1472–1529). These innovations point towards a number of more dynamic and onto-generatively significant additions to Ruist self-cultivation, suggesting how these self-critical moral reflections might go beyond merely personal reflections to become a hermeneutics of suspicion in relationship to forms of social or cultural moral disorientation. Those contributions were first highlighted in Huáng Zōngxī's account of his teacher's influences in the last section of his lengthy *Míng Rú xuéàn* 《明儒學案》 (2008, 1507–1598). Very notably, his approach to whole person cultivation countered a quietistic stream in the teachings of Wáng Yángmíng and a number of his followers that some considered to be Buddhistic rather than Ruist in nature. Though our purpose here is not to work through the comparison of the two Ruist scholars "four sentence teachings" (四句教) which capsulized and highlighted these differences (Huáng 2001; Struve 2003, 405–408; Liú 2008; Dù 2009), what we will do here is to indicate the dynamic and onto-generative orientations of Liú Zōngzhōu's teachings in this realm that have direct relevance to our concern for overcoming personal and familial forms of vengeance.

Seeking to avoid extremes that either identified everyday values as the standard for right and wrong, good and bad, or led to a spontaneous willfulness that was

78   *Lauren Pfister*

socially chaotic, Liú Zōngzhōu countered the quietistic and Chán 禪 Buddhistic
tendencies of those alternative Ruist interpretations by arguing for foundation for
whole person cultivation in the (Struve 2003, 407) united heart-mind-and-nature
(心性) (Liáo Jūnyù 2008), which was always engaged in moral environments, but
had a transcendent will which was able to discern the absolute nature of good and evil
within "the self-controlling, good-impelling, principled will of heaven-in-
humankind". As a consequence, his four sentence teaching provided a transcendent pivot in the authentic will which provided a self-critical and transcendent
hermeneutic perspective to guide morally engaged conscientious acts of knowing
(良知). His version of the four sentence teaching as a consequence was presented
as follows (Dài Liǎnzhāng et al. 1996):[15]

有善有惡者心之動　　When the heart-mind is moved, there is good and evil.
好善惡惡者意之靜　　When the authentic will is quiet, it appreciates good and
　　　　　　　　　　hates evil.
知善知惡者是良知　　Innate moral knowledge is the knowing of good and evil.
為善去惡者是物則　　Principles governing all matters entail acting for the good
　　　　　　　　　　and eschewing evil.

The general orientation of this teaching is summarized by Lynn Struve as follows: "the force of moral will, radiating outward from the subjective heart-mind
into the world of affairs, is the link between our infinite and finite selves and,
therefore, must be made central to the theory and practice of self-cultivation"
(Struve 2003, 407). Liú applied this self-conscious awareness through a critical
self-appraisal (省察) which pivoted on the basis of a transcendent moral enlightenment and could be applied to all realms of life.[16] Struve summarizes the practical impact of this moral understanding drawn from Liú Zōngzhōu's account of
whole person cultivation:

> Those transgressions are laid out in a six-level scheme (derived from the
> stages of moral effort in the *Great Learning*), with universally condemned
> social sins at one end and the most subtle movements of private thoughts
> and emotion at the other.
>
> (Struve 2003, 407)

It is precisely this kind of a self-critical moral cultivation which would reject the
social chaos caused by familial or personal revenge and could lead towards a more
critically understood set of Ruist ethical traditions, promoting a more compassionate and embracing form of humane cultivation.

Concluding reflections

In the course of this chapter we have indicated how causes for revenge have
been and continue to be advocated within Chinese culture. It is a matter which
drives more legalistic forms of filial ethics and the harsher sides of *guānxī* 關

係obligations into perpetrating acts of vengefulness which lead often to personal self-destruction, relational embitterment, and social chaos which may even include inter-generational expressions of revenge. We have tried to indicate from classical Ruist sources why the principle of blood revenge, particularly in relationship to those who murder one's closest relatives (based originally on a patriarchal form of extended family) were justified, and so to explain why there was a manifest ambivalence between moral cultivation and legal restrictions in the context of vengeance justified on the basis of familial honour and filial obligations. Even from recent studies which draw on sources from the Qīng dynasty (1645–1911), it is clear that punishment of these vengeful acts, even when not considering the mental status of the agent of personal revenge, did not overcome the inherent cultural ambivalence energized by the conflicting roles of ritual obligations of ethical children and relatives and the punitive threats of imperial law.[17] That this and other forms of vengeance would act independently of any legal restrictions is exactly the point which threatens collective reconciliation of any sort, and so we have sought to identify ways in which the cycles of violence created by these putatively justified forms of revenge could be readdressed.

Our strategy for readdressing these matters has involved several steps. First of all, we have suggested that there may be good reasons for doubting the authenticity of the teachings placed in the mouth of Master Kǒng and found in *The Record of the Rites*. We have tried to argue this by referring to alternative ethical principles found in the most reliable source for Master Kǒng's teachings, the *Analects*. Not restricting ourselves to this source, we have explored the moral leverage which the engaged transcendent vision of moral will offers within the teachings of the Míng Ruist scholar, Liú Zōngzhōu. Within this alternative to Wáng Yángmíng's four sentence teaching is a form of transcendent moral enlightenment which argued for a critically accessible and self-reflective ethical awareness which could critique even the most pervasive of social problems and promote their elimination.

On this basis of these alternative interpretive traditions within Ruist texts and schools, therefore, the very popular and persistent interests in pursuing revenge within contemporary Chinese culture can be addressed and overcome by means of reference to both classical and traditional forms of Ruist ethics, one that seeks to "overcome evil with humane cultivation".

Notes

1 Out of the more than 930 pages of this total book, these two categories dealing with preternatural spirits occupy 294 pages of text. When another category referring to "animal revenge" (動物復仇) is included, the total comes to 373 pages. To see that more than a third of all revenge stories deal with agents who are not merely human deserves further reflection, and so we will discuss this factor further on in this chapter.

2 These appear as the first, fourth, and ninth categories in Wáng and Liú 1997, 1–82, 450–505, 869–930; the ranking also suggesting the relative honour or degree of justification assumed for these various categories on the basis of patriarchal understandings of extended family structures and the putative rational

80 *Lauren Pfister*

awareness and motivations (as opposed to irrational ones) motivating the perpetrators. This is not made explicit by the editors, but indicates something of the unspoken ethical hierarchy taken up even within these literary contexts.

3 Significantly, this is the second category within the work, suggesting both its prominence and its relative ethical attractiveness.

4 Here the practical implication of embodying the virtuous demands of filial piety involve a militant opposition against the murderer of one's nearest kin, and so it is justified as a requirement within the ethical responsibilities which Ruist propriety would entail.

5 I have inserted a contemporary Pinyin version for the name of the disciple, and used "Master Kǒng" to replace Legge's "Confucius". A Chinese version of this classical passage can be found in Qīng dynasty scholar Sūn Xīdàn's edition of the *Lǐjì jíjiě* or *Collected Explanations to the Record of the Rites* (1989, 200–201).

6 See specific discussion of this complication related to filial virtue and revenge in Táng and Zōu (2005, 26–30).

7 One very recent example in English is Fàn 2010. In this work, Fàn promotes the positive function of "Confucian rituals" and their employment of "shame" as a practices which "teach and train individuals to interact with each other in proper, cooperative ways" (177). Fàn's particular form of "familism" continues to promote a strong concern for inter-generational family virtues but never mentions this alternative tradition that is linked directly to the expression of filial care for parents, even though he spends a significant amount of effort to discuss the value of filial piety (95–99). For Fàn this is such an important aspect of family virtues that he will not countenance alternatives to adult children caring for their parents (such as placing them in retirement homes or other facilities for the elderly, 89–95). Yet it is precisely this kind of "principled filiality" which motivates familial forms of vengeance.

8 Legge was not the first to note this ethical problem; his sinological predecessor, Sir John Davis, had discussed it before him and received Legge's appreciation and approval. See the full discussion in Legge (1893, 110–111).

9 See the explicit discussion of a hierarchy of these four virtues in the *Mèngzǐ* 4A:27.

10 Here I am purposefully phrasing my thoughts in the form which occurs in the New Testament book of Romans, where it states, "Do not be overcome by evil, but overcome evil with good" (Romans 12:21).

11 See *Analects* 12:13, where Master Kǒng states that though he would not prefer to have litigation, "when hearing litigation, I am like other men".

12 See Matthew 5:43 and its context.

13 D. C. Lau, trans., *Mencius* (Harmondsworth: Penguin Books, 1983), p. 195.

14 Hé Zuòkāng et al., trans., *Mencius* (Beijing: Huayu Jiaoxue Publisher, 1999), p. 461.

15 This version of Liú's four sentence teaching is found in Liú 1996, 459. It varies from the version found in Huáng (2008, 1517), where the fourth and last line of the teaching various in two characters from the four sentences found in the aforementioned collection. I assume that this may be Huáng's error in recording the statement. The English renderings are those of this author.

16 Insights regarding this dimension of Liú Zōngzhōu's teachings have been gained from Hán (2009, 238–240). There is also here a Ruist transcendent vision of reality which includes an ultimate subject paralleling something like deity in mono-theistic traditions, and so paralleling similar conceptual matters in the pre-imperial Ruist teachings of Master Kǒng, but this need not be emphasized here in order to highlight the special moral achievement which we are describing within this late Míng scholar's account of whole person cultivation.

17 Discussed from an angle inspired by Foucault's deconstructionist strategies, the article by Gabbiani illustrates how punitive laws against those who committed parricide were meted out during the Qing dynasty even in spite of the fact that some were mentally incompetent. Their punishment was death by dismemberment. Gabbiani also admits that the phenomenon of parricide was not, therefore, eradicated; in ways that indicate further justification of James Legge's generalization, he explains that cases of parricide continued to be notable until after the advent of the 1911 revolution and the establishment of Republican China. Consult Gabbiani (2009, 334–392).

References

Chén, Ēnlín 陈恩林. 1998. "論公羊傳復仇思想的特點及經今古文復仇說問題" [On the Characteristics of Revenge in Gōngyáng Commentary and Problems with the Theoretical Basis for Revenge in the Old and New Text Versions of That Commentary]. *Social Science Front* 2, 135–145.

Dài, Liǎnzhāng and Guāng Wú 戴璉璋　吳光, eds. 1996. 刘宗周全集 (第二册) [The Complete Works of Liú Zōngzhōu, Vol. 2]. Taipei: Institute of Chinese Literature and Philosophy.

Dalby, Michael, Lì Wáng and Bīnbīn Wèi 王立 魏彬彬, trns. 2002. "傳統中國的復仇與法律" [Revenge and Law in Traditional China (I)]. *Journal of Dāndōng Teachers College* 24(3): 5–10, 20.

———, trns. 2003. "傳統中國的復仇與法律 (续)" [Revenge and Law in Traditional China (II)]. *Journal of Dāndōng Teachers College* 25(1): 1–4.

Dù, Bǎoruì 杜保瑞. 2009. 劉蕺山的功夫理論與形上思想 [LiúZōngzhōu's Theory of Moral Cultivation and His Metaphysical Ideas]. Yǒnghé: Huā Mù Lán Culture Publishing.

Fàn Ruìpíng 范瑞平. 2010. *Reconstructionist Confucianism: Rethinking Morality after the West.* Dordrecht: Springer.

Gabbiani, Luca. 2009. "Pour en finir avec la barbarie: Folie et parricide in Chine à la fin de l'ère impériale." *T'oung Pao* 95: 334–392.

Guō, Qíyǒng 郭齐勇. 2004. 儒家伦理争鸣集: 以 "亲亲互隐" 为中心 [A Collection of Essays about Contentions within Confucian Ethics: Focused on the Problem of "the Mutual Protection of Familial Relatives"]. Wǔhàn: Húběi Education Publishing.

Hán Sīyì 韓思藝. 2009. "From the Debate on Sin and Wrongdoing to the Ways of Regeneration – A Comparison of *Qike* (*The Seven Victories*) and *Renpu* (*Human Schematic*)." [In Chinese] PhD dissertation, Hong Kong Baptist University.

Henderson, John B. 1991. *Scripture, Canon and Commentary: A Comparison of Confucian and Western Exegesis.* Princeton, NJ: Princeton University Press.

Huáng, Mǐnhào 黄敏浩. 2001. 劉宗周及其慎獨哲學 [Liú Zōngzhōu and His Philosophy of Being Cautious When in Solitude]. Taipei: Student Book.

Huáng, Zōngxī 黄宗羲. 2008. 明儒學案 (下册) [Míng Rú Xué Àn, Case Studies of Rú Scholars in the Míng Dynasty, Vol. 2]. Beijing: Zhonghua Book Co.

Legge, James. 1893. *The Chinese Classics.* Vol. 1. Prolegomena.

———, trns. 1986. *The Sacred Books of the East.* Vol. 27. New Delhi: Motilal Banarsidass.

Lǐ Lóngxiàn [Lee Lung-hsien]李隆獻. 2005. "復仇觀的省察與詮釋 – 以《春秋》三傳為中心"[Observations and Interpretations of Relationships of Vengeance – Focused on the Three Commentaries to the Spring and Autumn Annals]. *National Taiwan University's Academic Bulletin for Chinese Literature* 22(6): 99–150.

82 *Lauren Pfister*

———. 2008a. "兩漢魏晉南北朝復仇與法律互涉的省察與詮釋"[Observations and Interpretations of the Mutual Interactions between Vengeance and Law in the Two Hàn Dynasties, as well as the Wèi Jìn and the Southern and Northern Dynasty Periods]. *National Taiwan University's Academic Bulletin for Literature, History and Philosophy* 68(5): 9–78.

———. 2008b. "隋唐時期復仇與法律互涉的省察與詮釋"[Observations and Interpretations of the Mutual Interactions between Vengeance and Law during the Suí and Táng Periods]. *National Cheng Kung University's Academic Bulletin for Chinese Literature* 20(4): 79–110.

———. 2010. "先秦至唐代鬼靈復仇事例的省察與詮釋"[Observations and Interpretations of Cases Related to the Vengeance of Spirits from the Pre-Qín Period to the Táng Dynasty]. *Literature and Philosophy* 16(6): 139–202.

———. 2011. "先秦至唐代復仇型態的省察與詮釋"[Observations and Interpretations of the Attitude toward Punishing Vengeance from the Pre-Qín Period to the Táng Dynasty]. *Literature and Philosophy* 18(6): 1–62.

Liáo, Jūnyù 廖俊裕. 2008. 道德實踐與歷史性: 關於蕺山學的討論 [On Moral Practice and Historicity: On the Discussions of Liú Zōngzhōu's Works]. Yǒnghé: Huā Mù Lán Culture Publishing.

Liú, Hòuqín 刘厚琴. 1994. "論儒學與兩漢復仇之風" [On Ruism and the Prevalence of Revenge during the Western and Eastern Hàn Dynasties]. *Qílǔ Xuékān* 2, 62–66.

Qiū, Fēng and Jiànwǔ Wāng 邱锋 汪建武. 2008. "春秋公羊傳復仇論淺議" [Initial Discussions about Revenge in the Spring and Autumn Annals and Its Gōngyáng Commentary]. *Journal of Húběi Normal College – Philosophy and Social Sciences* 28(6): 75–79.

Struve, Lynn. 2003. "Liu Zongzhou (Liu Tsung-chou)." In *Encyclopedia of Chinese Philosophy*, edited by Antonio S. Cua, 405–408. New York and London: Routledge.

Sūn, Xīdàn 孫希旦. 1989. 禮記集解 [Collected Explanations to the Record of the Rites]. Běijīng: Zhōnghuá Book Co.

Táng, Hónglín and Jiǎnfēng Zōu 唐红林 邹剑锋. 2005. "儒家'孝治'對'血親復仇' 的揚抑" [Ru Scholars Use of "Ruling by Reverence to Elders" in Overcoming and Prohibiting "Familial Revenge"]. *Journal of Níngbō University – Humanities* 18(6): 26–30.

Wáng, Lì 王立. 1995. "孔子與先秦儒家復仇觀初探" [Initial Investigations of Master Kǒng and Pre-Qín Ruist Viewpoints on Revenge]. *Kǒngzǐ Yánjiù* 3, 20–24.

———. 1998. 中國古代復仇文學主題 [Main Themes within Chinese Ancient Literature Dealing with Revenge]. Chángchūn: Northeast Normal University Press.

Wáng, Lì and Wèiyīng Liú 王立 刘卫英, eds. 1997. 中國古代復仇故事大觀 [A Grand Overview of Chinese Ancient Stories about Revenge]. Shànghǎi: Xuélín.

Zāng, Zhīfēi 臧知非. 1996. "春秋公羊學與漢代復仇風氣發微" [On the Spring and Autumn Annals and Its Gōngyáng Commentary Regarding Proofs of the Popularity of Taking Revenge during the Hàn Dynasty]. *Journal of Xúzhōu Normal College – Philosophy and Social Sciences* 2, 23–28.

6 Repentance as a post-philosophical stance

Tanabe Hajime and the road to reconciliation

Dermott J. Walsh

> Metanoetics possess profound significance as a philosophy for the present turning point in history. History is calling on people of all nations to practice *zange* in order to build up societies of fellowship. This is how I understand the meaning of Philosophy as Metanoetics.
>
> – (Tanabe 1986, 296)[1]

Introduction – situating the text

In 1946 the Japanese Philosopher Tanabe Hajime 田辺元 (1885–1962) published his *magnum opus*, a work entitled *Philosophy as Metanoetics* (*Zangedo toshite no tetsugaku*, 懺悔道としての哲 学). This text attempted to critique the fundamentals of philosophical discourse via an adaptation of Shin Pure Land Buddhist concepts, especially the idea of "repentance" (*zange* 懺悔). Tanabe then links this idea to another Pure Land Buddhist notion, that of "other-power" (*tariki* 他力) in an attempt to provide a new start for philosophy in the post–World War II era.

The core assumption of the text is that philosophical problems cannot be considered in the abstract and are simultaneously and urgently linked to the existential. A personal transformation is required before one can engage meaningfully with the world in a philosophical manner. Tanabe's focus on the existential importance of the experience of radical repentance in the form of *zange* is not unknown to the western world. Figures such as Augustine, Socrates and Pascal, amongst others, are also associated with conversion as a category that borders philosophy and religion.[2]

The purpose of Tanabe's text is twofold: first, it is a public recognition of his failure to fulfil his duty as a philosopher during World War II. Tanabe points to this issue in the Preface when he speaks of the dilemma he faced during the war period:

> I myself shared in all these sufferings of my fellow Japanese, but as a philosopher I experienced yet another kind of distress. On the one hand, I was haunted by the thought that, as a student of Philosophy I ought to be bringing the best of my thought to the service of my nation, to be addressing the

84 *Dermott Walsh*

government frankly with regard to its policies towards academic thought and demanding a reexamination, even if this should incur the displeasure of those currently in power. . . . On the other hand, there seemed something traitorous about expressing in time of war ideas that, while perfectly proper in time of peace, might end up causing division and conflicts among our people that would only further expose them to their enemies.

(Tanabe 1963, 3–4, 1986, 1).

Tanabe's admission had little impact, largely due to its unfortunate timing. His public act of repentance was lost amongst a plethora of such calls for national repentance, with several "opportunistic Politicians" leading the way.[3] The fact that Tanabe had written much of the text before the end of the war did little to set his sentiments, however genuine, apart from the mass.

The second purpose of the book is philosophical. Tanabe felt that worldwide warfare was proof not only that he had failed in his duty as a philosopher but also that the entire project of philosophy needed to be reconfigured. Thus Tanabe set about re-reading the history of (western) philosophy via the idea that reason was no longer an adequate guide and that a more ethically potent alternative had to be sought. It is this alternative, repentance in the guise of the Shin Buddhist inspired concept of *zange*, which forms the core concept of the book. He points to the experience of *zange* as a means to reinterpret existence, once we have come to understand the limits of rationality through a discourse he calls "absolute critique" (*zettai hihan* 絶對批判). Unfortunately this intriguing aspect of Tanabe's work has often been overshadowed by questions concerning his wartime political activity.

While Tanabe's position on wartime politics cannot be simply brushed aside, it is unfair to emphasize this aspect of his thought at the expense of the issues raised in *Philosophy as Metanoetics*. Tanabe presents a challenge to standard western approaches to ethical problems and suggests that his new method will lead to a reconfiguration of the concept of philosophy in the future. This new method will be based upon the experience of radical repentance, an experience so profound that one's entire philosophical foundations may well be turned upside down. *Zange*, a term Tanabe borrows from Buddhism, comes thus to represent both a concept that opens up new and radical horizons of thought, and also an experience which is akin to a religious conversion.

The purpose of this chapter is to outline clearly what is novel in Tanabe's thought, while also dealing with some of the criticisms which have been levelled at Tanabe's text. I will show that while Tanabe overemphasizes the existential at the expense of the philosophical, there is still much in Tanabe of relevance today.

The meaning of *zange* in Tanabe's thought

Tanabe's understanding of the term *zange* is both complicated and controversial. Ueda Yoshifumi has pointed out that Tanabe's use of the term differs fundamentally from how it is understood in the Japanese Shin Pure Land Buddhist

Analysis of philosophy as metanoetics 85

tradition, from which he draws Inspiration (Ueda 1990).[4] However, if we look to the text itself we see that Tanabe's "way of metanoia" (*zangedo* 懺悔道) is a compound of three aspects: confession, conversion and repentance. When referring to confession, Tanabe uses the Japanese term *kokuhaku* 告白, a word that can mean "confession" in a religious context, but is also used in everyday life. This contrasts with Tanabe's choice of *zange* for repentance. Tanabe could have used the everyday Japanese word for repentance, *kokai* (後悔), rather than the explicitly Buddhist term *zange*. This indicates that it is not an ordinary case of repentance; he is referring to something radical and life changing which goes beyond what is understood by the everyday term.

The third aspect of the "way of repentance" is "Conversion". Tanabe points out that "Metanoia can mean both conversion and repentance " (Tanabe 1963, 21, 1986, 6) using the term *zange* for repentance and *kaishin/eshin*, (迴心) for "conversion". The Japanese word *kaishin/eshin* refers to conversion in a specifically religious context. Interestingly, reading the first character of the compound as *kai* suggests a conversion to Christianity, while reading the same character *e* suggests a conversion to Buddhism. Tanabe may well be exploiting this ambiguity to suggest that the conversion is not to a specific religion but to a new mindset or outlook. Regardless, both conversion and confession are necessary, but not sufficient, conditions for the possibility of genuine repentance and the transformation of perspective that occurs when one follows the "way of metanoia". Within this triad, however, it is *zange* that is most important (Tanabe 1963, 18, 1986, 2). Without *zange*, one cannot follow the "way of metanoia"; the subject cannot undergo conversion or confession without first experiencing true repentance.

While Tanabe may wish to stress the unique intensity of his version of repentance, we can still compare his understanding with modern accounts. For example Etzioni (1997, 9–10) outlines the three characteristics of repentance as follows: an expression of true remorse (confession or *kokuhaku*), the desire to do penance (repentance or *zange*), and the desire to re-structure one's life to ensure no repeat of the action which led to the required act of repentance in the first place (Conversion or *kai/eshin*) (Etzioni and Carney 1997). The key difference between Tanabe and this more standard interpretation rests with the issue of what motivates repentance in the first place. Usually, we repent when we are unable to tolerate the fact of our own guilt. Tanabe does not consider this a genuine form of repentance. Repentance as an act of will is doomed to failure: "the tenacity of ego cannot be avoided in any act brought about directly by will. This is our radical evil" (Tanabe 1963, 180, 1986, 155). This is why an ordinary act of repentance is not sufficient; it must be radical repentance; in other words, it must be *zange* as Tanabe understands it. Self-will cannot force the subject to repent, as it is this very self will that is the root cause of our moral deficiency. Furthermore, in the case of *zange* we are not simply repenting of one or even a number of deeds; rather we assume a repentant attitude towards the entire course of our lives. Tanabe insists that such a radical change of perspective is beyond the power of our own self will to instigate. Thus for Tanabe, there is a further aspect

86 *Dermott Walsh*

to radical repentance, and that is the realization of the futility of our own ego-fuelled efforts to repent. In order to ensure true and total repentance, one must look elsewhere, to the concept of "other-power".

Self-power and other-power

For Tanabe, the path of reason and the path of *zange* represent two different means of approaching the world, roughly equivalent to the Pure Land Buddhist distinction between "self-power" (*jiriki* 自力) and "other-power" (*tariki* 他力). For this distinction Tanabe draws on the work of the Japanese Pure Land Buddhist Shinran 親鸞 (1173–1263): "instead of interpreting Shinran's teaching in a philosophical manner, I have it in mind here to remold philosophy as metanoetics, to start afresh on the way of philosophy by following Shinran's religious path" (PM: 20/ THZ, Vol. 9: 32). Shinran is central to Tanabe's thought, but this is not the same as suggesting that Tanabe is accurately representing Shinran's Buddhism. Tanabe acknowledges himself that his philosophy seeks to incorporate a whole range of different elements:

> Metanoetics does not always and of necessity adhere to the doctrine and tradition of Pure Land Buddhism. It is rational in terms of its demand that ethical theory provide *zange* with its distinctive foundation. In this sense, it is closer to Christianity. At the same time, it is obvious that the *kyogyoshinsho* of the Pure Land is fundamentally metanoetic in motivation. This is why it has been my guide. Still, I would insist that my metanoetics developed its distinguishing traits under the inspiration of both sources and cannot be strictly identified with either. As a product of my own experience it cannot but be colored by personal history, and this I regret. I cannot exercise my own *zange* otherwise than in this metanoetic philosophy of mine.
> (Tanabe 1963, 204–205, 1986, 221–222)

This is a key passage, and it refers back to criticisms of Tanabe by Buddhist Studies scholars such as Ueda. To suggest that Tanabe has misinterpreted Shinran is not in itself a terminal problem for his philosophy. Those who suggest otherwise are veering perilously close to the genetic fallacy of critiquing the origins of a theory rather than its content. Tanabe's philosophy is certainly inspired by Shinran but is not designed to present the historical or philosophical reality of Orthodox Shin Buddhism as one would expect say from a Buddhist scholar. Shinran's thoughts are a foil for Tanabe's creative process. To take Tanabe to task for an inaccurate representation of Shinran misses the point entirely. We can, however, draw an interesting parallel regarding timing. Shinran's use of *zange* was in response to the wide-ranging belief that Japan was in the age of *mappo* 末法, the age of the degenerate Dharma. For Shinran, all previous ethical systems had proven to be a failure and must be rejected in the face of the challenge presented by the times. Controversially, this also included rejection of the Buddhist monastic codes, the *vinaya*. The major political and social upheavals of the times, as well as a series of

Analysis of philosophy as metanoetics 87

natural disasters, provided the backdrop and justification for this radical position. Such a radical stance mirrors Tanabe, who suggests that the horrors of World War II warrant a similarly far-reaching and fundamental reorientation of ethical norms.

The distinction between the self-power route of reason and the other-power route of *zange* also serves a second purpose, suggesting an egalitarian element to the experience of *zange*. Rather than presenting a religion for philosophers, or a philosophy of religion, Tanabe is suggesting that *zange* is an aspect of human nature; every individual has the potential to experience it:

> From everything that I have said so far, it should be clear that the ethical metanoetics I am proposing may also be considered a 'total koan', rooted in the essential structure of reality. It is not restricted to saints and sages, but is one koan in which ethics and *zange* are made directly accessible to anyone possessed of conscience. It is a gate to religious life for ordinary ignorant persons.
>
> (Tanabe 1963, 125, 1986, 127–128)

This distinction between the "path of saints and sages" and that open to the ordinary and ignorant, of which Tanabe regards himself as one, is a cornerstone of his work, and is also reminiscent of Shinran. For Shinran, opening up religious and ethical experience to those in society who are not scholars or monks was a key aspect of his teaching and of his success, especially in the Kanto region of Japan. Tanabe also maintains an egalitarian view, except for him the targets are philosophers and intellectuals. Other-power does not discriminate on the basis of one's intellectual ability. The key point is that one has a repentant attitude that is not bound to ego and that will thus be open to receive other-power. With this in mind, Tanabe envisages *zange* as a societal phenomenon open to all, rather than a merely private experience. This is, for Tanabe, one of the aspects of his thought that crucially distinguishes it from Zen 禅, which he regards as a self-power philosophy (Tanabe 1963, 180, 1986, 188). Yet the influence of Zen remains in Tanabe's philosophy, with the idea of a self "resurrected" and thus transformed through a combination of other-power and its encounter with Absolute Nothingness, a move that combines both Pure Land and Zen aspects. The influence of the latter is particularly obvious with Tanabe's interpretation of the function of absolute nothingness. The realization of the fundamental nothingness at the centre of our existence allows us to fully participate in the world of praxis, without hindrance from the artificial sense of a rational self that can understand and interpret the world through the action of its ego.

Tanabe's use of the ideas of self-power and other-power marks a clear distinction between those who have yet to experience radical repentance and those who are still relying on their own self. A description of the route of self-power through reason takes up a large part of Tanabe's text. Tanabe suggests that both existentially and philosophically we can no longer rely on rationality as it is normally

88   *Dermott Walsh*

understood. Once we realize that rationality is no longer ethically viable we are on our way to the realization of a repentant attitude. Tanabe narrates this story of the failure of reason via a re-reading of the history of western philosophy, what he terms the "death of reason" due to "absolute critique" (*zettai hihan*, 絕對批判). This concept embodies the key critical aspects of Tanabe's text, and it is to this that we now turn.

The death of reason in absolute critique

For Tanabe, World War II presents a critical challenge to the Kantian ideal of a rational fulcrum to the philosophical enterprise.[5] What we can be sure of, however, is that reality itself does not conform to any preconceived rational limits. Tanabe here echoes Hegel's famous criticism of Kant, when he suggests that Kant failed to embrace the radical conclusions that his postulation of the antinomies of reason inevitably led. Thus philosophical thought is in a bind; the philosopher cannot transform her thought into praxis, as the assumption that reality is fundamentally rational is no longer tenable. Tanabe suggests that this explains why philosophy remains abstract and unable to perform its duty of providing feasible answers to both personal and societal questions. This failure was at the root of inability of philosophical discourse to dissuade the world from war. Tanabe is thus pointing to a classical problem in philosophy – the gap between theory and praxis, a problem that is perhaps the key issue for the entire Kyoto school of philosophy. Tanabe suggests that our ethical and philosophical selves cannot be transformed until we have come to realize the folly of our reliance on reason and allow ourselves to be transformed by *zange*:

> The only way for philosophy to achieve this goal of total transformation is for the autonomy of reason, the motivating force of philosophy, to become dead-locked in the self-awareness of its own incompetence. In its despair of self power – that is metanoesis – reason can be led to self surrender via 'Other power', until at last it revives as a philosophy of "effortless naturalness" (*musa honi* 無作法爾) beyond all opposition of self and other.
>
> (Tanabe 1963, 37, 1986, 27)

Tanabe terms this critique of reason "absolute critique" (*zettai hihan*, 絕對批判). If one prioritizes the rational at the expense of other-power, "effortless naturalness", a state free of the radical evil inherent in ego and beyond all dichotomies, cannot be reached.

The death of reason through absolute critique serves several purposes within the scheme of Tanabe's philosophy. First, there is the philosophical significance of the discourse as a critique of the history of western philosophy; second, it suggests that the realization of the fallibility of reason and our inability to act in an irrational world is a key factor in pushing us to the brink of the repentant attitude. Once we realize that the world is not rational we may fall into a morass

Analysis of philosophy as metanoetics 89

of self-doubt or even depression. Thus we realize the necessity for radical repentance and the need for other-power to make this happen.

Second, this critique of reason provides a key contrast between the pre- and post-*zange* mindsets. Tanabe points to the fact that post-zange we come to a new understanding of reason. Critics such as Jamie Hubbard (1990, 372) asked how we can continue to engage in questions concerning the validity of propositions in either Philosophy or Religion post-*zange*, if reason is no longer the benchmark (Hubbard 1990)?[6] Certainly this is a justified criticism, but Tanabe's basic position is still defensible. Tanabe can claim it is legitimate to use reason to reach the point where reason is no longer useful. The vagueness in Tanabe's account emerges with attempts to explain this post-*zange* rationality. Seemingly it is both broader and more fluid; what that amounts to is a rationality untainted by concerns of the ego. Tanabe suggests this in the following passage: "the reason that dies in the depths of absolute critique is not resurrected in the same form as before, as reason whose principle is self-identity" (Tanabe 1963, 61, 1986, 55).

This characterization of reason suggests that Tanabe may have made a technical error in considering reason and logic as equivalents, even directly saying so in certain parts of the text (Tanabe 1963, 53–54, 1986, 44–45). While this move enables him to fight off the kind of critique suggested by Hubbard, it also presents a problem for his characterization of reason and what it actually is that he deems to have failed in the philosophical enterprise. There are two key differences for our purposes between reason and logic: first, logic is used entirely in the abstract to judge the validity of arguments and does not present a major factor in practical decision making (indeed, one might even call it irrational to use formal logic in an attempt to decide the moral course of action); a second problem, suggested by the earlier, is that the boundaries of reason are much broader than those of logic, and thus to conflate the two is to treat reason to much tougher standards of correctness than is feasible in moral decision making. Nonetheless, the basic tenor of Tanabe's position seems fair; all Tanabe is suggesting is that our rational faculties are radically changed by the experience of *zange*, and once we have this experience of repentance, we need a new sense of what is rational in order to more accurately describe reality. The seismic personal transformation one undergoes during *zange* cannot possibly leave something as central as rationality untouched. Such a view has radical implications, especially for considerations in the field of ethics.

Ethical implications of Tanabe's thought

The impact of Tanabe's philosophy is wide ranging. First, while Tanabe's text orients us somewhat with regard to philosophy in the past, we are left to speculate on how philosophy as a discipline should be configured in the future. Tanabe's insistence that philosophy be considered a form of life suggests that much of what we may consider philosophy now, metaphysics and epistemology, for example are not genuine philosophical issues. It appears the nature of action is the main concern of the philosopher post-*zange*, hence what we consider ethics takes centre

90 *Dermott Walsh*

stage. The post-*zange* stage is concerned not with theory but with practice; philosophy can no longer be considered a discipline concerned with conceptualization and analysis. The normative judgement Tanabe makes regarding philosophy prior to radical repentance holds equally true of pre-*zange* existence in a general sense. Tanabe is clearly condemning pre-*zange* existence as misguided in comparison to the truth revealed in the experience of *zange*.

Tanabe illustrates the changes to ethical life which occur post-*zange* when he makes reference to "the action of no-action" (*musa no sa*, 無作の作) and "naturalness" (*jinen hōni*, 自 然法爾) in the following passage:

> The confrontation of ethics with radical evil cannot avoid facing antinomy and arriving ultimately at *zange*. The self that has been forced to let go of itself in metanoesis is then restored to itself. . . . In this way the antinomies are resolved without being dissolved, and the road-less transit of "the action of no action" (*musa no sa*, 無作の作) becomes manifest as a "naturalness" (*jinen honi* 自然法爾) that surpasses all opposition between good and evil. The gate impassible for *jiriki* becomes passable through *tariki*.
>
> (Tanabe 1963, 124, 1986, 127)[7]

The dualities of right and wrong, of good and evil, of rational and irrational, are no longer applicable. The requirement of rational consideration in the pre-*zange* stage taints every act with ego, even those that may initially appear morally acceptable. In contrast, there is an inevitability surrounding ethical action in the post-*zange* framework; with the removal of ego, the root of radical evil, one can act in accordance with "naturalness" – a concept that appears in one form or another in all of Buddhism, Confucianism and Taoism – adhering to the correct order of things as they are. Consideration of how to act is no longer tainted by false dichotomies. In fact, once one has undergone *zange*, we philosophize in the act of doing, rather than extrapolating from doctrines. Philosophy is no longer centred on abstract reasoning but on the ability to act, removing the gap between theory and practice that Tanabe sees as having beset the history of philosophy.

This is the ethical end-point envisaged by Tanabe, the ability to act in a morally correct way in accordance with "naturalness", almost instinctively doing what is right without the requirement of rational consideration.

This idea of morality bears similarity to the work of other thinkers, not least that of his teacher Nishida Kitaro 西田幾多郎 (1870–1945). In his *An Inquiry into the Good* (*zen no kenkyu* 善の研究) (1911) Nishida is also concerned with bridging the gap between theory and praxis. One of Nishida's main influences regarding this issue is the Neo-Confucian thinker Wang Yangming 王陽明 (1472–1529), particularly Wang's idea of "the Unity of knowledge and Action" (Chn. *chi xing ho-i*, Jpn. *chigyodoitsu*, 知行同一). Yet the route followed by Tanabe and Nishida to achieve this goal is entirely different. Nishida's Zen-inspired philosophy is from Tanabe's perspective infected with self-power and is thus open only to whom Tanabe calls "saints and sages". Moreover, given that the ego is the cause of radical evil, relying on the self to uproot the self is for Tanabe entirely

Analysis of philosophy as metanoetics 91

unfeasible. If we want to reach the point where an individual actor without ego acts in accordance with "naturalness", there must be a thorough transformation brought about by other-power, bringing us to the realization of radical repentance. This eliminates the need to philosophically muse on ethical problems at all. Instead one demonstrates understanding via action, through the ability to act in "naturalness". Thus having experienced *zange* becomes a necessary condition for those who wish to understand the ethics of "naturalness"; the sphere of interpersonal discussion surrounding ethics in the post-*zange* stage precludes the possibility of understanding for those who have yet to experience *zange* themselves. This issue brings to the fore one of the major problems which faces Tanabe's philosophy: the nature of both interaction and discourse between those who have repented and those who have not.

Concluding reflections on Tanabe's philosophy of repentance

Tanabe's philosophy is both challenging and original, and thus it is no surprise that he has left many questions unanswered. Some of the questions we may state without further elaboration: for example given the similarities, why not simply follow Shinran's version of Buddhism rather than Tanabe's philosophy? Another question one may ask is how do philosophers who have not experienced *zange* communicate with those who have? It seems as if pre-*zange* life is merely something deluded in comparison to life once one has experienced radical repentance.

A broad-ranging problem, however, is evident with the issue of how *zange* is understood as a concept in comparison to as an experience. It seems clear that undergoing the process of radical repentance in the manner understood by Tanabe is a very serious and profound experience for the individual. Tanabe has taken this experience and suggested that it has a dual function as both an existential experience and a concept. However, it seems clear that for Tanabe describing the existential experience and its impact is much easier than explaining the logical effect of radical repentance as a concept. By placing the experience rather than the concept of repentance at the centre of his philosophy, Tanabe has left himself open to a number of objections, both from a philosophical and an existential perspective. We have a description of a mental process leading to an experience and then a description of how the experience alters our lives. However, we have no conceptual understanding of what repentance actually signifies other than its significance as an experience, no means to understand the evolution of the concept from pre- to post-*zange*. It may be helpful here to contrast Tanabe's approach with that of Descartes, who de-personalizes and conceptualizes his radical doubt so as to facilitate its use as a philosophical concept rather than a description of a private conversion. With *zange*, the means to assess its validity as a concept is denied to us: those who have not experienced radical repentance are incapable of commenting. It is hard to avoid the conclusion that *zange* is akin to a religious conversion, a conclusion that Tanabe would certainly wish to avoid for fear of reducing his philosophy to an unorthodox form of Buddhism. Tanabe

92   *Dermott Walsh*

himself acknowledges such a possibility, but suggests that he has no experience of enlightenment so cannot comment on any similarities to the experience of *zange* (Tanabe 1963, 122, 1986, 125).

Tanabe's failure is rooted in his assumption that theory needs to be reduced to praxis. By failing to find adequate room for theory, Tanabe has inserted an experience into a philosophical discussion, leaving us with the idea of action as "naturalness" which is conceptually incompatible with many of our previous ethical assumptions. Tanabe has provided no means by which we in the pre-*zange* stage can conceptually account for how the experience of radical repentance results in an overriding of dichotomies such as good and evil. We are thus left with a situation where only a small group of those who have had this experience can truly understand the ethical world.

Tanabe could have avoided many of these issues if he had made a concerted effort to present repentance as a concept both pre- and post-*zange*. Ideally Tanabe could have presented the rational basis for the concept and how it functions within the current boundaries of ethical thought, followed by a conceptual analysis of the radicalization of repentance in *zange* and its status and functionality vis-à-vis the new sense of rationality. Such a discourse may have charted the development of the concept of repentance, facilitating dialogue between pre and post-*zange* philosophers by providing a working comparative model. Moreover, providing a sense of how the concept of repentance evolves through pre-*zange* into the radical post-*zange* stage lessens the stark contrast between those who have experienced radical repentance and those who have not, as we can access at least a conceptual understanding even if an experiential one remains lacking.

From the perspective of reconciliation, Tanabe presents an intriguing model. On the one hand, he has made a very radical claim: to repent is to *start* on the path of philosophizing. In emphasizing that repentance has both a practical and a theoretical aspect, he suggests that repentance leading to reconciliation is not just a simple matter of apologizing and asking for forgiveness; rather it requires an existential transformation and an acknowledgement of how not just one's actions, but one's entire philosophical mindset while doing the action needs to be reconstituted. However, the suggestion that somehow this repentance comes from outside of us, from "other-power", may provide an obstacle to reconciliation. We expect repentance to follow a period of soul searching, of actively acquiring a corrected moral vision. For Tanabe, it is simply a case of waiting for other-power to act upon you, thus absolving the guilty of the need to repent and take personal responsibility. Perhaps radical repentance through "self-power" is a happy medium: responsibility cannot be shirked by the individual, but at the same time, the individual remains open to the radical power of true repentance, a necessary condition for reconciliation.

Tanabe envisaged a world where radical repentance is transformative, where one cannot repent piecemeal. It must be a whole-hearted transformation that leaves no aspect of our existence untouched, an experience which results in the casting aside of previous paradigms and a complete re-fashioning of one's mindset. While we have critiqued Tanabe on a number of technical details, the overriding tenor of his thought must be borne in mind: repentance is a serious philosophical issue, and thus by extension is the process of reconciliation with which it is linked. When approaching issues of reconciliation, one must ensure a sound philosophical basis, for what Tanabe has taught us is that repentance and reconciliation are not just issues for philosophy, they are its main concern. For Tanabe, philosophy is a practical matter, and repentance is at its core. In our efforts to affect reconciliation, it may well be the overriding tenor of Tanabe's thought, rather than the details, which will provide inspiration for a new generation of philosophers.

Notes

1 All subsequent quotations will be from this text and will be accompanied by references to the Japanese edition of Tanabe's complete Works (Tanabe 1963).
2 Tanabe himself suggests that Socrates as "the most authentic of all philosophers" and that the Athenian was following the "Way of Metanoetics" (Tanabe 1963, 29, 1986, 16). The full quote in Japanese is as follows「古代に於いて哲学者の典型なるソクラテスは、その無知の知反語を以て懺悔の途を歩んだのである。」
3 See Takeuchi's "Translator's Introduction" to *Philosophy as Metanoeitcs*, p. xxxvi: "I find it unfortunate that its publication in the immediate post-war period . . . should have overshadowed its true origins and caused it to be absorbed into the general atmosphere of mass appeals for national repentance being generated by opportunistic politicians."
4 Ueda concludes his analysis (1990, 134–135) by suggesting that Tanabe has not utilized, at least correctly, a single concept from Shinran.
5 "The Critique of Pure Reason cannot provide the ultimate standpoint for philosophy that Kant claimed for it . . . reason is left exposed to antinomies which can only rend it asunder and cast it into a state of absolute self-disruption . . . reason that tries to establish its own competence by means of self-criticism must finally, contrary to its own intentions, recognize its final self-disruption" (Tanabe 1963, 51–52, 1986, 43).
6 I will refer to Hubbard's critique again later in the chapter.
7 Tanabe borrowed the Japanese phrase *jinen honin* from Shinran, see Tanabe (1986, 299), note 2. In English language scholarship, the concept is discussed in Abe (1991, 166).

References

Abe, Masao. 1991. *A Study of Dogen: His Philosophy and Religion*. New York: New York State University Press.
Etzioni, Amitai and David E. Carney, eds. 1997. *Repentance: A Comparative Perspective*. Lanham: Rowman and Littlefield Publishers.
Hubbard, Jamie. 1990. "Tanabe's Metanoetics: The Failure of Absolutism." In *The Religious Philosophy of Tanabe Hajime*, edited by Mark Unno and James Heisig, 360–382. Berkeley, CA: Asian Humanities Press.
Tanabe, Hajime 田辺元. 1963. *Zangedo toshite no tetsugaku*, 懺悔道としての哲学. In *Tanabe Hajime Zenshu*. Vol. 9. Tokyo: Chikuma Shobo.
———. 1986. *Philosophy as Metanoetics*. Translated by Takeuchi Yoshinori. Berkeley, CA: University of California Press.
Ueda, Yoshifumi. 1990. "Shin Buddhism and Metanoetics." In *The Religious Philosophy of Tanabe Hajime*, edited by Mark Unno and James Heisig, 117–134. Berkeley, CA: Asian Humanities Press.

Part II

Regional experience and comparison

7 Reconciliation theories and the East Asian peace

Alan Hunter

The military parade held in Beijing on 3 September 2015 relayed several political messages on the complex relations between China and Japan. Since 1949 China's military parades have always been held on 1 October, the National Day which commemorates the founding of the People's Republic. The 3 September was chosen specifically to celebrate the seventieth anniversary of victory over Japan and the end of World War II. The parade was strongly supported throughout the country by broadcasts, posters, interventions to stabilize the stock market and the creation of two new national holidays: 3 September itself, and the 13 December as a tribute to the victims of the Nanjing Massacre of 1937.

International participation was mixed. Alongside many leaders from developing countries, an important guest was Mr Ban Ki-moon, Secretary-General of the United Nations. His office had rejected a strong protest from the Japanese government, stating that 'it was important to recognise China's wartime sacrifice and learn the lessons of history' (McCurry 2015). The US and most European leaders declined to attend, apparently feeling that the parade was more a marker of China's recent military assertiveness than a peaceful commemoration.

So in one sense, the parade seemed to be confirmation of continuing tension and hostility between China on the one hand and Japan and its Western allies on the other. However, the picture is more complex. In April 2015, China's leader Xi Jinping and Japanese Prime Minister Abe had held a tentatively conciliatory meeting. This meeting was followed by a 3.000-strong Japanese delegation to China in May, and a productive bilateral meeting of finance ministers in June. Perhaps the real intention of the parade was more to strengthen Xi's position in domestic politics, in the midst of his difficult anti-corruption campaigns, and a signal to the outside world that China is now strong, self-confident and ready to move on from any self-presentation as 'victim' of the war into a new era as the leading power in Asia: a position which Japan and the US have little choice but to accept. By the end of September, Xi was in Washington for a summit with President Obama that led to no breakthroughs but achieved some minor agreements. No armed conflict but no deep reconciliation seems to be a theme of East Asian politics.

98 *Alan Hunter*

Reconciliation theories

East Asia is in many respects an extremely successful part of the world.[1] Health-care, welfare, employment, transport and technical infrastructure are generally good, governments are stable, and there have been no armed conflicts since the end of the Korean War in 1953. School students in Korea, Japan and the major Chinese cities were among the best in the world in the 2012 OECD analysis of achievements in mathematics, science and reading. Universities in Tokyo, Seoul, Beijing, Shanghai and other cities rank high by international measures. These are significant achievements, especially considering that the countries were devastated by wars between 1937 and 1953; that China was one of the poorest nations in the world for much of the twentieth century; and that the states were split by Cold War politics, with Japan, Korea and Taiwan in the US camp facing North Korea and China.

With the exception of North Korea, its countries are intimately connected by tourism, investment, trade and popular culture, and all countries host significant immigrant communities from their neighbours. Much of the region's culture is still derived from a classical Chinese heritage, although its influence may be less than in earlier generations. Cultural overlaps include Buddhism, Confucianism, poetic and calligraphic sensibilities, martial arts and many other shared resources. The strategic game of Go alone has more than 40 million players, with top championships hotly contested between Japanese, Chinese and Korean players.

Yet the region is also experiencing a massive increase in military expenditure. There is much angry rhetoric between China and Japan, and confrontations between the two countries over disputed territory have triggered dangerous incidents. The rhetoric is not restricted to government statements but is amplified in vitriolic Internet-based nationalist propaganda involving millions of citizens, occasionally translated into street violence; while public opinion surveys in both China and Japan show a majority mutual dislike and mistrust. In the light of theoretical perspectives on reconciliation, what precedents and theories might be useful in understanding this persistence of antagonism? Why do the deep and angry sentiments between Japan and China exist, despite the shared heritage, high levels of education and mutually beneficial economic activity? And what contributions might the East Asian experience make towards reconciliation theory and practice in other parts of the world?

Peace and war in East Asia are of critical importance to the whole world as well as to the peoples of the region. Among other reasons, the world's second and third largest economies, Japan and China, are located here as neighbours; and the United States is deeply engaged with their economies, and also with security, including nuclear issues. From the dynamics of the region we can also learn much about reconciliation or, more specifically, conditions that are not conducive to it.

Lederach (1999) formulated the idea that reconciliation between former enemies might take place if several factors were brought into public settlements. For example there needs to be a restoration of justice; truth about the past events needs to be brought to light and acknowledged; peace, security and economic

Reconc. theory and the East Asian context 99

reconstruction need to take place; and former enemy societies need to develop a culture of forgiveness. These four factors will always be to some extent in a state of tension with each other and also, some cultures, some countries and some regimes will be more interested in pursuing one rather than the others. Other definitions include Johan Galtung's 'process of healing the traumas of both victims and perpetrators after the violence, providing a closure of the bad relation. The process prepares the parties for relations with justice and peace' (Galtung 2001, 3). Hizkias Assefa (1999, 4) argued that reconciliation differs from all other conflict-handling mechanisms by way of its methodology:

> Tthe essence of reconciliation is the voluntary initiative of the conflict parties to acknowledge their responsibility and guilt . . . the parties are not only meant to communicate one's grievances against the actions of the adversary, but also engage in self-reflection about one's own role and behaviour in the dynamic of the conflict.

Reconciliation is an imperfect term in many contexts, since it implies a restoration of an intimate relationship that suffered a rupture of some kind. In fact, many populations that have learned to live together without armed conflict had previously been isolated from each other or lived in chronic conflict. Terms for 'reconciliation' in different languages and cultures also carry different connotations. Still the term is widely used now to refer to relationships that have moved beyond emergency peacekeeping and cessation of armed conflict to deeper, broader and more friendly interactions with a former enemy. Reconciliation in this sense has been of central importance both after civil conflicts, as in South Africa and Spain; and after international wars, for example World War II. In terms of stable peace and deep reconciliation, the exemplars cited most frequently are Germany-France and Germany-Poland. Many other pairs or groups of countries, though, have moved from armed conflicts to much more friendly relationships, for example the UK and most of its former colonies; the US and Vietnam; Greece and Turkey; Chile and Peru. Chinese scholar He (2009, 12) observed:

> The traumatic experiences of a state usually originate in protracted, destructive conflicts with external actors. Such conflicts not only cause massive combat casualties, but also often involve gross violations of human rights and even national annexation, territorial loss, or pillaging of important national resources. Besides, states suffer the psychological wounds of humiliation while enduring horrendous physical damage. These historical injustices generate deep-rooted collective sorrow and grief that become national trauma, predisposing former enemy states to mutual enmity. To attain reconciliation is to overcome such enmity stemming from the traumatic past.

There are various typologies of international peace and reconciliation in the works of Boulding (1978), Galtung (1996), Kacowicz (2000) and Kupchan (2010); He (2009, 17) consolidated many of the observations to illustrate a

100 *Alan Hunter*

transition from 'non-reconciliation', through friction and rapprochement to 'deep reconciliation'.

After a survey of literature, Brounéus (2003, 20) arrived at core reconciliation themes shared by many scholars and practitioners: reconciliation involves mutual acknowledgement by former enemies of past suffering; changing of destructive patterns of interaction between former enemies into constructive relationships, in attitudes and behaviour; a process towards sustainable peace. Her study is mainly focused on reconciliation within societies that have suffered civil wars, but the working definition she provides is useful for the context of international reconciliation in East Asia:

> Reconciliation is a societal process that involves mutual acknowledgment of past suffering, and the changing of destructive attitudes and behaviour into constructive relationships toward sustainable peace. In other words, reconciliation mainly focuses on remembering, changing, and continuing with life in peace. Reconciliation does not require forgetting, forgiving, or loving one another.

Geopolitics and memory politics

As well as reconciliation scholarship, a 'neo-realist' paradigm of international relations is relevant to approaching the East Asian context, despite its repeated gloomy predictions of an 'inevitable' regional war that have not yet materialized. Realist paradigms maintain that nation-states are most likely to maintain peaceful, harmonious relations where they share security, strategic, political and economic interests. They are likely to experience conflicts with states in rival alliances, especially in situations where rising powers challenge an existing power-structure. Important perceptions of potential rivals include their military capabilities, resources and hostile intentions. Representative authors include Rock (1989), Walt (1990) and Waltz (2008). There are many sub-variants of realist theory but, on the whole, relations between formerly enemy states after a military conflict are considered as likely to improve from some kind of security alliance; for example mutual agreement to cooperate against a perceived threat from a rival power grouping. The acceptance of West Germany into NATO in 1955 doubtless facilitated its acceptance by other West European nations.

However, scholars such as He argued that stable peace, or deep reconciliation, needs to be based on a more profound understanding and goodwill between former combatants; without it, security alliances may be fragile. He used phrases such as 'sustainable mutual understanding and trust' (2009, 4), 'emotions and actions that spring voluntarily from the societies involved' (2009, 14) and 'a feeling of mutual closeness and sometimes affection, or at least mutual empathy' (2009, 20).

There is precisely a lack of 'mutual understanding and trust' in East Asia, especially between the Chinese and Japanese, though also impacting on both countries' relations with North and South Korea. A realist perspective on Sino-Japanese antagonism should certainly be considered seriously, as the two countries are, in

Reconc. theory and the East Asian context 101

fact, integrated in different regional and global security alliances. Realists might suggest that citizen rapprochement is not very likely or even particularly significant under these circumstances.

This fact alone, however, could not come close to explaining the anger, mistrust and suspicion that pertains between both the populations and the political elites. For that, one has to turn to the history of Japanese militarized aggression against China and Korea for the fifty years between 1894 and 1945 and, in the Chinese view, Japan's singular failure to apologize and provide compensation for, or even acknowledge, the depth of destruction it inflicted on China as well as other peoples of Asia.

In Chinese argument, often supported by Koreans and others, Japan has consistently manipulated historical records both in terms of public policy and specifically in its teaching of history in schools. Chinese commentators allege that brutal massacres in China are referred to in Japanese documents simply as 'incidents'; military occupation as a civilizing mission; there has been systematic distortion of history to whitewash atrocities. These allegations are reinforced by perceptions of other Japanese public behaviour related to the legacy of the period: failure to compensate women forced to work as sex slaves for the Japanese military; visits by senior politicians to shrines where Japanese war criminals are venerated; failure to return territories occupied by force of arms when China was weak. Meanwhile the Japanese have different but significant grievances: the Chinese always fail to acknowledge Japanese apologies and compensation; they do not recognize Japanese contributions to ousting Western imperialism from Asia or its massive aid and investments to the region; the Chinese manipulate and exaggerate wartime incidents to lever advantages in contemporary negotiations.

One Chinese scholar describes the outcome as a 'huge perception gap':

> China and Japan both view themselves as the victim and the other as the aggressor. Each party sees itself as peaceful, while the other state is aggressive and revisionist. Both also have bubbled conspiracy theories against the other, placing doubt on each other's intentions.
>
> (Wang 2013, 11)

As we address the first question of the Introduction concerning the persistence of mutual antagonism, the question of memory politics is central. At its most extreme, the Japanese attitude can be characterized as evasive denial. However, such statements are simplistic: senior Japanese politicians have made numerous formal public apologies, as have religious and civil society groups. It is not only the *substance* of any apology or lack of apology that prolongs the antagonisms: it is the political manipulation of the agenda by many of the actors concerned.

Power transitions

Power transitions have long been considered a strong predictor of armed conflict, especially where a dominant hegemonic power is challenged by a rising power,

102 *Alan Hunter*

or alliance. In the East Asian 'context' for possible reconciliation, or lack of it, two geopolitical power transitions are prominent. The first is the US loss of unrivalled political and security leadership, despite the Obama administration's recent attempt at reinforcing its engagement with the Asia Pacific; the second major transition is the rapid decline of Japan as economic superpower.

US hegemony in Asia

There is an obvious case to argue that the dominance of the US-led security alliance in Asia is currently threatened by the rising power of China. The US started its expansionist policies in the Asia Pacific after the 1898 war with Spain, when it annexed Guam and the Philippines, later maintaining a naval presence in the region from bases in China. For decades after 1945, the US was indisputably the hegemonic power in Asia including East Asia: its Cold War strategy included the construction of major bases throughout the continent and the installation of client or at least friendly regimes in major countries.

If one excludes the tragedies of the massive fatalities inflicted by US forces in Vietnam, Cambodia and Laos, one could argue that overall, the 'pax Americana' served Asia reasonably well: for example the numerous tensions embedded in the China-Taiwan or North-South Korea relationships have been contained. But in the past decade, US power in the region has been undermined by two sequences of events. The US launched wars with such disastrous consequences in Iraq and Afghanistan that its international reputation was severely damaged and its population, at least according to some analysts, has lost its appetite for further loss of life and funds to military adventures. At the same time, China was successful in forming regional and even global alliances to construct a network of ties with a wide variety of countries, including resource-rich states to feed its industrial economy and Japan, the richest US ally in the region, continued its relative decline.

The Obama administration did promise a renewed focus on the Asia Pacific and a shift in the balance of military resources away from West to East Asia, as tacit recognition of its chronic failures in the Middle East. Nevertheless, in virtually all respects, China now equals or is superior to the US across the region. The exception, however, is vital. In advanced military technology and power-projection, China is still a generation behind the US, despite massive recent investments in its armed forces. The Chinese have long known that a war with the US, or with a strong neighbour backed by the US, would be catastrophic. Its top leadership would, therefore, be extremely cautious about pushing anti-Japanese rhetoric to a point where they cannot back down from armed conflict, and this constraint may mean playing a difficult game with the forces of populist nationalism should they be demanding military action, for example over the Senkaku Islands.

Overall it seems that East Asia hosts exactly the kind of power transition that 'realist' theories would predict as most likely to engender armed conflict: a weakened hegemon challenged by a rising power. It will need much wisdom in Beijing and Washington, and their allies, to negotiate a safe and constructive way forward.

China-Japan

From the 1970s to the 2000s, Japan was economically the most successful country in Asia, and the second largest economy in the world, a status it retained till about 2012. It enjoyed technological leads over its neighbours, with brands such as Honda, Sony and Toyota becoming world leaders through exports and also through manufacturing operations in the US, Europe and elsewhere. The Japanese developed some of the world's best healthcare, welfare and educational systems, and their security was assured by an unconditional US guarantee; in exchange for which the Japanese government provided land for military bases and funding to the US government.

However, the situation has transformed remarkably and dramatically in the past twenty years: China achieved an overall growth rate of some 10 per cent per annum at least, while Japan largely stagnated, suffering the impact of high costs, economic mismanagement, over-borrowing and lack of resources.

Moreover, since the 1950s, Japan has been a client-state of the US, dependent on its patron for military protection, and in return being an unquestioning supporter of all US military and strategic priorities including the wars in Iraq and Afghanistan. For decades, this patron-client relationship was little challenged in Japan but rather taken as axiomatic by generations of Japanese politicians. In 2012 the first signs of doubt among the elite did appear in two books by a former senior figure in the Japanese Foreign Ministry, Magosaki Ukeru, titled *The Truth of Postwar History* and *Politicians Crushed by the US*. Magosaki argued that Japan failed to develop an autonomous position in the region precisely because of the Japanese political elite's complete servility towards US power. A small minority had argued for changes such as closer ties with neighbours, reduction in US bases and in funding provided to the US military, and implicitly an acknowledgement of China as the new rising power in Asia. However, they were successfully marginalized and politically eliminated, so by 2014 the Japanese foreign policy and diplomatic community was still completely oriented to support of US power.

Overall, with the relative decline of both the US and Japan in the region, China has emerged as the world's second economy, the leading country in Asia, and the centre of a largely successful network of alliances and cooperative agreements with countries around the world from Asia though Africa and Latin America. It has also upgraded its armed forces, now capable of robust military action, should any be required, against almost any country except the US.

Trauma politics

Any historiography is imperfect and could be criticized for bias or exaggeration. Establishing details of incidents such as battles or civilian deaths under occupation is especially complex. Nevertheless, if Chinese historians wish to demonstrate 'fifty years of Japanese aggression' it would be hard to argue with them except as to details. Japanese aggression against China possibly ranks among the very worst atrocities of the twentieth century, on a similar scale to deaths

104 *Alan Hunter*

by famine and purge in Stalin's Soviet Union or those of Nazi occupations in Poland and elsewhere. Among the most salient were the annexation of territories such as Taiwan and 'Manchuria' in 1895 and 1931 and military occupation of much of North, East and South China between 1937 and 1945. The casualties of this occupation are unknown, but estimates are in the range of 15 to 20 million dead and uncountable devastation of infrastructure. There was no valid reason or even pretext for the annexations, which were planned and implemented by extreme nationalists in control of the Japanese armed forces, with apparently very little opposition within Japan. Some specific aspects of the occupation such as the conscription of sex workers, biological experiments on live prisoners, and rape and execution of civilians are particularly notorious. The eventual withdrawal of Japanese troops following surrender in August 1945 also left China impoverished, divided and militarized, which led to the civil war between nationalists and communists from 1945 to 1949.

There is no reason to doubt that the Chinese population was very deeply traumatized by these experiences; but there are perhaps questions to consider now, seventy years after the departure of Japanese troops from China, without which one cannot start to address the basic dynamic between China and Japan.

Among Chinese perceptions and arguments are the following:

- Japan has never acknowledged or fully apologized for the atrocities of this period.
- Japanese have brainwashed subsequent generations of school children by sterilized accounts of the occupation in textbooks.
- Japanese leaders periodically visit the Yasukuni shrine in Tokyo, where the remains of convicted war criminals are enshrined, as a symbol that the nation rejects Chinese trauma.
- Attempts to secure financial compensation, for example by former sex slaves, have always been blocked by Japanese courts.
- The Diaoyu/Senkaku Islands were annexed in 1895, and Japan has since manipulated international meetings to avoid returning them.

That is overall there has been no concerted effort to make amends for the disgraceful record and, on the contrary, the Japanese population maintains an implicit state of denial. Not surprisingly, Japanese perceptions are often very different, if not the opposite.

- The Japanese government, Parliament, Prime Ministers, and numerous senior public officials have apologized to China, Korea and other countries on many occasions. The Japanese state especially made use of 1995, the fiftieth anniversary of the ending of the war, to issue formal state-level apologies. The Chinese government and state-controlled media have always chosen to ignore such apologies and failed to make them known to the Chinese public.

- The Japanese war record is known to the Japanese public through museums and exhibitions, school textbooks, Internet materials and many other channels.
- Visits to Yasukuni shrine have been made only by persons in their private capacity, never endorsed as official business.
- International treaties accepted and signed by China have confirmed that full war reparations have already been paid and that the Senkaku Islands are Japanese territory. Attempts by pressure groups to secure extra compensation through the Japanese legal system are a matter for courts, not for the government.
- Japan donated a vast amount of funds for China's development especially in the 1980s and 1990s, without which China would never have taken off as economic power. The scale of this assistance has never been acknowledged.
- China continually raises unreasonable, threatening demands against Japan and brandishes the war record as blackmail.

Surveys of public opinion, meetings of political leaders and other indicators in both countries do indicate fluctuations over periods of time, but the overall picture is quite clear: the populations of both countries cordially dislike each other, and politics between the two countries is marred by distrust and angry rhetoric. China and Japan have the economic potential to be two world-leading economic powers, geographically and culturally close in one of the world's most successful regions. Full cooperation could have massive benefits. Instead, they appear to struggle to avoid military conflict over tiny islands; there are periodic outbreaks of overt civic hostilities; overall cooperation is generally poor despite much economic activity. We find here an example of failed, or at least very troubled and partial, reconciliation.

Reconciliation dynamics in East Asia

Given the experiences of reconciliation in Europe and elsewhere, how do we explain this failure of, or constraints on, reconciliation? And what do we learn that might be of interest in other contexts?

First, from a basic 'realist' frame, the lack of reconciliation is predictable and reasonable. For most of the preceding decades, China and Japan have been in different security alliances. Still, these alliances did not come to open military hostilities at any point, and likewise China and Japan refrained from armed conflict with each other. They are thus at a state of 'shallow peace', which is at least far better than the armed conflict that many had predicted.

Second, although there have been some hints, discussions and preliminary moves towards regional institutions across East Asia, or Northeast Asia, so far none have materialized. There is no region-level security institution remotely similar to NATO, nor an economic one similar to the EU. However, the first signs of serious discussions on a free trade area emerged in 2012, with the start

106 *Alan Hunter*

of a series of talks on a China-Japan-South Korea Free Trade Agreement. It was encouraging that the fourth meeting was held in Seoul in March 2014 despite acute political tensions.

Third, there has been little evidence of a vision for reconciliation from political leaders in either China or Japan. At best, certain political leaders have worked hard for pragmatic cooperation on certain areas such as economic exchanges and investments, and some important summits have established precedents of avoiding force or arms. It seems that precisely a *lack of reconciliation provides domestic political advantages* in both countries. In Japan, the main political party can continue its support for US agendas in Asia without appearing to make concessions to Beijing; in China, the communist party can continue to promote its record in the heroic struggle against occupation and imperialism and incidentally provide an outlet for popular nationalism and a pressure point against Japan. This position stands in sharp contrast to the successful reconciliation between Japan and Singapore, a city-state that also suffered extreme brutality and mass killings under Japanese rule in the 1940s. Loo (2013) demonstrated that this reconciliation was achieved almost entirely by government and commercial interests, with no particular assistance from 'memory politics' groups.

Fourth, there is a relatively low level of activity by religious groups, NGOs or other non-state actors in both Japan and China. Several authors have argued that it is precisely this kind of activity in Europe that spread the concept of reconciliation between former combatants throughout the continent with decades of religious and youth exchanges, veterans meetings, memorializations, art and cultural activities and so on, all of which made the reconciliation agenda acceptable to politicians also. Horvat (2007) argued that the weakness of civil society in Japan especially has led to lack of action on this agenda.

Though relations between the two states have been particularly tense since the renewed confrontation about the Diaoyu/Senkaku Islands in 2010, there were some periods before 2010 when the governments appeared to be building bridges, and even in difficult years the two foreign ministries have held constructive meetings. For example in Cambodia in July 2012, Foreign Ministers Yang Jiechi and Koichiro Gemba agreed on a wide range of issues, including on the need to 'improve national sentiments':

> Both sides shared the recognition that based on the current sentiments of the people of Japan and China, great improvement of such sentiments is required. From such a view point, both parties shared views on accelerating adjustments for the early launch of a "Japan-China People-to-People Exchanges Council", an inter-governmental council to structurally expand and strengthen exchanges between the people of Japan and China.
>
> (Ministry of Foreign Affairs of Japan 2012)

Is the lack of reconciliation problematic? Or may we just accept the fact that the two populations appear to not like each other, while their respective politicians engage in sometimes angry rhetoric? China and Japan have shown for seven

Reconc. theory and the East Asian context 107

decades that they can avoid the mass mutual destruction of modern warfare, while trade and investment between the countries has continued despite occasional breakdowns through political pressures. One argument in favour of reconciliation is that it makes war between two nations 'unthinkable', which certainly sounds an attractive benefit, and one imagines there are other benefits in terms of cultural synergy, ease of communication and so forth. However, an effective system of crisis management might equally render war between China and Japan extremely unlikely, if not completely 'unthinkable'. The 'failure' of reconciliation would then be limited perhaps to undefinable 'opportunity costs' rather than concrete disadvantages. But if the respective populations and their political representatives appear to feel comfortable with a certain level of cooperation, would it just be projecting Euro-centric values, or the specific and non-reproducible aftermath of one European war, onto East Asia to demand 'deep reconciliation' there?

Conclusions

As a conclusion, I will consider the East Asian, and specifically Sino-Japanese, 'reconciliation' dynamic. First the relationship between China and Japan appears to be a strong case study of a concept highlighted by Heo (2012), namely, 'hereditary enemies'. Heo suggested that some nations may be locked into chronic, bitter, intractable negative relations which take generations to heal, if ever. She takes China and Japan as an example of three major components of 'hereditary enemies': traumatic historical events in the past, hostile public mood in the present and fear and distrust of future actions. Such antagonism would inevitably need very favourable conditions to soften. Heo suggested some essential components would be systemic support from third parties, positive steps with neighbours in the region and domestic political commitment. Overall, the US has perhaps been a relatively positive outside influence on both Japan and China; however, the 'neighbourhood' has various other tensions and few signs of regional institution building and as I will re-cap, domestic politics in both countries is if anything anti-reconciliation.

Geopolitically, Japan is firmly embedded in its security alliance with the US and among other issues, committed to support Taiwan against attack by China. Japan's leaders claim their nation is threatened by China's growing military power; China maintains that the US has a strategy of encircling it with naval and air bases, the biggest of them in Japan.

However, security politics are possibly not the main, certainly not the only, source of tension. I would highlight here an argument of Weissmann, that there are specific dynamics in East Asian political culture which allow the region to function well in most respects, including in the avoidance of armed conflict; but which are not based on institutions or behaviours derived from West Europe. They include a tacit understanding between elites, messaged by back-channel or private communications rather than public meetings and announcements; international relations preserved as an exclusive domain of government rather than welcoming civil society contributions; and emphasis on pragmatic economic

108 *Alan Hunter*

activity rather than transnational bureaucracy. The East Asian leaders, if confined to managing purely military issues, could quite possibly continue to implement a northerly version of this 'ASEAN way' of soft regionalization, elite consensus building, and informal but decisive contacts between top leaders. (Weissmann analyzed regional dynamics involving Korea and Taiwan rather than China-Japan to illustrate these points.)

The perspective of conflict prevention is relevant and important here. It may well be generations before Chinese and Japanese transform their antagonism and bitter memory politics to anything like 'warm mutual understanding'. The catchphrase often used by politicians and media characterizes their relationship as 'hot economics and cold politics' since enterprises have managed to sustain and grow the extremely high volume of trade between the countries despite all the political rhetoric. Mutual suspicion has until now de-railed progress towards formal regional architecture, but again ASEAN has shown that informal pragmatism can work as effectively as more formal, legalistic, Western models of cooperation. East Asia can certainly stand decades of tension and rhetoric between China and Japan; arguably the main disadvantage would be the theoretical 'opportunity cost' for example the loss of putative benefits from a regional 'common market' of some kind. East Asian cultures are known for their Long-Term Orientation, that is a willingness to persevere patiently and to wait for solutions in the perhaps distant future. In one empirical study, China and Japan were the most 'patient' countries in the world, with European, African and North American nations among the least (see the Gofstede Cultural Dimensions Project 2014). Maybe 'deep reconciliation' would take place between China and Japan in the next couple of centuries; that is not long to wait. But a war between China and Japan would be disastrous. An urgent task for researchers, politicians, journalists, military personnel and anybody else would be to work towards the prevention of armed conflict between these two nations.

Note

1 There are no fixed definitions of the terms "East Asia", "Northeast Asia" or "Southeast Asia". For the purpose of this chapter, I use East Asia to refer to the Peoples Republic of China (China), Taiwan, Japan, the Republic of Korea (Korea) and the Democratic People's Republic of Korea (North Korea). A detailed discussion of names used for the regions of Asia is provided by Weissmann (2009, 15–16). I use the term "region" here referring mainly to geography and shared cultural heritage; the chapter focuses on relations between China and Japan.

References

Assefa, Hizkias. 1999. 'The Meaning of Reconciliation'. In *People Building Peace: 35 Inspiring Stories from around the World*, edited by Paul van Tongeren, 37–45. Utrecht: European Centre for Conflict Prevention.

Boulding, K.E. 1978. *Stable Peace.* Austin, TX: University of Texas Press.
Brounéus, K. 2003. *Reconciliation Theory and Practice for Development Co-Operation.* Stockholm: SIDA.
Galtung, J. 1996. *Peace by Peaceful Means Peace and Conflict, Development and Civilization.* Oslo; London; Thousand Oaks: International Peace Research Institute; Sage Publications.
———. 2001. 'After Violence, Reconstruction, Reconciliation, and Resolution: Coping with Visible and Invisible Effects'. In *Reconciliation, Justice, and Coexistence: Theory and Practice*, edited by Mohammed Abu-Nimer, 3–23. Lanham: Lexington Books.
Gofstede Cultural Dimensions Project. 2014. "Long-Term Orientation|Clearly Cultural." http://www.clearlycultural.com/geert-hofstede-cultural-dimensions/long-term-orientation/. Accessed 15 Jul. 2014.
He, Y. 2009. *The Search for Reconciliation: Sino-Japanese and German-Polish Relations since World War II.* Cambridge; New York: Cambridge University Press.
Heo, S.E. 2012. *Reconciling Enemy States in Europe and Asia.* New York: Palgrave Macmillan.
Horvat, A. 2007. "A Strong State, Weak Civil Society, and Cold War Geo-Politics: Why Japan Lags Behind Europe in Confronting a Negative Past." In *Rethinking Historical Injustice and Reconciliation in Northeast Asia*, edited by Gi-wook Shin, Soon-won Park and Daqing Yang, 216–234. New York: Routledge.
Kacowicz, A.M. (ed.) 2000. *Stable Peace Among Nations.* Oxford: Rowman and Littlefield.
Kupchan, C. 2010. *How Enemies become Friends: The Sources of Stable Peace.* Princeton, NJ: Princeton University Press.
Lederach, J.P. 1999. *Building Peace: Sustainable Reconciliation in Divided Societies.* Washington, DC: United States Institute of Peace Press.
Loo, T.M. 2013. "Historical Reconciliation in Southeast Asia: Notes from Singapore." In *Inherited Responsibility and Historical Reconciliation in East Asia*, edited by Jun-Hyeok Kwak and Melissa Nobles, 81–99. London: Routledge.
McCurry, J. 2015. "Ban Ki-moon Rejects Japanese Criticism of Him Attending China's Victory Day." http://www.theguardian.com/world/2015/aug/31/ban-ki-moon-rejects-japanese-criticism-of-him-attending-chinas-victory-day. Accessed 15 Jul. 2014.
Ministry of Foreign Affairs of Japan. 2012. "Japan-China Foreign Ministers' Meeting (Overview)." http://www.mofa.go.jp/region/asia-paci/china/meeting1207_fm.html. Accessed 15 Jul. 2014.
Rock, S.R. 1989. *Why Peace Breaks Out: Great Power Rapprochement in Historical Perspective.* Chapel Hill, NC: University of North Carolina Press.
Walt, S.M. 1990. *The Origins of Alliances.* Ithaca, NY: Cornell University Press.
Waltz, K.N. 2008. *Realism and International Politics.* New York: Routledge.
Wang, Z. 2013. "Perception Gaps, Identity Clashes." In *Clash of National Identities: China, Japan, and the East China Sea Territorial Dispute*, edited by T. Arai, S. Goto and Z. Wang, 11. Washington, DC: Wilson Center Asia Program.
Weissmann, M. 2009. *Understanding the East Asian Peace: Informal and Formal Conflict Prevention and Peacebuilding in the Taiwan Strait, the Korean Peninsula, and the South China Sea 1990–2008.* Gothenburg: Distributed by School of Global Studies, Peace and Development Research, University of Gothenburg, Gothenburg.

8 Challenges of teaching international reconciliation in Japan and Korea

A comparative perspective

Seunghoon Emilia Heo

Make me an instrument of Your peace.
Where there is hatred, let me sow love;
where there is discord, unity;
where there is despair, hope.
Grant that
I may not so much seek to be consoled as to console;
to be understood as to understand.
For it is in giving that we receive;
it is in pardoning that we are pardoned.[1]

Do not do to others what would cause you to suffer if it were done to you.[2]

I still remember my first class in Japan when my students asked me: "*Sensei*, Japan is such a peace-loving country. Why are Koreans and Chinese angry at us?" I also remember what my students said in Korea: "What is wrong with them? Why are they not apologizing for their misdeeds?" There was little space for any reflection why the other side does not think the way we do. Teaching peace and reconciliation in Japan and Korea is not an easy experience. Most of my students had something to say either to blame the other side or to defend one's position. However, the classroom often became silent when I asked, "What is needed to rebuild a broken relationship?" or "What contribution can we make to transform an enmity relation into a friendlier one?"

If international reconciliation studies has become popular in the academia and received much media coverage in 2015,[3] it does not go the same way in the higher educational institutions. Besides the lack of interest among the younger generation, not many universities offer courses that allow students to think about the meaning of reconciliation between countries from an interdisciplinary approach as well as various ways of rebuilding their broken relations from a global perspective.[4] Since I started teaching reconciliation studies at universities, my "journey" towards reconciliation has met new challenges that I have not known much as a researcher: does the commitment in research and in teaching go in pair? Is the intellectual debate with scholars transferable to the one with students in the classroom? Do reconciliation studies help reconciliation? To what extent can scholars contribute to reconciliation through teaching and research?

In order to address these central questions, the present chapter takes education as one of potential resources for reconciliation – the interaction between professors and the younger generation through teaching. By focusing on three major challenges of teaching international reconciliation in Japan and in Korea, I will argue that education can be an effective resource for reconciliation depending on the purpose as well as the method of teaching. I will show that if we want our younger generation to play an active role in promoting reconciliation, it is crucial to create a locus where youth can learn current issues through the eyes of others in order to understand why the other side does not think the same way one does. In addition, it is also important to offer them an opportunity to think and share their reflections, not only with their compatriots but also with youth from their neighbouring countries.

Does "teaching reconciliation" contribute to reconciliation?

The first challenge of teaching I have been facing with relies upon the question "why do we teach reconciliation?" Scholars have different motivations, reasons and purposes of engaging themselves into their academic research. Just like in natural sciences, most approaches in social sciences, especially in International Relations or Political Science, actively discourage personal involvement by the researcher. The more we distance ourselves from the research topic, the more the outcome is perceived as scientific or objective, if objectivity is something that exists in social science. Still, we do have a personal relationship with our research field: the reason we decided to become a researcher, the reason we became interested in a particular subject, the way we formulate our research puzzle, the way we conduct research and analyze the world. Simply put, "research is all about a person's engagement with an issue" (Brigg and Bleiker 2010, 779). Throughout a series of interviews and conversations I have made during international conferences, I noticed that many reconciliation scholars choose their empirical cases that have something to do with their own origin/nationality, if not, a cultural affinity they share with. Some told me, for instance, that they fluently speak the local language, spent their childhood in the region or simply hold a genuine passion in a certain country. The academic motivation that leads them to develop their argument certainly varies. But some of us share a common concern: does research on reconciliation affect reconciliation happening in our world? Is our research helping policy makers find a better way to reconcile? Do all the excellent debate and discussion made at academic conferences resonate beyond the ivory tower?

For some scholars, especially historians, this reflection does not have much value since the duty of a researcher is to provide knowledge, not prediction. For others, especially political scientists, policy recommendation is an essential part

112   *Seunghoon Emilia Heo*

of research (Levy 1997). In my case, professional experience in foreign services and international organizations pushed me to make a connection between theory and reality around the following question: does my intellectual reflection contribute to promoting reconciliation in unreconciled cases around the world? This puzzle went further when I started teaching at universities: does the research outcome I share in the classroom help students become interested in reconciliation studies and eventually incite them to become an agent of reconciliation themselves? I realized that education could or could not become an essential resource for reconciliation depending on the answer I provide here. Through my teaching experience in Japan and Korea, I discovered that I have been looking at my student not only as a subject to transfer my knowledge but also as a potential candidate to become a protagonist of reconciliation. In other words, my research subject on the paper became alive in my professional life. Having observed the lack of interest among students in reconciliation studies, my purpose of teaching became clear over time: to help students understand their own role in promoting international reconciliation by introducing various unreconciled or reconciled cases around the world, by raising the awareness of its importance, and by making them see issues from the eyes of "others".[5]

Teaching reconciliation thus can contribute to "real" reconciliation if researchers (professors) do not stop at knowledge transfer by sharing their research outcome but also consider our students as potential candidates to become one day the agents of reconciliation themselves. This reflection around the question "why to teach?" links us to the question "how to teach?" in order to meet our teaching purpose.

Why do we compare European cases to Northeast Asian ones?

The second challenge of teaching deals with the utility of comparing empirical cases in the classroom. In an attempt to provide a plausible explanation, if not a possible solution, to the not-yet-reconciled cases of international reconciliation, academia has been focusing on comparing Europe with Northeast Asia, in other words, German and Japanese foreign policy of reconciliation with their respective neighbouring countries. Many scholars explored how Germany and Japan have attempted to reconcile with the past to highlight the contrast between public expressions of guilt and denial,[6] national leaders' behaviour, the impact of US foreign policy, political elites' national mythmaking, the history textbook controversy, government-civil society relationship, and governmental influence in creating official historical narratives (Buruma 1995; Horvat 2007; Lind 2008; He 2009; Berger 2012; Gardner-Feldman 2012). In recent years, the number of academic conferences on comparative reconciliation studies has also multiplied.[7] A comparative approach does offer useful insights. But it needs to be done with care, especially when it comes to *why* to compare.

One of the risks the Europe versus Asia approach encounters is focusing too much on success/failure dichotomy. The rather embarrassing research outcome has not positively affected politicians and the larger public in the Northeast Asian region since it often ends up with falling back into the vicious circle of accusation-denial. During his official visit to Norway, former South Korean president Lee Myung-bak (2012) emphasized that the only way for Asia to reconcile is to follow the European way, true self-reflection and apology, applying moral terms such as "universal ethics" or "global norms". Current president Park Geun-hye (2012) pointed out a specific political figure, German Chancellor Willy Brandt, to praise his reconciliatory gesture towards Poland in 1970. The mass media has repeatedly used this episode to the extent that most Koreans now know who he is although not many could identify current German Chancellor Angela Merkel. I noticed that my Korean students, strongly influenced by the media, often use European cases for one purpose: to criticize the "other" for not having done the same. Brandt's kneeling down, Queen Elizabeth's hand shaking with former IRA commander Martin McGuinness in 2012, and the British foreign secretary William Hague's speech addressed to Kenya in 2013 were all used in their in-class presentation to *blame*.

When it comes to the Japanese case, the opposite is often observed. I sometimes encouraged my students to participate in seminars or international symposiums that invite reconciliation scholars from all over the world. But I soon noticed that they experienced a strong backlash against the comparative approach. In June 2015, Waseda University organized a special symposium on "Reconciliation and Cooperation in Europe after World War II" with French, German, Dutch, Polish, and British Embassies in Tokyo. A lot of Japanese university students were present in order to listen to various experiences of Franco-German, Polish-German, and British-former colonies reconciliation processes. However, there was a sense of disenchantment in the conference hall when a scholar concluded that there seems to be no hope for Asia today compared to all the great success European countries have made since the end of the Second World War.

The comparative method we use in research does not necessarily have the same impact when applied in the classroom. If we wish to help the younger generation critically think about their own role to promote reconciliation, we need to use cases in a way that allows them to learn the issues through the eyes of "others".

What makes us believe what we believe?

The third challenge is the issue itself: international reconciliation relates past, present, and the future. Teaching reconciliation, therefore, meets inherent difficulty since the current generation in Japan and Korea has not experienced the traumatic historical event that remains unresolved today. We are not *remembering*, as we cannot remember what we have not experienced. Instead, we shape our perception on the basis of what we have learned from school, what we have seen from the media, and what we have heard from older generations. This ongoing interaction between the past and the present becomes even more challenging as each home country attempts to influence our understanding by choosing ways of remembering the past in order to create an official version of national and international history, especially through school curricula and media.

114 *Seunghoon Emilia Heo*

According to two research surveys I conducted this year, I found out that the degree and the variety of knowledge sources our students are exposed to largely affect the way they assess their home countries' role during World War II. Furthermore, it also influences the way they perceive their love-hate relations with former enemy states.[8] While a clear majority of German students rate their knowledge about World War II as "deep" or "very deep", Japanese and Korean students do not think they have sufficient knowledge. The net outcome of knowledge gap may not be that surprising. However, their World War II narratives showed that the diversity of knowledge sources allowed German students to carry various ways of understanding the past – including self-critical assessments, which remains heavily homogeneous and non-critical in the Japanese and Korean case.

If all German, Japanese, and Korean students chose high school education to be the most important source of their knowledge (93.2%, 88.3%, and 82.5% respectively), the variety of sources largely differed. As one example, German students noted that aspects of World War II history were covered not just in their history lessons but also across a variety of different subjects such as literature, music, religion, philosophy, and politics/economics, whereas 98% of Japanese respondents and 68.2% of Korean respondents answered history class only, which often remains an elective. German students displayed a wider variety of knowledge sources such as school trips to museums or memorials, daily conversation with their friends or acquaintances, books, ARTE (a Franco-German joint TV channel), and joint history textbooks. Japanese and Korean students are not provided with many other sources except oral stories from their grandparents, NHK and online sources (Wikipedia or Yahoo Japan) for Japanese students and TV news, war movies (*Schindler's List, La Vita è Bella, Saving Private Ryan*) and online sources (Wikipedia or Naver Korea) for Korean students. No wonder their perception about the past I observe in my classes sounds so similar that I almost thought they copied their answers from one another.

This reality makes it challenging to teach international reconciliation, especially whenever I try to conduct a conversation or debate with and among students around conflicting issues in the Northeast Asia. As Japanese and Korean students are exposed to different sources that each country provides with through school curricula and media, their voice is rather homogenous about any argument I raise in my class alongside their nationality. It is not surprising to see the black-white contrasting conclusion in their research paper when it comes to Takeshima/Dokdo island dispute. Students mainly collect information from their own governmental sources or online news they read in their own language. In Japan, I often encourage my students to use Korean official sources (translated into English) or other international sources as well. In Korea, I ask my students to tell me whether their argument would have remained the same if they had been born Japanese. Although I told them that our argument loses credibility if it can easily change depending on the nationality, they sometimes looked at me not as their professor any more but as the "other" side.

Two to tango approach

For those who are committed to engage their students into reconciliation challenges through teaching, I suggest focusing on the following aspect in order to overcome the three major obstacles mentioned earlier: to help students see reconciliation issues through the eyes of "others", which I name here a *two to tango* approach. Just like the expression "It takes two to tango," reconciliation implies two sides. The beauty of the tango does not depend on how perfectly you make your own step or master your skills. It rather relies on how well you feel and understand your partner through eye contact, body gesture, and hand pressure in order to make your next move. Reconciliation goes the same way. You do not unilaterally deliver a message. It is not like "I said what I wanted, I am done!" When you talk, you care about the reaction of your counterpart. You listen even though you do not want to. Mutual dialogue requires practice and patience. Motives, gestures, and forms of reconciliation vary from one another. But not all initiatives lead to *real* reconciliation. Reconciliation means first to properly face the wound between and among the offender and the offended. It means not only to be ready to open the dark side of the self but also to be ready to listen and to try to understand the pain of the other. Reconciliation, therefore, requires two-way efforts to *transform* a relationship from enmity into amity, in other words, a constant interactive process between the past and the present as well as between the self and the other. The teaching method I have been applying is two-fold: First, to break one's own way of thinking, second, to focus on the *transformational* aspect of reconciliation.

I usually start my class asking my students to share their understanding of the term 화해, 和解, or 仲直り, which means reconciliation in Korean and Japanese languages. Although I do not refer to any specific case, it is interesting to observe that most of my Korean students mention the word apology (reconciliation means to properly apologize) whereas most of my Japanese students talk about 水に流す, a Japanese expression meaning "to let bygones be bygones". To my Korean students, I raise a second question: "do you make efforts to rebuild a relationship? If yes, how? If no, why?" The most popular responses I receive are as follows: "I sometimes feel like I want to make a first step but I am afraid that my pride will get hurt"; "Because I think nothing is going to change, I prefer keeping a certain distance. It makes my life easier"; "When a relationship is broken, I do not make efforts to rebuild since I have other friends with whom I can spend more time".[9] With my Japanese students, I often conduct a role-play game. I create a situation where I become the aggressor and my students become the victims of a war in which they lost a part of their family. I ask them again what forgiveness or "let bygones be bygones" means in this situation. One student told me after the class that she would like to rewrite her paper as she realized that she would never let her pain go untold.

When it comes to case studies, I avoid using a Europe versus Asia approach. Instead, I take an actor-focused approach to explore skills, resources, and ideas

116 *Seunghoon Emilia Heo*

that bring about successful or failed outcomes of reconciliation. Few examples are as follows:

Historians

A collaborative work of historians from both countries is a telling example that helps students see the reconciliation issue from various angles: Benjamin Stora and Mohammed Harbi, Gilles Manceron and Hassan Remouan, or Jean-Louis Levet and Mourad Preure among others in the Franco-Algerian reconciliation process.[10] I also explain how some episodes around the joint history textbook commission, especially in the Polish-German, Franco-German, and Turkish-Armenian cases, prove that an active way of listening is required to better understand the past from the other point of view (Heo 2014, 5–6). This approach incited curiosity among students to make further research on how certain aspects of history is taught and learned in their neighbouring countries.

Artists

A piece of art such as novel, picture, film, or theatre has been always beneficial to lead my students into reconciliation studies. To introduce the Polish-Russian reconciliation process, I often refer to the Polish filmmaker Andrzej Wada's *Katyn*. In Japan, students could have time to think and learn about the meaning of national victimhood. In Korea, students could broaden their perspective and compare the role of civil society in Poland (Russia), Armenia (Turkey), and Algeria (France) with the one in Korea (Japan). When it comes to literature, Simon Wiesenthal's *The Sunflower*, for instance, helped students from both countries to think about the notion of collective responsibility about the past.[11]

Religious actors

Religious value has become a crucial element to be explored in my class. Students often consider religion as the main cause of conflict, division, and war and not much as a factor that can contribute to promote reconciliation. I regularly use Frieberg's (2010) work in my class to highlight the importance of religious actors as well as media professionals. For my students, especially Koreans, who immediately think about Willy Brandt when they learn about the Polish-German reconciliation process, this approach helped them discover that bottom-up reconciliation exists as well. Furthermore, students brought about other religious values than apology and forgiveness (Christianism) they consider beneficial to promoting reconciliation: 慈悲 (mercy) or oneness from Buddhism, 德 (virtue), 情 (affection), 和 (harmony), or a sense of community from Confucianism. The inter-confessional dialogue process between Polish Catholic Church and German Protestant Church has also affected students to think about the potential of inter-religious dialogue between Korean catholic communities and Japanese Buddhist communities.

From my teaching experience, I realized that our students rarely took the time to think about how to *rebuild* a broken relationship with their neighbouring countries. Furthermore, Japanese and Korean students had little awareness of themselves as potential agents of reconciliation while German students offered various original ideas when asked about the role of youth to promote reconciliation (Bode and Heo 2017). By focusing on political and social actors committed to transforming enmity into amity beyond national borders, students can broaden their understanding of reconciliation and further explore how their counterpart sees the same issue from another perspective. For this reason, it is crucial for our younger generation to be exposed to various ideas and have a locus to think and share their reflections, not only among themselves but also with youth from their neighbouring countries.

Is there any hope in Asia?

Depending on the purpose and the method of teaching, education can be an effective tool for reconciliation. I feel a strong responsibility of promoting international reconciliation not only as a scholar but also as a professor through teaching and research activities. Each discipline including theology, history, law, political science, and international relations has certainly its own contribution to provide to reconciliation studies. As an international relations scholar, I am convinced that my life commitment is to help the younger generation see the issue from the eyes of others as a first step to reconciliation. Without any willingness to understand the difference, there will be no true dialogue. It is, indeed, a tough journey. I sometimes wonder why I chose reconciliation or *rebuilding* a broken relationship, as I prefer saying. Talking about reconciliation practically means to constantly stay inside the world of hatred and discord in order to understand how to *transform* an enemy relation into a friendlier one. The reason why I continue my journey of reconciliation is that I see hope in my students. It has been only three years since I started teaching reconciliation in Japan and in Korea, not without frustrating moments. But I answer yes to the question I have received so many times at academic conferences "Is there any hope in Asia?" For I do see hope in them[12]:

> I'd like to say I always appreciate from deep in my heart your sincere efforts inside/outside class and caring approach to students and I feel sorry and terrible to see you suffer and get hurt so much in doing what you aim to achieve. Maybe I couldn't understand much of pain and suffering you really are dealing with since I have not been there standing up before students and trying to involve them in issues of reconciliation whoever they are. But I can tell you, what I learned about reconciliation in your class at Sophia University became my lifetime question and also a mission. Yes, some would rather hate their enemy, keep an absolute distance from it or just ignore it maybe because it seems easier to stay in a broken relationship just keep blaming the other out of hatred or not interacting honestly with each other and 'hurting

each other any more' out of mistrust or fear. However, there are and will be some people that get hurt or feel insecure and terrified in a broken relationship. To stop this vicious circle, we need to be brave enough to get out of our own comfort zone and tackle the past and causes. Maybe somebody should take a challenging initiative, which might be criticized, or even worse paid little/no attention after all. This certainly is accompanied by a lot of pain and hard work, even at the interpersonal level, but overcoming them is essential and will be a stepping-stone. I believe you are pulling it off and your voice is reaching our minds, even if not everyone at the moment, and heard by God and it will be! I'm really glad I was in your class and want to be there again!

(N, Japan)

I want to learn more about the past. I hated history class since it was all about memorizing. But I want to understand how Korean and Chinese friends learn about our past, and also why we learn different things. Maybe I will start reading sources from outside my country.

(A, Japan)

I have never had a chance to think about reconciliation. I learned how to blame but not how to transform the relationship. I always thought that Takeshima is our land and Koreans are illegally asking for it. But I wonder how I would see the issue if I were born Korean.

(M, Japan)

I am sometimes surprised myself how angry and furious I can become about something I have not even experienced myself just by watching a TV news about Japan. I am Korean but I am also Catholic. I would like to see how sharing and forgiveness work between nations.

(C, Korea)

I have good Japanese and Chinese friends. So I thought everything going on between our nations does not consider me. But now, I feel like there is something more I should do.

(K, Korea)

Anti-Japanese feeling cannot justify my ignorance about Japan or Japanese history. For that reason, I started learning Japanese language and study their history. I would like to become a journalist. I am a bit pessimistic about the role of journalism in reconciliation. But I do believe that their role is crucial after I learned about German-Polish actors in your class. We are too much influenced by what media tells us. When I am ready, I would like to suggest that we should also think about forgiveness. Forgiveness goes along with apology. I don't know how but that is my dream.

(L, Korea)

Teaching international reconciliation 119

We often try to convince others to make them believe what we believe. We also easily give up working together when we think others will never change their way of thinking. However, with my students, I discover that our "journey" towards reconciliation is a step-by-step process. By making efforts to understand the difference and trying to see the issues from the eyes of others, we discover our way of dancing tango. We may not know where this journey is going to lead us. But my experience tells us that finding one piece of puzzle together is worth enough spending our lifetime even though we do not know how the whole puzzle looks like when completed one day.

It is perhaps easier to break a relationship than rebuild a broken one. It is perhaps easier to hate someone we once loved than to love someone we once hated. Not everyone can reconcile. In 2015 we commemorated not only the seventieth anniversary of the end of World War II. We also commemorated the fiftieth anniversary of the diplomatic relations between Germany and Israel as well as Japan and Korea. I hope that our younger generation, at least our students, can seize this opportunity to learn *how to tango*.

Notes

1 Selected sentences from *Peace Prayer of Saint Francis*.
2 From an early collection of Buddhist teaching, *Udana-Varga* 5:18.
3 2015 marks the seventieth anniversary of the end of the Second World War, the one hundredth anniversary of the Armenian genocide, the fiftieth anniversary of the diplomatic relations between Germany and Israel as well as between Japan and the Republic of Korea.
4 By "interdisciplinary", I mean a theoretical reflection on the term reconciliation from religious, philosophical, psychological, legal, sociological and political perspectives. By "global", I mean a comprehensive analysis of empirical cases ranging from Europe, Africa, the Middle East to Americas and Asia. For a further analysis of theoretical and empirical frameworks of international reconciliation, see Heo (2012).
5 I teach two courses entitled "Peace and Reconciliation Studies: A Global Perspective" and "International Love-Hate Relations" in the undergraduate programme at Sophia University (Tokyo) since 2012 and at Ritsumeikan Asia Pacific University since 2016, as well as at the School for Politics (MPPU) at Korean national assembly since 2010. The assessment is based on my own experience and does not apply to other scholars' case.
6 Reasoning behind these arguments was frequently based on Benedict's (1946) contested guilt cultures vs. shame cultures thesis.
7 To name but a few, "Political and Societal Leadership in Encouraging Reconciliation: A Comparison of Japanese and German Foreign Policies in Their Neighbourhoods" organized by AICGS Johns Hopkins University, Berlin, October 2013; "Political Reconciliation in Comparative Perspective" organized by Hong Kong Baptist University, Hong Kong, June 2014; A tandem symposium held at the same time in Korea and in Japan: "Post-WWII Reconciliation and Cooperation: Lessons for East Asia" organized by European Embassies and Asan Institute, Seoul, June 2015 and "The 70th Anniversary of the End of World War II: Reconciliation and Cooperation in Europe after World War II" organized by European Embassies and Waseda University, Tokyo, June 2015; "Commemorating the 50th anniversary of diplomatic relations between Germany and Israel as

120 *Seunghoon Emilia Heo*

well as Japan and the Republic of Korea" organized by Konrad Adenauer Stiftung and Focolare movement, Korean national assembly, October 2015.

8 To get access to the perception of the past, especially World War II, that German and Japanese students have, Bode and I devised an online survey with 19 open or multiple choice questions, sub-divided into three thematic parts: World War II knowledge and sources, World War II narratives, and international reconciliation issues. We shared this survey among our professional networks from May to August 2015, which led to 133 and 155 responses from German and Japanese students, respectively. When it came to Korean students, I started conducting the same online survey in September to be completed in December 2015 (currently received 57 responses). For an in-depth analysis of our findings, see Bode and Heo (2017).

9 These responses were collected during my lecture on "Political and social actors contributing to promote international reconciliation" at the school for politics, Korean national assembly, 31 October 2015.

10 See Naylor's contribution in this volume.

11 Other examples include *Le silence de la mer* by Vercors (Franco-German relations), *Blood Brothers* by Elias Chacour (Israeli-Palestine relations), *Ce que le jour doit à la nuit* by Alexandre Arcady, and *Indigènes* by Rachid Bouchareb (Franco-Algerian relations).

12 Selected answers from student evaluations after my teaching at Sophia University since 2012 and at the School for Politics (MPPU) at the Korean national assembly since 2010.

References

Benedict, Ruth. 1946. *The Chrysanthemum and the Sword: Patterns of Japanese Culture*. Boston, MA: Houghton Mifflin Company.

Berger, Thomas U. 2012. *War, Guilt, and World Politics after World War II*. Cambridge: Cambridge University Press.

Bode, Ingvild and Seunghoon Emilia Heo. 2017. "Choosing Ways of Remembering: Comparing Student Narratives about World War II in Germany and Japan. International Studies Perspective (Oxford). http://isp.oxfordjournals.org/content/early/2016/12/27/isp.ekw011.

Brigg, Morgan and Roland Bleiker. 2010. "Autoethnographic International Relations: Exploring the Self as Source of Knowledge." *Review of International Studies* 36: 779–798.

Buruma, Ian. 1995. *The Wages of Guilt: Memories of War in Germany and Japan*. London: Atlantic Books.

Frieberg, Annika. 2010. "Catholics in Ostpolitik? Networking and Non-State Diplomacy in the Bensberger Memorandum, 1966–1970." In *Searching for a Cultural Diplomacy*, edited by Jessica Gienow-Hecht and Mark C. Donfried, 109–133. Oxford: Berghahn Books.

Garder-Feldman, Lily. 2012. *Germany's Foreign Policy of Reconciliation: From Enmity to Amity*. Lanham, MD: Rowman & Littlefield.

He, Yinan. 2009. *The Search for Reconciliation: Sino-Japanese and German-Polish Relations since World War II*. Cambridge: Cambridge University Press.

Heo, Seunghoon Emilia. 2012. *Reconciling Enemy States in Europe and Asia*. New York: Palgrave Macmillan.

———. 2014. "Between Tokyo and Berlin." *AICGS Issue Brief.* American Institute for Contemporary German Studies: The Johns Hopkins University.

Horvat, Andrew. 2007. "A Strong State, Weak Civil Society, and Cold War Geopolitics: Why Japan Lags Behind Europe in Confronting a Negative Past." In *Rethinking Historical Injustice and Reconciliation in Northeast Asia*, edited by Giwook shin, Soonwon Park and Daqing Yang, 216–234. London: Routledge.

Lee, Myung-bak. 2012. "President's Special Lecture at the University of Oslo." *Blue House News*, 11 Sep.

Levy, Jack. 1997. "Too Important to Leave to the Other: History and Political Science in the Study of International Relations." *International Security* 22(1): 22–33.

Lind, Jennifer M. 2008. *Sorry States: Apologies in International Politics.* Ithaca, NY: Cornell University Press.

Park, Geun-Hye. 2012. "A Plan for Peace in North Asia." *Wall Street Journal*, 12 Nov.

9 Altered states of consciousness

Identity politics and prospects for Taiwan-Hong Kong-mainland reconciliation

Edward Vickers[1]

Hong Kong and Taiwan share much in common. They are culturally, linguistically and ethnically overwhelmingly 'Han'; were detached from the Qing Empire during the nineteenth century; became symbols of China's 'humiliation' by foreign imperialists; and have been the object of nationalist calls for 'reunification'. Both have also experienced, during the past thirty years, an upsurge in local identity consciousness, complicating efforts to draw them back into the motherland's embrace. Important historical and political differences condition identity discourse in each society, with implications for reconciliation with the mainland. Most obviously, while Hong Kong's reunification with China was effectively accomplished in 1997, Taiwan remains *de facto* separate. A troubled post-colonial retrocession is nonetheless another experience shared by these 'pseudo-states', though in Taiwan's case this was overtaken, and overshadowed, by the ramifications of China's Civil War and the global Cold War. The history of both societies demonstrates that political reunification in itself does not imply reconciliation with the Chinese mainland or with mainlanders.

The continuing divisiveness of relations with mainland China has been underlined in recent years by Hong Kong's 2012 protest over a 'Moral and National Education' initiative (Morris and Vickers 2015) and the 'Umbrella' and 'Sunflower' movements of 2014 (in Hong Kong and Taiwan respectively). In both societies, schooling has been a key battleground for struggles between different visions of local identity and of its relationship to political, ethnic or cultural Chineseness. But attitudes to the mainland and mainlanders are shaped at least as much by experience outside the classroom as by discourse within it. This chapter traces the evolution of identity consciousness in Taiwan and Hong Kong, analyzing its relationship both to official education policy and to developments beyond the school gates. It shows that, in these societies, shifts in the curricular representation of identity have often reflected preceding changes in popular consciousness, rather than producing them. A key insight – that should be obvious to political leaders, but clearly is not – is that top-down efforts to mould identity, when they go against the grain of lived experience, tend further to alienate estranged communities, rather than reconciling them.

Meanings of being Chinese in the modern world

In the early twentieth century, many observers doubted whether, as Thorstein Veblen put it, 'the Chinese are properly to be spoken of as a nation' (1917, 5). Such doubts were shared by many early Chinese nationalists, for whom awakening a sense of nationhood was rendered urgent by the manifold threats to the integrity and sovereignty of the Qing Empire. Over the past century, successive regimes have striven to transform former Manchu imperial subjects into citizens of a Chinese nation-state. Chinese nationalism shares with its Indian counterpart an attachment to a vast and diverse imperial successor state wrapped in the mantle of an anti-imperialist founding myth. This contradictory legacy helps explain the difficulty for contemporary elites of managing elements within their imagined national community who experience Chinese dominance as a manifestation of continuing colonialism or imperialism (Vickers 2009a).

China's imperial elites saw themselves as the custodians of the definitive universal civilization, epitomizing all that was wisest and best in human thought and experience. This rendered the encounter with upstart European, and later Japanese, imperialists all the more shocking and humiliating, prompting anguished questioning of the very viability of a civilizational legacy now seen as parochially 'Chinese'. But what alternatives existed? From around the turn of the twentieth century, many Chinese nationalists saw Japan as offering a compelling prescription: for elites, intensive training in modern Western science, technology, administration and the military arts; for the masses, schools to drill a citizenry regimented in the service of a strong, united state.

How similar, though, were visions of Chinese and Japanese nationhood during the early twentieth century, when Japan posed the greatest threat to China's sovereignty and integrity? Mitter argues that Chinese nationalism was 'more secular and civic'; visions of 'Japaneseness', by contrast, were rooted in an irrational, primordialist, 'blood and soil' romanticism, associated with fascistic notions of spiritual superiority and racial purity (2013, 48). However, the idea of China as a racially circumscribed (if not 'pure') community has always been a strong ingredient in nationalist thought (Dikotter 1990), reinforced by the traditional emphasis on ancestral bloodlines. To this day, in discussions of Chinese nationhood, ethnic and civic, or spiritual and secular schools of thought contend.

However 'Chineseness' is characterized, conceptions of modern nationhood in China – as elsewhere in East Asia – have been profoundly shaped by a teleology of modernization and by an essentially neo-Darwinian worldview. Both Nationalists and Communists have portrayed the nation as an imagined community of progress, with industrialization and technological advancement promising growing prosperity to all. At the same time, internal and external threats have been invoked to underline the importance of the state's role in maintaining national unity and security. But today the promise of indefinite material progress seems less plausible than it once did. As in Europe, North America and much of the 'developing' world, anxiety about the threat posed by external or global economic forces to

124   *Edward Vickers*

jobs and incomes has prompted a growing urge to raise the drawbridge against 'outsiders' – often defined in ways that subvert official discourses of nationhood. The relationship between such impulses and the shifting politics of identity in contemporary Chinese societies is a central theme of this chapter.

Taiwan

Historical background

Definitions of what it means to be Chinese in the modern world have nowhere been more vigorously contested than in Taiwan. Nationalist attempts to portray it as a bastion preserving Chinese tradition against Communist barbarism were allied to assertions of the island's 'immemorial' Chineseness (Vickers 2007). But Taiwan's history is rather more complex; substantial Chinese settlement only began under Dutch rule in the early seventeenth century, and it was only in the 1680s that the island was incorporated within the Qing imperium. The significance of the half-century of Japanese rule (1895–1945) for Taiwanese culture and identity is especially hotly debated. Although the island's experience of Japanese colonialism was relatively benign, Taiwanese were entangled in Japan's wars and subjected to enforced assimilation (Ching 2001). The 1945 retrocession to China was greeted with general jubilation. It was not the experience of Japanese rule itself that made many Taiwanese 'separatists'; in 1945, most were convinced of their 'Chinese' identity, if only hazily aware of its political implications (Cabestan 2005). It was subsequent tensions between 'natives' (*benshengren*) and exiles from the mainland (*waishengren*) that sowed the seeds of a sense of Taiwaneseness constructed vis-à-vis China as 'other'. The Kuomintang's (KMT's) White Terror and four decades of repressive Martial Law caused many 'native Taiwanese' to see colonial subjection to Japan as preferable, in retrospect, to second-class citizenship under the Nationalists.

That most Taiwanese are ethnically and culturally 'Han' creates difficulties for those 'separatists' who conceive of nationhood in ethno-cultural terms – leading some to stake somewhat tenuous claims to indigenous (i.e. non-Chinese, Austronesian) ancestry. Many have sought to portray the island as primordially 'multicultural', citing Dutch, Spanish and Japanese as well as indigenous legacies. But the lived experience of Taiwan as a political community separate and radically different from the mainland also provides the basis for a sense of local belonging defined more in civic than in ethno-cultural terms.

Official identity discourse in the Martial Law era

Intent on countering the deracinating effects of Japanese colonialism, the KMT prescribed a programme of intensely nationalistic education (Vickers 2007). With the Communists championing 'New Culture' on the mainland, the Nationalists rallied to the defence of China's ancient civilizational glories, combining commitment to economic modernization with a backward-looking, essentialist conception of Chineseness. Intellectual underpinning came from neo-Confucian traditionalists such as the historian Qian Mu (Dennerline 1988), but such visions reflected the gulf between émigrés pining for the motherland and a local population for whom 'China' was an abstraction. Nor were tales of Communist infamy calculated to inspire enthusiasm for reunification with a distant and alien mainland.

Also alien was the medium for such messages. Mandarin was the sole language of instruction in Taiwan's schools, with use of Hoklo or Hakka (not to mention Japanese) outlawed. In addition to language and literature, instruction in history and Sun Yat-sen's *Three People's Principles* spelt out the nature and meaning of Chinese citizenship. Schooling portrayed an essentialized national subject traceable to an immemorial past. At high school level, Taiwan's own history featured only in a final textbook chapter celebrating the KMT's achievements in developing its 'base for the recovery of the mainland' (Vickers 2007).

Fantasies of a triumphant KMT return to the mainland were irretrievably discredited by the Sino-American rapprochement of the 1970s – though textbooks maintained the fiction for a further quarter-century. However, the remarkable growth of Taiwan's economy, and a rapid rise in living standards, lent the regime a significant measure of performance legitimacy. As a prosperous and increasingly well-educated *benshengren* middle class agitated for democratization, Chiang Kai-shek's son and successor, Chiang Ching-kuo, felt sufficiently confident to concede gracefully. In 1986, Chiang permitted the newly formed Democratic Progressive Party (DPP) to contest elections, and the next year he ended Martial Law. On his death in 1988, he was succeeded by the native-born, Japanese-educated Lee Teng-hui. Death and democracy were loosening the grip of the old mainlander elite.

Under Chiang the younger, a notable thaw had taken place in cross-Strait ties. Aged KMT veterans were finally permitted to visit the motherland, and Taiwanese entrepreneurs began to invest there – though with direct links still banned, bilateral traffic was routed through Hong Kong. Hong Kong was also tasked with piloting the 'one country, two systems' arrangement Deng Xiaoping had originally proposed for Taiwan. Direct experience of the mainland revealed to Taiwanese the chasm in wealth, institutions, norms and habits that separated them from their national compatriots (Roy 2003). Nevertheless, the mainland's liberalization seemed to warrant cautious optimism regarding prospects for eventual reconciliation.

Taiwanese nativism and educational politics

In this respect, 1989 marked a parting of the ways. Subsequent pressure on the Taiwanese authorities to reinforce the island's freshly minted civil liberties was intense – with the Tiananmen Incident reminding some of Taiwan's own experience of KMT repression, fuelling calls for atonement and commemoration. During the 1990s, President Lee proved adept at harnessing and articulating

126 Edward Vickers

the growing consciousness of Taiwanese distinctiveness, aided by the bellicose posture adopted by the Communist authorities on the mainland (Vickers 2007).

Shifts in historiography, meanwhile, reflected growing 'nativist' consciousness and intellectual liberalization. A new generation of scholars – many foreign-educated – questioned both the methodology and state-centric assumptions of nationalists or neo-Confucian classicists. For example Wang Ming-ke (1997) argued for an analysis of Chinese history from the margins, examining the relationship between 'historical memory and communal identity'. In Academia Sinica, the study of Taiwan had for decades been subsumed within the 'Institute of Chinese History', but in 1993 a 'Preparatory Office' for an 'Institute of Taiwan History' was inaugurated (Heylen 2001). This became an important centre for the practice of a 'scholarly native history' (Morier-Genoud 2010), conceiving of identity as constructed, shifting and contingent (see also Vickers 2009a).

Related to such historiographical shifts were wider moves to promote the study of Taiwan, in the context of what was felt to be an 'increasingly tenuous relationship with mainland China' (Hughes and Stone 1999, 980). By the end of the 1990s, learning about Taiwan started in Year 2 of elementary school, while study of China began only in Year 5 (982). Provision of 'mother-tongue education' (in Hoklo and Hakka) spread in response to popular pressure. Despite talk of 'layered identities' partly aimed at soothing outraged conservatives, the Taiwanese 'layer' was increasingly prioritized. Mandatory study of the *Three People's Principles* was abandoned, to be replaced by civics courses that were both more liberal and more rooted in the local context. Reformers engaged in Deweyan-sounding talk of the need to promote the critical 'political literacy' required by a globalized, diverse and increasingly democratic society (Hughes and Stone 1999, 990–991).

Nevertheless, established paradigms of nationhood and identity died hard. Lee Teng-hui's vision of an inclusive 'community of destiny' (*shengming gong-tongti*) was challenged on two flanks: by Chinese nationalists and Taiwanese 'fundamentalists' (Cabestan 2005, 10). The latter mimic the primordialist tropes of Chinese nationalism, applying them to Taiwan (Vickers 2007). Taiwanese and Chinese 'fundamentalists' also share a conviction of their community's unique victimhood. The discourse of 'national humiliation', a powerful theme of modern Chinese nationalism (Cohen 2009), has been used by both the KMT and the Communists to claim moral superiority for China and underline the need for national strength. Many Taiwanese nationalists similarly assert their blameless victimhood, at the hands of the Dutch, Qing and Japanese, as well as the KMT, while stressing the need to defend the resulting 'multiculturalism' against further external (i.e. Chinese) depredation. But this victimhood narrative features significant blind spots. One relates to the history of relations between Chinese settlers and indigenous Austronesian tribes (Vickers 2009a), another to the suffering of mainland Chinese during the Asia-Pacific War (Vickers 2013).

Identity politics and mainland-Taiwan relations under Ma Ying-jeou

The 'fundamentalist' vision of Taiwanese identity purveyed by Chen Shui-bian's DPP administration (2000–2008), while appealing to its core supporters, prompted widespread anxiety over relations with China as well as resentment amongst those still sentimentally attached to the motherland. The latter included many senior figures in the KMT which, after its 2008 election victory, sought to restore elements of Chinese nationalist orthodoxy (Vickers 2010). These culminated in an early 2014 announcement that school textbooks for history had deviated from the precepts of the ROC constitution and would have to conform (see Vickers 2014).

As well as illustrating how little had changed in politicians' educational ideas, such terminological tussles may also have been linked to efforts to placate Beijing, in the context of cross-Strait trade negotiations. The mainland government has in recent years used its economic leverage to pressure Taiwanese authorities not only to tone down separatist rhetoric on the island itself but also to distance themselves from Tibetan or Uyghur separatists (Rowen 2014, 72). However, given Taiwan's now deeply entrenched political and institutional pluralism, such attempts to muzzle public debate tend only to further undermine Beijing's image.

Meanwhile, demographic shifts appear to be working against pro-unification forces. Surveys show a steady growth of 'Taiwanese' consciousness, particularly marked during periods of KMT rule (1996–1999 and 2008–2016)[2] and strongest amongst the young. For the population as a whole, National Cheng Chi University data show an isolated spike in 'dual identity' responses around 2005, perhaps reflecting hopes of a respite in cross-Strait tension following the mainland tour by former KMT chairman, Lien Chan (NCCU 2013). However, the steady fall in both 'Chinese-Taiwanese' and 'Chinese' identification then resumed, despite – or because of – growing economic reliance on the Chinese mainland. This seems at first sight paradoxical, since the KMT's electoral victories in 2008 and 2012 were largely attributable to popular desire for better relations with China.

Notwithstanding improved cross-Strait ties, on growth, unemployment and income inequality, the post-2008 KMT administration compares poorly to its predecessor. The global financial crisis after 2008 is clearly one factor. Nevertheless, the DPP's 'economic nationalism' helps account for its subsequent electoral revival. Growing integration with the mainland is perceived by many as threatening their jobs and livelihoods. While in 2008 and 2012 most voters seemed inclined to trust President Ma to do a better job of managing relations with China, in local elections most favoured the DPP's messages on social justice – emphatically so in the autumn of 2014, when anti-mainland sentiment was further heightened by the spectacle of Hong Kong's 'Occupy' movement.

Qi's 2008 data indicated particularly strong support for an economic 'open door' to mainland China amongst younger and better-educated individuals – precisely the demographic most self-consciously 'Taiwanese', and which, in 2014, took to the streets in its thousands to oppose extending cross-Strait commercial ties (Qi 2013). It seems that, for many Taiwanese, young or old, economic reliance on the mainland has deepened faster and further than they anticipated. Also unforeseen was the huge influx of mainland tourists that followed the relaxing of restrictions on cross-Strait travel. This has dramatically reversed the previous pattern of interaction with the mainland. Recent research suggests that, far from promoting reconciliation, discomfort at the political leverage that the tourist trade affords Beijing, and concerns over the distribution of the resulting benefits, are producing 'greater social and cultural alienation among Taiwanese' (Rowen 2014, 72). At the most banal level, the deviant personal habits of mainland tourists also alienate locals – a risk acknowledged by the mainland newspaper, *Wen Wei Bao*, which published a list of 'Ten don'ts for mainland tourists in Taiwan' (Shi 2011).

Economic integration thus appears to have reinforced popular determination to defend Taiwan's effective political autonomy. China's increased wealth accentuates perceptions of the mainland as threatening, while growing domestic inequality prompts suspicion that mainland trade disproportionately benefits elites. However Taiwanese identity and its relationship to 'Chineseness' are conceived, old notions of Chinese culture as unchanging, monolithic and invested in a single state have been radically discredited. Multiculturalism and democratic pluralism distinguish a 'Taiwaneseness' constructed in opposition to homogenous, totalizing and state-defined Chinese nationalism. In this context, the KMT's own attempts to associate closer cross-Strait ties with assertions of Chinese nationhood have become, for many, just one more source of alienation.

Hong Kong

Historical background

Until the nineteenth century, Hong Kong, like Taiwan, was a sparsely populated outpost on China's imperial periphery. But unlike Japanese colonialists, keen to incorporate Taiwan within a 'Greater Japan', the British valued Hong Kong primarily as a gateway to China. The point was not to Anglicize the inhabitants, but to use them to profit from the China trade. Locals were actively encouraged to maintain links with their ancestral homeland. Many elites identified strongly with China, while often seeing Hong Kong as a model or conduit for ideas or institutions useful to national salvation. The colony provided refuge for rebels and dissidents from the mainland, including Sun Yat-Sen. Involvement in mainland politics could be two-way; as anti-imperialist Chinese nationalism took hold during the 1920s and 1930s, Hong Kong also witnessed strikes and boycotts. It was involved, too, in China's war with Japan, experiencing invasion and brutal occupation.

Division from the mainland came only after China's Civil War, which brought a vast influx of refugees to Hong Kong. Whereas Taiwan's post-war newcomers lorded it over a far larger native population, Hong Kong's, by the 1950s, constituted the overwhelming majority of local inhabitants. Post-war Hong Kong was thus largely defined by the trauma of exile from the mainland.

The rise of 'Hongkongese' consciousness

Even then, mainland politics continued to spill over the border. The 1950s saw KMT-CCP street fights, and in 1967 Red Guard-inspired riots rocked the colony. While the KMT in Taiwan pursued anti-Communist nation building, the British embarked on no similar enterprise in Hong Kong. They extended diplomatic recognition to Beijing, while also maintaining commercial and cultural ties with Taiwan. Meanwhile, to maintain domestic tranquillity, they sponsored a depoliticized vision of timeless Chineseness, in which the largely refugee population was content to acquiesce.

Ironically, China was perhaps less immediately present in day-to-day life in Hong Kong than in Taiwan. Taiwanese consciousness fed off friction with a mainlander elite insistent that Taiwan *was* China. In Hong Kong, by contrast, enhanced civic consciousness emerged in movements demanding greater recognition for cultural and linguistic, if not political, Chineseness. An educated younger generation, raised in Hong Kong, and cognizant of the norms of British governance, engaged in targeted public protest. Expressions of Chinese patriotism were a means of asserting collective dignity – unrelated to CCP or KMT politics. Meanwhile, a vibrant Cantonese popular culture celebrated a local lifestyle detached from considerations of statehood.

But if many Hongkongers preferred to forget Beijing, in Beijing they were not forgotten. The Communist Party covertly sponsored various leftist organizations and maintained a substantial local support base. Until the 1970s, Hong Kong served as China's principal link to the outside world. This prompted many to assume that the colony's political separation would be indefinitely tolerated. However, the post-Mao leadership was keen to establish its nationalist credentials. And whereas Taiwan remained the great prize, Hong Kong – militarily indefensible and ruled by a distant and increasingly disinterested Britain – was much easier prey.

The Sino-British Joint Declaration of 1984 set the stage for the colony's retrocession. Deng Xiaoping himself promised that 'Hong Kong people' would rule Hong Kong. But while Taiwan was experiencing real democratization, Hongkongers waited to be informed of their future governing arrangements. China's liberalization offered some hope, but as in Taiwan (Cabestan 2005), direct experience of the mainland sharpened the sense of local distinctiveness. During the 1980s, mainlanders were widely ridiculed as ignorant country bumpkins but also feared as a backward, alien horde threatening to overwhelm the gleaming capitalist citadel on their doorstep.

Both fear of and commitment to China were crystalized in the local response to Tiananmen. Vast demonstrations reflected passionate Chinese patriotism but also profound anxiety regarding Hong Kong's own future. As Pepper (2007) argues, the 1989 events contributed crucially to a lasting polarization of local opinion. On the one hand, a pan-Democrat camp, led by veterans of the anti-colonial campaigns of the 1970s, rallied to a vision of Hong Kong defined by civil rights and the trappings of democracy. On the other, a pro-Beijing camp, comprising traditional leftists and collaborationist businessmen, clove to a Beijing-focused

130 Edward Vickers

patriotism. As in Taiwan, schooling became a crucial battleground for these rival visions.

Education and identity discourse

Hongkongers' lukewarm patriotism has often been attributed by pro-Beijing elements to the 'brainwashing' effects of colonial education. As in Martial Law Taiwan, the official prescription for this condition involves reacquainting locals with Chinese culture and traditions. However, pre-retrocession schools, in fact, conveyed a highly conservative, even chauvinist, vision of Chineseness (Luk 1991). In the 1950s, associates of Qian Mu were deliberately co-opted to draft depoliticized curricula. Hong Kong's Chinese History and Literature syllabi were politically neutered versions of their Taiwanese counterparts (Vickers 2005).

Profound, if depoliticized, Chinese ethno-centrism pervaded the curriculum and resonated strongly with many locals. Meanwhile, consciousness of Hong-kongese distinctiveness was rooted primarily in popular culture, rather than con-structed through schooling. Nonetheless, the civic values seen as constitutive of the local lifestyle – the rule of law, civil liberties, the importance of civic activism (Kaeding 2011) – were reflected in, and encouraged by, aspects of the curricu-lum. As the transition to Chinese rule loomed, calls intensified for a more politi-cized approach to citizenship education. But confronted with conflicting political pressures, and sensitive to their own lack of legitimacy, the authorities resorted to symbolism (Morris and Vickers 2015).

The lack of an electoral mandate differentiates Hong Kong's government, pre- and post-1997, from Taiwan's, even though both operate in a context of relative media freedom and civil liberty. This imposes intense and contradictory pressures on curriculum developers, as revealed in the contrasting curricular treatment of local history in post-1997 Hong Kong and Taiwan. Taiwanese texts have offered a vision of a strongly distinctive multicultural community, but Hong Kong's have emphasized the Chineseness of local society (Vickers 2005). As Chief Executive Tung Chee-hwa put it, 'I am Chinese, my home is Hong Kong' (cited by Hughes and Stone 1999, 985). A declared official intention to cultivate critical political literacy conflicted head-on with an obligation to promote Chinese nationalism.

While both Hong Kong and Taiwan adopted a 'layered' approach to the teach-ing of identity during the 1990s, the 'national' was prioritized over the local dimension in Hong Kong, and the reverse in Taiwan (Hughes and Stone 1999, 981). This divergence has since widened. Hong Kong officials have increasingly behaved as if their 'post-colonial status bestowed a popular mandate for nation building. 'National education' has encompassed, *inter alia*, museum exhibitions, student tours to the mainland, military-run 'boot camps', patriotic rituals in schools and regular broadcasts of the national anthem (Vickers 2011).

In education as in other areas, the hand of Beijing has become steadily more significant, or visible. A significant turning point came in 2003, when massive protests scotched the introduction of an 'anti-subversion' ordinance. In 2007, President Hu Jintao called for 'more emphasis on National Education', and a

'Task Group' subsequently cited the propensity of locals to prioritize their 'Hong Kong' over their 'Chinese' identity as a problem requiring rectification (TGNE 2008, 9, cited in Vickers 2011). The proposed solution was a new compulsory school subject: *Moral and National Education* (MNE). However, draft textbooks for this, published in 2012, were redolent of mainland-style political education. The ultimately successful movement to oppose MNE was largely led and organized by high school students: precisely the generation subjected to the post-handover government's various attempts at nation building (see Morris and Vickers 2015).[3]

Recent trends in public opinion and Hong Kong-mainland relations

Trends in identity consciousness have been more complex than in Taiwan, evincing a growing polarization between so-called 'pro-China' and pan-Democrat camps. Chan (2014), for example, found evidence for both increased 'pride and affinity' in relation to 'Chinese cultural icons', but also increased resistance to such symbols of Chineseness. Prior to around 2010, some data suggested a slight rise in self-identification as 'Chinese', but most locals have consistently preferred to identify themselves as Hongkongers or 'Hong Kong Chinese' (HKTP, cited in Kaeding 2011).

Meanwhile, Hong Kong identity itself has been conceptualized in increasingly diverse ways. In the 1990s, prominent elements included an exuberantly consumerist 'lifestyle', Hong Kong's status as an 'international city', and assumptions of superiority vis-à-vis the mainland (Turner 1995). Matthews, Ma and Lui (2007) argued that consumerist values extend to an instrumental rather than sentimental conception of citizenship. Acquiring a passport was for many just another shopping expedition. Identity conceived in these terms was only shallowly rooted, if at all, in consciousness of local history or heritage. However, recent developments – popular movements to protect heritage landmarks, and perhaps the recent fashion amongst some protesters for waving colonial-era British flags[4] – suggest something of a shift in this respect.

There are inklings in Hong Kong today of the sort of nostalgia for a semi-mythologized colonial era exhibited by Taiwan's nativist movement. A marked reversal in relations with the mainland lends credence to a sense that Hong Kong's best days lie in the past. In 2003, facing an economic downturn, the local administration signed a Closer Economic Partnership Arrangement (CEPA) with Beijing – billed as salvation from a solicitous motherland. But, as in Taiwan, the terms of trade are widely perceived as mainland-dictated and the benefits unevenly shared. No longer simply ridiculed as rustic hayseeds, mainlanders have come to be feared as privileged elites threatening the local way of life – with the connivance of collaborationist tycoons. Meanwhile, a constant influx of new mainland immigrants replenishes the ranks of self-consciously 'Chinese' Hongkongers, provoking tension with established residents and reinforcing 'pro-' and 'anti-Beijing' polarization (Chan 2014).

132 *Edward Vickers*

Nonetheless, some recent research may, in fact, have over-estimated pro-China sentiment and under-estimated anti-mainlander resentment (Kaeding 2011; Chan 2014). Kaeding cited a sharp rise in identification with China in 2008, but this coincided with the Beijing Olympics (HKTP, cited in Kaeding 2011). HKTP's early 2014 survey found that younger and more highly educated respondents were far more likely to prioritize 'Hong Kong's identity as plural and international' over 'China's historical and cultural identity' (over 80% of those in the 18–39 age group gave this response, and 70%–80% of those with an undergraduate or higher degree) (HKTP 2014). And while the same survey showed a narrow majority of local residents opposed to the then nascent *Occupy Central* movement, a substantial majority of young people supported it (between 60%–70% of those ages 18 to 29). This suggests that local youngsters share with their counterparts elsewhere concerns about the amassing of wealth by a cross-border elite and its implications for employment and income distribution.

Similar concerns were shared by young participants in Taiwan's 'Sunflower Movement', who occupied Taipei's government buildings in early 2014. Their strategies and messages drew on Hongkongese experience in ways that underlined the values and cultural bonds shared by these societies. However, Hongkongers remain not only more polarized but perhaps also less ready to acknowledge their community's cultural or ethnic diversity. Kaeding observes the 'invisibility' of the long-standing Indian presence, but a more significant blind spot relates to Filipina domestic workers. Their role sits awkwardly with many Hongkongers' sense of themselves as sturdy, self-reliant toilers, exploited by a privileged and unaccountable elite.

Mainland perspectives

When Mao's China was championing global anti-capitalist revolution, in Hong Kong and Taiwan Chinese tradition was invoked to legitimize a colonial or authoritarian-nationalist *status quo*. But today, many young Hongkongers and Taiwanese see China as a principal source of capitalist exploitation. In tandem with this role reversal, a Communist Party anxious to shore up its legitimacy in a post-socialist era has embraced a conservative, traditionalist vision very similar to the old KMT orthodoxy. Confucius has been rehabilitated, along with his latter-day cheerleaders (including Qian Mu); so too has the KMT itself, its contribution to China's anti-Japan struggle now warmly praised (Mitter 2013). The Soviet collapse lent urgency to a renewed emphasis on national unity and strength, buttressed by calls to remember past 'humiliation' at the hands of foreigners. Anti-imperialism is the prism through which official visions of Hong Kong or Taiwanese history are almost invariably refracted (Vickers 2009b).

Chinese university students are far from uniformly nationalistic, though urban youth appear more sceptical than their rural counterparts regarding China's overall situation and prospects (Sinkkonen 2013). However, when it comes to attitudes towards 'the Taiwan question', virtually all agree on the imperative of preventing Taiwanese independence, by military means if necessary (Sinkkonen

Taiwan-Hong Kong-mainland reconciliation   133

2013, 1059). The year after Sinkkonen's data was collected (2007), Taiwan was opened to mass tourism from the mainland. Many mainland visitors have contrasted experiences of spontaneous hospitality there with the atomized, mistrustful quality of life in China (e.g. Wang 2013).[5] Some idealize Taiwan as a repository of values and customs irrevocably lost on the Chinese mainland: 'I have to thank Hong Kong and Taiwan,' declares the popular blogger, Han Han, 'for protecting Chinese civilization' (cited in Rowen 2014, 63). But the PRC authorities also endeavour to ensure that mainland visitors are screened from contact with ideas considered heterodox back home (Rowen 2014). The volume of traffic to and from Hong Kong renders such quarantining impossible; there, local hostility often provokes incredulity and resentment amongst mainlanders primed to see the region as just another part of China (see Xu 2015).

When it comes to Hong Kong and Taiwan, mainlanders' views thus seem strongly conditioned by the officially sanctioned narrative. This associates China's state with a Han *minzu* ('race'/ethnicity) and culture seen as singular and essentially timeless; sub-national identities are perceived and experienced as more fluid than, and strictly subordinate to, a Chineseness defined in these terms (Joniak-Luthi 2013). Like Taiwanese during the Martial Law era, mainlanders are still taught to see Chinese civilization as essentially peaceful and China's expansion as the outcome of harmonious cultural osmosis. The possibility that China, the quintessential victim of colonialism, might itself engage in colonial-style oppression seems unthinkable. More plausible is the claim, made by mainland officials, that Hongkongers or Taiwanese who assert a distinctive local identity have simply been 'brainwashed' by foreign forces and require patriotic re-education to reawaken them to their true identity (Morris and Vickers 2015).

Conclusion

Prasenjit Duara has argued that an opportunity to 'rescue history from the nation' was missed in early twentieth-century China, when a federalist, pluralist vision of nationhood might have emerged (Duara 1995). However, the depredations of foreign imperialism helped to reinforce the conviction that the integrity and sovereignty of a unitary state must be upheld at all costs. China's twentieth-century experience of war and occupation exhibits similarities with that of Eastern Europe, where the ravages of the conflict were particularly intense, and where the subsequent imposition of Communism helped entrench xenophobic attitudes and authoritarian habits. As Communism, with its internationalist tenets, was discredited, and as Europe's multi-national states fell apart, the scene was set for the rise of rival and uncompromising ethno-cultural nationalisms.

The collapse and Balkanization of the Soviet Union and Yugoslavia prompted profound anxiety amongst elites in mainland China, reinforcing a conviction of Western malevolence (Vickers 2009b). Since the 1990s, the stock official response to unrest on China's periphery has been to ramp up patriotic education and further restrict local autonomy. This is the broader context for recent attempts at enhancing 'national education' and restricting press freedom in Hong Kong and

134   *Edward Vickers*

for accusations that pro-democracy protests amount to a '*Gangdu*' movement for independence (Chan 2014).

Such language invokes an analogy with the *Taidu*, or Taiwanese independence movement – but this is misleading. Even in Taiwan, strong 'Taiwanese' identification by no means necessarily implies support for outright political independence. Taiwanese and Hongkongers alike are aware of the dangers of provoking a Beijing regime assured of public support on the mainland for any crackdown on 'separatism'. This has been especially so in Hong Kong, where, even in the absence of anti-subversion legislation, allusions to Taiwan are generally avoided by mainstream pan-Democrats (though a youthful 'nativist' movement has recently arisen that dispenses with such taboos). In Taiwan, meanwhile, Deng Xiaoping's original hope that Hong Kong might demonstrate the benefits of the 'one country, two systems' formula has become an embarrassment for pro-unification forces. During its successful presidential campaign of 2004, the DPP ran advertisements featuring a photograph of Hong Kong's hapless Chief Executive, Tung Chee-hwa, with the caption: 'we are electing a president, not appointing a Chief Executive'. And during the 2012 campaign, DPP candidate Tsai Ing-wen backed up her criticisms of the Economic Cooperation Framework Agreement (ECFA) by claiming that Hong Kong's similar CEPA agreement had brought increasing inequality there (Qi 2013, 1037). Taiwan's 2016 elections, which resulted in a sweeping DPP victory and Tsai's installation as President, came in the midst of signs of growing attacks on Hong Kong's civil liberties (including abductions of publishers to the mainland). These did nothing to shore up Taiwanese support for closer rapprochement with the People's Republic, but issues of inequality, jobs and falling growth, related to the KMT's perceived tethering of the island to a now-stuttering Chinese economy, ultimately doomed the governing party at the ballot box.

Concern over rising inequality is an increasingly prominent theme of public debate in all these Chinese societies. Many Hongkongers, Taiwanese and some urban Chinese appear to share a sense that life in their communities is in important respects becoming worse rather than better. For the wealthiest or most fortunate, whose prospects are increasingly detached from those of their fellow-citizens through access to transnational education, employment and finance, the promise of a better life remains. But for those left struggling with increased overcrowding, pollution, competition and declining real wages, the teleology of modernization – a fundamental premise of Chinese nationalism – may be wearing thin. As belief in progress erodes, this raises the premium on defending what 'we' already have against the depredations of outsiders. In this sense, anti-mainlander sentiment in Hong Kong and Taiwan is analogous to anti-immigrant sentiment in contemporary Europe or to urban Chinese resistance to equal citizenship for rural migrants.

Many in Hong Kong, and even Taiwan, still retain an idea of themselves as in some sense 'Chinese'. But growing socio-economic inequality and increasing economic dependence on China have reinforced hostility towards integration with the mainland. On one level, therefore, reconciliation requires convincing

Taiwanese and Hongkongers that engagement with China can deliver broadly shared benefits for their societies, without undermining their way of life.

However, this is not a sufficient condition for building trust. Communist ideologues may still believe that the economic 'substructure' determines the cultural 'superstructure', and that separatist identities reflect 'false consciousness'. But the fundamental barrier to reconciliation is that Beijing's vision of a unified China can accommodate neither the reality of plural conceptions of Chineseness, nor its political implications. Nationalist rhetoric and displays of intolerant authoritarianism only exacerbate the alienation of many Hongkongers and Taiwanese – especially the young. The Party has invested so heavily in its rigid 'One China' vision and has been so successful in popularizing it, that any attempt to promote a more plural, confederal model might well undermine its legitimacy. Ultimately, though, it is hard to imagine a lasting reconciliation with Hong Kong and Taiwan unless a broader, more inclusive and more liberal vision of 'China' takes hold.

Notes

1 My thanks to Tim Summers for his comments on an earlier draft of this chapter.
2 Perhaps for slightly different reasons in each case; in 1996–1999, the KMT President, Lee Teng-hui, was increasingly emphasizing "Taiwaneseness" in his public statements and policies (e.g. on education), distancing him from many members of his own party. After 2008, the KMT administration of Ma Ying-jeo more consistently pursued warmer ties with the mainland.
3 Many of this generation, taught to revere China's national anthem, have in recent years made a habit of booing it at matches played by Hong Kong's international football team.
4 In early 2014, the short film *Hong Kong will be destroyed in 33 Years*, a major YouTube hit, invoked iconic images of the pre-1997 era (Kai-tak Airport reopened, planes flying over Kowloon rooftops), while fantasizing about a future of fresh air, open space and, above all, self-rule.
5 It should be remembered, however, that postings by mainland tourists criticizing their Taiwanese hosts are perhaps likely to be quickly removed by official censors anxious to promote cross-Strait harmony and solidarity.

References

Cabestan, Jean-Pierre. 2005. "Specificities and Limits of Taiwanese Nationalism." *China Perspectives* 62: 2–14.

Chan, Chi-kit. 2014. "China as "Other": Resistance to and Ambivalence toward National Identity in Hong Kong." *China Perspectives* 2014(1): 25–34.

Ching, Leo T.S. 2001. *Becoming Japanese: Colonial Taiwan and the Politics of Identity Formation*. Berkeley, CA: UC Press.

Cohen, Paul A. 2009. *Speaking to History: The Story of King Goujian in Twentieth-Century China*. Berkeley: University of California Press.

Dennerline, Jerry. 1988. *Qian Mu and the World of the Seven Mansions*. New Haven, CT: Yale University Press.

Dikotter, Frank. 1990. *The Discourse of Race in Modern China*. Hong Kong: Hong Kong University Press.

136 *Edward Vickers*

Duara, Prasenjit. 1995. *Rescuing History from the Nation*. Chicago, London: University of Chicago Press.

Heylen, Ann. 2001. "From Local to National History: Forces in the Institutionalization of a Taiwanese Historiography." *China Perspectives* 37: 39–51.

HKTP (Hong Kong Transition Project). 2014. "Constitutional Reform: Consultations and Confrontations." *Briefing Paper*. Hong Kong Baptist University.

Hughes, Christopher and Robert Stone. 1999. "Nation-Building and Curriculum Reform in Hong Kong and Taiwan." *The China Quarterly* 160: 977–991.

Joniak-Luthi, A. 2013. "The Han *Minzu*, Fragmented Identities and Ethnicity." *Journal of Asian Studies* 72(4): 849–871.

Kaeding, Malte. 2011. "Identity Formation in Taiwan and Hong Kong: How Much Difference, How Many Similarities?" In *Taiwanese Identity in the 21st Century: Domestic, Regional and Global Perspectives*, edited by Gunter Schubert and Carsten Storm, 258–279. Routledge: London

Luk, Bernard H.K. 1991. "Chinese Culture in the Hong Kong Curriculum: Heritage and Colonialism." *Comparative Education Review* 35(4): 650–668.

Matthews, Gordon, Ma, Eric Kit-wai and Lui, Tai-lok (2007). *Hong Kong, China – Learning to belong to a Nation*. London and New York: Routledge.

Mitter, Rana. 2013. *China's War with Japan, 1937–1945: The Struggle for Survival*. London: Allen Lane.

Morier-Genoud, Damien. 2010. "Taiwanese Historiography: Towards a 'Scholarly Native History'." *China Perspectives* 2010(3): 79–91.

Morris, Paul and Edward Vickers. 2015. "Schooling, Politics and the Construction of Identity in Hong Kong: The "Moral and National Education" Crisis in Historical Context." *Comparative Education* 51(3): 305–326.

NCCU (2013). *Taiwanese/Chinese Identification Trend Distribution in Taiwan, 1992/06–2015/12*. Taipei: National Cheng Chi University Election Research Center. http://esc.nccu.edu.tw/app/news.php?Sn=166#. Accessed 22 May 2016.

Pepper, Suzanne. 2007. *Keeping Democracy at Bay*. Lanham, MA: Rowman and Littlefield.

Qi, Dongtao. 2013. "Globalization, Social Justice Issues, Political and Economic Nationalism in Taiwan: An Explanation of the Limited Resurgence of the DPP during 2008–2012." *The China Quarterly* 216, December 2013: 1018–1044.

Rowen, Ian. 2014. "Tourism as a Territorial Strategy: The Case of China and Taiwan." *Annals of Tourism Research* 46: 62–74.

Roy, Denny. 2003. *Taiwan: A Political History*. Ithaca, NY: Cornell University Press.

Shi, Yong-qi. 2011. "Dalu ren qu Taiwan bu neng zuo de 10 jian shi" ("Ten Things that Mainlanders Visiting Taiwan Cannot Do"). *Wen Wei Bao*, 14 Jan.

Sinkkonen, Elina. 2013. "Nationalism, Patriotism and Foreign Policy Attitudes among Chinese University Students." *The China Quarterly* 216, December 2013: 1045–1063.

Turner, Matthew. 1995. "60s/90s: Dissolving the People." In *Hong Kong Sixties: Designing Identity*, edited by Matthew Turner and Irene Ngan, 13–34. Hong Kong: Hong Kong Arts Centre.

Veblen, Thorstein. 1917. *An Inquiry into the Nature of Peace and the Terms of Its Perpetuation*. New York: Macmillan.

Vickers, Edward. 2005. *In Search of an Identity: The Politics of History as a School Subject in Hong Kong, 1960s–2005*, 2nd ed. Hong Kong: Comparative Education Research Centre.

———. 2007. "Frontiers of Memory: Conflict, Imperialism and Official Histories in the Formation of Post-Cold War Taiwanese Identity." In *Ruptured Histories: War, Memory and the Post-Cold War in Asia*, edited by Sheila Miyoshi Jager and Rana Mitter, 209–232. Cambridge, MA: Harvard University Press.

———. 2009a. "Original Sin on the Island Paradise: Taiwan's Colonial History in Comparative Perspective." *Taiwan in Comparative Perspective* 2: 65–86.

———. 2009b. "Selling Socialism with Chinese Characteristics: "Thought and Politics" and the Legitimation of China's Developmental Strategy." *International Journal of Educational Development* 29: 523–531.

———. 2010. "History, Identity and the Politics of Taiwan's Museums: Reflections on the DPP-KMT Transition." *China Perspectives* 2010(3): 92–106.

———. 2011. "Learning to Love the Motherland: 'National Education' in Post-Retrocession Hong Kong." In *Designing History in East Asian Textbooks: Identity Politics and Transnational Aspirations*, edited by Gotelind Müller, 85–116. Abingdon: Routledge.

———. 2013. "Transcending Victimhood: Japan in the National Historical Museums of Taiwan and the People's Republic of China." *China Perspectives* 2013(4): 17–28.

———. 2014. "China-Taiwan History: No Textbook Answers." *East Asia Forum*, 21 Mar. 2014 (online).

Wang, Long-xiang. 2013. "'Dalu ren zai Taiwan' luxing Taiwan gei wo shang de san tang ke" ("'A mainlander in Taiwan': Three Lessons from My Trip to Taiwan"). http://www.want-daily.com/portal.php?mod=view&aid=74976. Accessed 1 Apr. 2014.

Wang, Ming-ke (1997). *Hua Xia Bian Yuan: lishi jiyi yu zuqun rentong* (China's Frontiers: Historical Memory and Communal Identity). Taipei: Yun Chen Ye Kan.

Xu, Cora Lingling. 2015. "When the Hong Kong Dream Meets the Anti-Mainlandisation Discourse: Mainland Chinese Students in Hong Kong." *Journal of Current Chinese Affairs* 44(3): 15–47.

10 Wrestling with the past
Reconciliation, apology and settling history in Australia and New Zealand

Giselle Byrnes

Historians and their publics rely on certain shared beliefs. One of these commonly held convictions, and a foundational paradigm of Western historical thought, is that history and progress are irrevocably interconnected and mutually entwined. We tend to assume that the present will be better than the past. It would be fair to say that, for most societies, the hope for a better future propels us forward. This conviction is, however, sorely tested when present and past collide. Nowhere is this more evident than when nations publicly apologize for historical injustices, excesses and indiscretions, especially those implemented under the globalizing reach of the nineteenth-century British imperial project. This chapter considers public gestures of apology and reconciliation at the level of the nation-state – in particular, the process of saying 'sorry' to Indigenous peoples in Australia and New Zealand – each of which may be understood more generally as attempts to respond to the aftermath and ongoing consequences of British colonization. It does this through examining what is termed here 'the ethics of public apologies'; this is an approach that considers the resources necessary for ensuring genuine and lasting apologies on the one hand, while being alive to the obstacles faced by protagonists on the other. The chapter approaches this analysis comparatively, through a very brief examination of the colonial histories of both countries, followed by a more detailed critique of each of the reconciliation and apology processes in question, particularly as they have developed over the last decade or so in Australia and the past thirty years in New Zealand.

Since the end of the Second World War, the impulse – by governments, institutions, nation-states and former regimes – to officially apologize and reconcile with victims for past wrongs (and, moreover, be *seen* to be doing so) has developed as a powerful global phenomenon. Governments and political elites around the world have felt compelled to publicly atone for historical injustices through processes of formal apology, civic acts of contrition and, in some cases, significant reparations. These injustices include, but are certainly not limited to, wartime atrocities, gross infringements of human rights and the failure to recognize and acknowledge Indigenous rights. The reparative efforts referred to here include the work of the Truth and Reconciliation Commission in South Africa and commissions of inquiry in other parts of Africa, Asia, South and Central America (and recently, North Korea); the Truth Commission established in Northern Ireland;

Australia and New Zealand 139

and processes addressing Indigenous rights in Canada, Australia, New Zealand and elsewhere (Leebaw 2011; Dwyer and Ryan 2012). In considering how and why Western states and institutions have sought to come to terms with their relationships with non-Western states and peoples, Mark Gibney and his co-authors go even further, labelling the late twentieth century the 'age of apology' (Gibney, Howard-Hassmann, Coicaud and Steiner 2007). More recently, Martha Minow, Priscilla B. Hayner and Melissa Nobles have critically examined responses to mass violence, truth commissions and the politics of official apologies (Minow 1998, Hayner 2001, Nobles 2008). Set against a broad international canvas, scholars from a range of disciplinary perspectives are now considering guilt and political redress, apology and 'truth-seeking' commissions, reparation in settler societies, as well as the philosophy and ethics of cultural devastation (Barkan and Karn 2006; Torpey 2006).

In post-colonial settler societies, the quest by Western nations to address 'historical injustices' is, it might be argued, part of a specific historical and cultural moment. While some issues are context and place specific, there are nonetheless general issues (such as the excesses of nineteenth-century colonialist ambition) that may be contextualized against an international milieu, which includes the global spread of reparations politics as well as transnational cooperation among Indigenous peoples in claims for political and legal rights. There is a broader sense too, in which efforts to reconcile past wrongs affect the way in which we understand memory and history in inter-generational as well as contemporary contexts; most current issues in terms of addressing Indigenous rights and justice have their roots in past historical actions. In summary, modern processes designed to address historical wrongdoings ultimately reveal how liberal democratic societies process, prioritize and politicize 'new' historical information.

It is worth briefly sketching the post-invasion (or white settler) histories of both Australia and New Zealand. While both countries share similar broad trajectories in terms of British invasion, annexation and settlement, the particular narrative associated with each makes them remarkably different. The key difference between the settlement experiences of New Zealand and Australia, with regard to the resident Indigenous populations, was the timing of colonization and the prevailing attitudes of the day. By way of illustration, in 1788, the continent of Australia was inhabited by hundreds of tribal societies of Indigenous people with diverse customs, laws and languages.[1] While the instructions provided to British navigator Captain James Cook in 1770 were to 'take possession of convenient situations' with 'the consent of the natives', the colonization of Australia effectively proceeded without any formal treaties being negotiated. While aboriginal Australians actively resisted the British invasion, especially in the early years of the occupation of the southeast of the continent, their status as the original occupants of the land was often unclear, both in legislation and in terms of social practice. Indeed, for most of the post-invasion history of Australia it was not entirely straightforward or clear if Indigenous Australians were adversaries (especially with regard to the authority over land use) or citizens of the Crown. Even when the latter seemed well understood, long-standing cultural attitudes, coupled

140   *Giselle Byrnes*

with entrenched assumptions around white race superiority, meant that any form of 'protection' offered by the settler society's legal system was hypothetical. Driven by an unwavering belief in the moral and legal righteousness of white systems, structures and modes of thought, colonial policy in the late nineteenth century transformed into state-sponsored protectionism; in part, it was argued, to defend the rapidly diminishing Aboriginal population from further bellicosity at the hands of white settlers. Official attention was, in the words of a contemporary axiom, directed towards 'smoothing the pillow' of the 'dying race'; an aphorism that fixed, in theory as well as in practice, the belief that the future for Aboriginal Australians was hopeless and that Darwinian competition was simply fulfilling its natural predestined order of events.

Through the first part of the twentieth century and through until the Second World War, official policies of protectionism continued to dominate Australian cultural policy towards Aboriginal Australians, along with efforts to cultivate and sustain 'whiteness'. This paved the way towards the vision of full-blown cultural assimilation, where Aboriginal people were to be just like 'whitefellas'. It is important to note here that through the period of early contact and colonization, as well as during the later eras of protectionism and assimilation, it was regular, condoned and systematic practice to remove Aboriginal children from their families and deposit them, by force if necessary, into institutionalized care. This long-standing policy, fed by benevolent state paternalism, had both long-term and inter-generational impacts that are still felt today. Indeed, it was not until the 1970s, following in the wake of the powerful decolonization campaigns of the 1960s and the highly publicized efforts of the American Black Power movement, that the Australian Commonwealth Government finally committed to an era of 'self-determination'. This ushered in a range of self-governance measures, with a particular focus on 'land rights' for Indigenous people. It is crucial to note, however, that while this resulted in a number of legislative measures designed to support Aboriginal self-determination, none of these were based on or allowed for the recognition of any form of underlying original Indigenous-owned title.

The question of whether native title existed in Australia was not, tested until 1971, when the Supreme Court of the Northern Territory rejected the proposition.[2] Two decades later, the matter of native title came before the High Court in the now well-known watershed *Mabo* case. The resulting decision, that native title, in fact, existed under the common law of Australia, resulted in huge legal, political and institutional disruption as well as signifying an important cultural and historical moment. The complex (Commonwealth) *Native Title Act*, which provided for the determination of land claims by Indigenous people through mediation, negotiation and litigation followed, facilitated by the National Native Title Tribunal and the Federal Court. The establishment of a national inquiry into the forced removal of Aboriginal children in 1995, only a few years after the Mabo decision, led many observers to draw a connection between these two historical processes. In the broad sweep of the Australian colonial experience, the two were, of course, intimately intertwined; land and people being inseparable in the Indigenous cultural and social context.

Australia and New Zealand 141

Despite its geographical proximity to Australia and its shared British colonial heritage, New Zealand has had a starkly different experience in terms of Indigenous rights. When Cook first visited New Zealand in 1769, he estimated the Indigenous Maori population as somewhere between 90,000 and 100,00 (Belich 1996; King 2003).[3] Contact with Europeans was sporadic through to the early nineteenth century, with sealers, whalers, traders and missionaries forging semi-permanent homes under the patronage of powerful Maori tribes, who were eager to trade and engage with the newcomers. However, by the late 1830s British designs on annexing New Zealand quickened, and in 1840 the Treaty of Waitangi was signed between Maori tribal leaders and the British Crown. In general terms, while the British conveniently saw this as a treaty of cession, the Maori signatories considered it a confirmation of their existing sovereignty, in exchange for them allowing British protection and the maintenance of law and order over the then small communities of resident British subjects. This vast difference in expectations (and this has shaped the subsequent historical trajectory of cultural relations in New Zealand) stemmed from the existence of two language versions of the Treaty, which contradicted each other.[4] Notwithstanding this confusion, both texts recognized the customary rights of Maori as the aboriginal inhabitants of the land and guaranteed to them native title rights at British common law. The Treaty of Waitangi also extended to Maori 'the rights and privileges of British subjects', legally absorbing the Maori population into the rapidly expanding white settler society. While native title to land was not always legally recognized by the Crown in New Zealand, it was confirmed as early as 1847 in a landmark legal finding.[5] This did not, however, prevent conflict over disputed land ownership and efforts to have land and other rights acknowledged have been strongly articulated by Maori from the late 1840s through to the present. Nonetheless, Crown recognition of native title in New Zealand initiated a debate over Indigenous rights, which would not emerge in Australia for another ninety years. It is worth noting too, that in 1867 four Maori seats were created in the young New Zealand settler parliament, formed just fifteen years earlier; a measure which, together with Maori population recovery and growth from the early years of early twentieth century, confirmed the status of Maori as 'almost white', and in the parlance of the day, a 'better sort of native'.

For the next 130 years, successive settler governments in New Zealand vigorously pursued policies of containment and 'amalgamation' in an attempt to comprehensively usurp and replace Maori customs, values and systems of land tenure. Despite the existence of the Treaty, and the sustained inter-generational efforts by Maori activists, educators and political leaders to remind the Crown of its obligations towards them, the document was effectively marginalized in public discourse and sanitized as a symbol of New Zealand's good race relations. Pakeha (white or European New Zealanders) tended to see the Treaty simply as an historical artefact, a relic of beneficence to Maori on the behalf of (their) humanitarian forebears. On the other hand, Maori were (and are still) inclined to see the Treaty variously as a sacred covenant, an emblem of broken promises

142 *Giselle Byrnes*

and as a touchstone for public and legal recognition of Maori autonomy and self-determination.

By the mid-1970s, decades of Maori activism and political protest in New Zealand, fuelled by international calls for the recognition of Indigenous rights, led to the establishment of a permanent commission of inquiry created under the *Treaty of Waitangi Act 1975*, known as the Waitangi Tribunal. This body was empowered to determine and interpret the principles of the Treaty and consider whether contemporary claims from Maori about transgressions by the Crown were legitimate and could be proven. A decade later, the Treaty of Waitangi Amendment Act 1985 extended the jurisdiction of the Tribunal to investigate historical claims concerning the actions of the Crown from 1840 to the present. Maori welcomed this latter amendment as the vast majority of claims had their roots in pre-1975 historical issues. As a result, many hundreds of claims flooded into the Tribunal with claimants seeking restitution for issues that had their origins in the late nineteenth or early twentieth centuries. It is worth noting too that the Waitangi Tribunal's investigations into Maori grievances under the Treaty are neither singular nor unique. Indeed, for many tribes, virtually every generation since 1840 has been involved in presenting some form of injustice regarding alleged Treaty breaches to the government of the day. In its forty-year history, the Tribunal has released over 100 reports on a variety of claims, from small claims through to multi-volume chronicles that have reframed the ways in which we conceptualize the nature of the Maori-Crown encounter in the post-1840 world. These claims cover land loss and the alienation or denial of a wide range of rights guaranteed to Maori under the Treaty of Waitangi.

While the history of Indigenous dispossession and the subsequent assertion of Indigenous sovereignty in Australia and New Zealand follow different narrative arcs, the revisiting of history through the lens of apology and reconciliation reveals particular congruities. The concepts of truth and evidence, fundamental hypotheses in the historians' toolbox, come under special scrutiny in the theatre of reconciliation claims. Moreover, the status of victim testimony and evidence presented in these forums provides particular clues into how political elites and governments consider recommendations to publicly reconcile history and 'right past wrongs'. For instance, in Australia, the 1992 *Mabo* decision was more than a finding of native title; it invited a reconsideration of Australia's colonial past in which the experience of Aboriginal people was (albeit partially) recovered. Drawing heavily on the work of revisionist historians such as Henry Reynolds, the High Court was commonly characterized as having 'rewritten history' in the *Mabo* case. In other words, the *Mabo* decision seemed to suggest a defining moment for post-colonial Australia. It is still seen as an important cultural moment in terms of the Australian narrative, a moment of uplift and hope (albeit largely unrealized) for aboriginal Australia. On the other hand, the Stolen Generations Inquiry in Australia, and its published report, *Bringing Them Home* (Commonwealth of Australia 1997), was controversial and disturbing. Unlike the native title process, it was not established to address specific legalistic matters but to engage in broader fact-finding and recommend general strategies for redress. The report argued that forced child separation had been widespread for a long period in Australian history, most often with devastating consequences for those removed and their distraught families and siblings. The report was honest and shocking, and many people were highly distressed by what they read. Most significantly, *Bringing Them Home* drew attacks from the far right of the political spectrum, specifically critiquing the Inquiry's conclusions that the child separation policies amounted to 'genocide'. This was seen by some commentators as a 'slur' on the work of well-meaning Australian administrators and threw into sharp relief questions around motivation and goodwill with the suggestion that historical actors needed to be read according to the context of their times (Manne 2001).

While in New Zealand, the Waitangi Tribunal and the larger settlement framework is also not strictly a 'truth commission', the issue of establishing 'truth' nevertheless looms large. As a quasi-judicial Commission of Inquiry, the Tribunal must ascertain the truth of what happened: it must identify who was involved, what was at stake and whether Treaty guarantees and promises were broken. Like the Federal Court in Australia, the Tribunal cannot recognize the coexistence of multiple accounts and alternate interpretations of the past but rather must prioritize one conclusive narrative. The Tribunal's narratives have tended to rely heavily upon the official documentary historical record. In more recent years, however, traditional oral evidence is playing a more prominent role: this material is presented in person by Maori elders and claimant witnesses before the Tribunal and is now subject to cross-examination, legal tests of witness credibility and, in some cases, audio-visual recording.

By virtue of its enabling legislation, the Waitangi Tribunal can only make findings and recommendations on any given claim (or group of claims) to the government of the day. The final arbiter of a claim – and the agency charged with drafting the official apology – is the Office of Treaty Settlements; ironically a Crown agency, albeit one expressly charged with providing advice on Treaty policy and strategy to the Minister for Treaty of Waitangi negotiations, consulting with and providing advice to claimants, in addition to taking responsibility for the implementation of Treaty settlements. The drafting of an official apology is the domain of this Office. While other critics have commented on the form and genre of these apologies, typically they are clear and unambiguous statements of regret, offered in full and final terms (Bellingham 2006). The apology is offered in order to seek closure for redress but also for the Crown to absolve itself and restore 'the honour of the Crown', a recurring theme in deeds of settlement. For the Crown, historical truth serves multiple functions: as a narrative of injustice, an absolution of wrongdoing, a restoration of honour and a narrative which promises to deliver 'justice' to claimants in the form of a settlement package.[6] In this forum, 'truth' is, therefore, the medium of forgiveness as well as the vehicle through which future economic development can be delivered. What is most apparent in Treaty discourse in New Zealand, however, is the *absence* of certain terms that are central to processes elsewhere in the world. In New Zealand, the term 'settlement' has supplanted references to 'reconciliation'; in the Crown's eyes, the settlement of grievances signifies a closure of the past and the beginning

144   *Giselle Byrnes*

of a new relationship between the Crown and Maori. This is more than mere semantics: language determines the mode of reparation. 'Settlement' carries with it a fiscal responsibility, while 'reconciliation', is a less easily defined, softer (and some might say, less binding) term.

Compared with the commission of inquiry, the 'truth' sought out by the courts is therefore contingent upon legal rules governing the way in which information is considered. Once a determination of fact has been made, it obtains the status of a 'truth'; upon the basis of which the rights and interests of the parties are then addressed. In the context of legal proceedings that arise from broader historical forces, such as Treaty transgressions in New Zealand or native title claims in Australia, there is a tendency for the decisions of judicial bodies to be obscured against broader historians' debates. In New Zealand, where the enterprise of researching and writing Waitangi Reports has more in common with the academic work of historians than does the functioning of the Federal Court of Australia, disjunctions as to the status of 'truth' have been the catalyst for criticism (Sharp 1997; Oliver 2001; Byrnes 2004). These critiques, however, share the assumption that the Tribunal, as a commission of inquiry, has not taken a neutral and 'objective' position, but has taken it upon itself to document and publicize Maori narratives of colonial and post-colonial resistance.

There are other public gestures that have engaged with the concepts of apology and reconciliation in New Zealand's recent history. The official public apology to the New Zealand Chinese community in 2002 by the New Zealand government was one such event. The then Prime Minister Helen Clark formally and publicly apologized to the descendants of those Chinese immigrants on whom a discriminatory poll tax had been enforced in the late nineteenth century. While not peculiar to colonial New Zealand, this practice was one of the most insidious ways in which past government administrators and their agents implemented a 'white New Zealand' policy. In the late nineteenth century, thousands of Chinese immigrants, lured to New Zealand by the prospect of a better life, were subjected to systematic economic and social discrimination which had left lasting effects on their families, their well-being and their ability to thrive (Ip, Murphy and Ho 2003).[7] The public apology acknowledged the personal cost of the policy and the ways in which Chinese people and their families had been affected. Notwithstanding the sentiments expressed in the apology, no doubt sincerely felt by the Prime Minister herself, the economic and political motivations of this gesture were abundantly clear.

Not content with issuing apologies to victims of Crown actions on New Zealand soil only, the state has also engaged in saying sorry to its former dominions. Later in 2002, Prime Minister Clark offered a public apology to Samoa for deaths arising from the 1918 influenza epidemic. This official apology included the admission that New Zealand's early administration of Samoa was incompetent and ineffectual, especially the decision by New Zealand authorities to allow a ship carrying passengers with the influenza virus to dock in Apia in 1918. This decision led to the deaths of more than one-fifth of Samoa's population, one of the world's worst outbreaks of the epidemic. The apology also referred to the

Australia and New Zealand 145

deliberate suppression of a local nationalist movement when the islands were under New Zealand administration and the arbitrary shootings of non-violent protestors in Apia by New Zealand police in 1929 (Tomkins 1992; Salesa 2009). The Prime Minister's statements in this apology included the hope that 'we' could 'move on' and put the past behind us, a popularly expressed sentiment. Here, history is seen as not only linear and progressive, but something to be momentarily embraced, then moved beyond and away from, a common trope in officially sanctioned apologies.

Public gestures of apology in the wake of either an imperial or colonial act – where the performance of being *seen* to make the apology is often considered as important as the apology itself – begs the question as to why. Why do governments and nation-states feel compelled to apologize for historical as well as contemporary crimes? What motivates the need to atone for the past in the present? The efforts by politicians and governments to atone for past wrongs might be read as efforts to appease or appeal to their constituencies; a cynical reading would suggest that such moves are often driven more by political expediency than moral outrage. A more generous view would submit that apologies offered on behalf of nation-states are genuine attempts to reconcile with the pain inherited from the past. Apologies that carry with them expressions of remorse and admissions of guilt have the capacity to be both confessional as well as healing spaces. Indeed, public authentic gestures of apology are often underwritten by a discourse of religiosity and motivated by a desire to seek atonement and (eventually) redemption.

There are, then, fundamental differences in the ways in which the Crown and 'white' majority settler governments and governing polities have acted towards the Indigenous populations in Australia and New Zealand in the past, many of which continue to reverberate in present policy debates. Perhaps one of the most startling differences between the two nations is that in Australia, native title was effectively extinguished upon the declaration of British sovereignty over the continent in 1788; on the other hand, in New Zealand, native title was recognized and, indeed, upheld by the existence of the Treaty of Waitangi since 1840. In recent years, too, Maori have had arguably a much greater level of access to Treaty-based rights, increased political representation and a significant visibility in the population at large. Put simply, the existence of the Treaty in New Zealand has tilted the reparation discourse slightly in favour of Maori: in other words, the *a priori* guarantee of native title and the Crown's duty to prove it remained faithful to the terms of the 1840 Treaty gives Maori claimants a platform and a place from which to speak. There is no equivalent in Australia.

However, these salient historical differences in native title rights and obligations ought not to obscure the clear similarities and parallels in contemporary efforts to address historical injustices. Both the native title process in Australia and the Treaty of Waitangi claims process in New Zealand place the onus of responsibility primarily on the Indigenous claimants to initiate a claim. Moreover, in both instances, legal methodology dominates the procedures and bureaucracies, thus actively marginalizing other ways of knowing, remembering

146 *Giselle Byrnes*

and recording the past. In both New Zealand and Australia, increased public and political awareness of Indigenous rights and land rights more generally has been due in large part to the tireless efforts of activists and leaders on both sides of the Tasman who have, for generations, continued to remind the dominant white settler state of its obligations towards them. In New Zealand, Maori have been particularly politically vocal in challenging the complacency of the voting electorate around the issue of race relations. Indeed, in recent years, Maori claimants, not content to simply be the recipients of public apologies and restitution packages, have insisted on responding to public declarations of regret by issuing their own 'statements of forgiveness', thus restoring the honour of the Crown on one hand – but also 'closing the conversation loop' on the other. This is in part aligned with Maori notions of reciprocity and exchange, forgiveness and obligation, representing a complex interplay between traditional notions of respect and self-identity with the contemporary realities of restitution politics.

While in both New Zealand and Australia, modern processes are in place to 'reply' to various allegations of historical wrongdoing; these processes are invested with more expectations of social good outcomes than they can realistically deliver. In post-colonial settler societies, public unease about revisiting the history of Indigenous-settler relations continues to fuel contemporary debates examining the ways in which Europeans came to colonize other peoples and places and the ethics of those historical processes. Accepting that certain historical events, acts and decisions were powerful determinants of present political and economic inequalities begs questions regarding the terms and conditions of continued occupancy. In Australia and New Zealand it is also clear that recent processes of reconciliation and settlement are informed by the belief that the past *needs* to be addressed before the nation can be redeemed and move forward into the future. For governing polities and elites, be it the Crown or state and federal governments, the absolution of past wrongdoing is central to the maintenance of a belief in progress. Most significantly, there are strong expectations on the part of the victims that the validation of claimant grievances will guarantee social justice and promise equality; in effect, that the principles of liberal democracy and free market philosophy – powerful discourses of progress – will necessarily right past wrongs.

Notes

1 Exact numbers are not known, but estimates range from 250,000 to 1,000,000.
2 The decision was *Milirrpum v. Nabalco Pty Ltd* (1971) 17 FLR 141.
3 James Belich indicates approximately 86,000, while Michael King estimates 100,000.
4 On the one hand, the English language version signed by the Crown unequivocally declared that the chiefs of New Zealand had 'absolutely and without reservation' ceded all their rights and powers of sovereignty. However, the Maori language version, which most chiefs signed, divided the powers of authority into two: kawanatanga (governorship), which went to the British, and rangatiratanga (self-determination or 'sovereignty'), which was to be retained by Maori.
5 The case was *R v. Symonds* (1847).

Most settlement packages include the return of assets, such as land, plus a cash settlement. The largest settlements, to the Ngai Tahu, Tainui and Taranaki tribes, are estimated at NZ$170 million each.

7 The Chinese Immigration Act was passed by Parliament in 1881, introducing a 'poll tax' of £10. Although the Minister of Customs could, from 1934, waive the poll tax, it was not officially repealed in New Zealand until 1944, long after a number of other countries had abandoned this punitive law.

References

Barkan, Elazar and Alexander Karn, eds. 2006. *Taking Wrongs Seriously: Apologies and Reconciliation*. Stanford, CA: Stanford University Press.

Belich, James. 1996. *Making Peoples: A History of the New Zealanders From Polynesian Settlement to the End of the Nineteenth Century*. Auckland: Penguin.

Bellingham, Julie. 2006. "The Office of Treaty Settlements and Treaty History: An Historiographical Study of the Historical Accounts, Acknowledgements and Apologies Written by the Crown, 1992 to 2003." MA thesis, Victoria University of Wellington.

Byrnes, Giselle. 2004. *The Waitangi Tribunal and New Zealand History*. Melbourne: Oxford University Press.

Commonwealth of Australia. 1997. *Bringing Them Home: Report of the National Inquiry into the Separation of Aboriginal and Torres Strait Islander Children from Their Families*. Australian Human Rights Commission (April).

Dwyer, Philip and Lyndall Ryan, eds. *Theatres of Violence: The Massacre, Mass Killing and Atrocity in History*. New York: Berghahn.

Gibney, Mark, Rhoda E. Howard-Hassmann, Jean-Marc Coicaud and Niklaus Steiner, eds. 2007. *The Age of Apology: Facing Up to the Past*. Philadelphia, PA: University of Pennsylvania Press.

Hayner, Priscilla B. 2001. *Unspeakable Truths: Facing the Challenges of Truth Commissions*. London and New York: Routledge.

Ip, Manying, Nigel Murphy, Bevan Lee and Elsie Ho. 2003. *Unfolding History, Evolving Identity: The Chinese in New Zealand*. Auckland: Auckland University Press.

King, Michael. 2003. *The Penguin History of New Zealand*. Auckland: Penguin.

Leebaw, Bronwyn Anne. 2011. *Judging State-Sponsored Violence, Imagining Political Change*. London and Cambridge: Cambridge University Press.

Manne, R. 2001. *In Denial: The Stolen Generations and the Right, Quarterly Essay 1*. Melbourne: Black Inc.

Minow, Martha. 1998. *Between Vengeance and Forgiveness: Facing History after Genocide and Mass Violence*. Boston, MA: Beacon Press.

Nobles, Melissa. 2008. *The Politics of Official Apologies*. Cambridge: Cambridge University Press.

Oliver, W.H. 2001. "The Future Behind Us." In *Histories, Power and Loss: Uses of the Past*, edited by Andrew Sharp and Paul McHugh, 9–29. Wellington: Bridget Williams Books.

Salesa, Damon. 2009. "New Zealand's Pacific." In *The New Oxford History of New Zealand*, edited by Giselle Byrnes, 149–172. Melbourne: Oxford University Press.

Sharp, Andrew. 1997. *Justice and the Maori: The Philosophy and Practice of Maori Claims in New Zealand since the 1970s*, 2nd ed. Auckland: Oxford University Press.

Tomkins, Sandra M. 1992. "The Influenza Epidemic of 1918–19 in Western Samoa." *Journal of Pacific History* 27(2): 181–197.

Torpey, John. 2006. *Making Whole What Has Been Smashed: On Reparations Politics*. Cambridge, MA: Harvard University Press.

11 Comparing Polish-German and Polish-Russian reconciliation efforts

Stanisław Bieleń and Krzysztof Śliwiński

The burden of historical injustices

Poland is among the countries that cite a geopolitical fate. Regardless of its own complex history, with no shortage of expansive wars, since the turn of the seventeenth and eighteenth century it has faced not only territorial claims from its strongest neighbours but also planned efforts to divide and liquidate it. Animosity, hostility or aggressiveness of neighbours is nothing special, but the scale of the phenomenon, which led to horrendous atrocities, is beyond the imagination of an ordinary person (Harasimowicz 2013, 21).

Poles themselves have sadly become the perpetrators. This refers both to the expulsions of Germans from the lands granted to Poland after World War II[1] and the atrocities against the Jewish population during the war as well as against those who survived the Holocaust and became the victims of anti-Semitic disturbances after the war. Therefore, it can be concluded that the traumatic legacy of World War II leaves a lasting mutilation of memory about the wrongs inflicted on each other in relations with almost all the neighbours – the Germans and the Russians, but also the Ukrainians, the Lithuanians and the Jews.

The wounds inflicted on Poland and the Poles by the Germans during World War II were particularly deep. No other country suffered such huge losses as Poland did during World War II. Warsaw was one of the most affected cities, attempting to fight the invader also through uprisings (the 1943 Ghetto Uprising and the 1944 Warsaw Uprising). Perhaps if the Poles had not resisted the occupation so firmly, they would not have suffered such enormous material and human losses.

Not only did Poland become the site of mass genocide, it was also subjected to division as a result of the Yalta and Potsdam decisions ending World War II in Europe. In fact, it was turned into a bargaining chip in the struggles between the great powers.

The processes of reconciliation with the largest neighbours – Germany and Russia – are thus about, on the one hand, the preservation of memory about the atrocities and human sufferings, bringing forgiveness and preventing such atrocities from happening again in the future. On the other hand, it is about making

Polish-German and Polish-Russian reconc. 149

an examination of conscience and admitting one's guilt. As pointed out by Anna Wolff-Powęska (2011, 13), an outstanding expert on Polish-German relations, "modern history is yet to see a case of mourning foreign victims by a nation or state on behalf of which crimes were committed." Hence, there can be no illusions about the possibility of finding a single model for reconciliation between nations. Experience shows that each new generation brings in its own issues and doubts and seeks its own ways of reconciling with history.

The road to Polish-German reconciliation

Due to Poland's dependence on the Soviet Union, after World War II the Poles could only cultivate the memory about the injustices wrought by the Germans, who murdered nearly 6 million people and took 2.5 million to Germany for forced labour (Karnowski 2009). It was a long wait for the memory about retaliation against the Germans, forcibly expelled to Germany from the areas east of the Odra and Nysa (Oder-Neisse) rivers (estimated at more than 11 million people), to be restored.[2] Władysław Bartoszewski, a hero of the resistance, a prisoner at the Auschwitz concentration camp, a participant in the fight against the communization of the country and foreign minister during the presidency of Lech Wałęsa, was the first to bring up the problem on the Polish side (see Hyodo 2007, 78–81). This arguably came from the understanding of the German trauma caused by the loss of 20 per cent of the German territory. Although the decisions on territorial shifts were made at the conferences of great powers, ultimately it was the Poles who lived in post-German homes of Wrocław, Szczecin and Olsztyn. For these reasons, German-Polish relations were not comparable in psychological and moral terms with any other neighbourly relations of Germany.

An enormous role in Polish-German reconciliation was played by ethical reflection derived from religion, which became a source of inspiration in politics. The first steps, arising from Christian premises, aimed at breaking the existing taboos and overcoming psychological barriers. They were initiated on the Polish side by two Catholic publicists and activists, Stanisław Stomma and Stefan Kisielewski, focused around the Catholic "Tygodnik Powszechny" ("General Weekly") and the Deputies' group "Znak" ("The Sign").[3] On the German side, an important trailblazing role in reassessing the view of mutual relations was in turn played by Protestant intellectuals from Tubingen, and also the Evangelical Church Council in Germany, whose Memorandum of 1 October 1965 came several months before the Polish bishops' message to German Catholic bishops. The issue of coming to terms with post-war realities, concerning shared neighbourhood in the new borders, constituted the most important problem on the German side, in light of the pressure from thousands of expellees from the lands now settled by Polish exiles from the Eastern areas, taken over by the Soviet Union. A huge role in this respect was played by representatives of German secular and clerical elites. They included Evangelical theologian Martin Niemöller and also Joseph Ratzinger. The Memorandum of the Bensberg Circle (1968) with their participation

150   *Stanisław Bieleń and Krzysztof Śliwiński*

was signed by nearly 200 intellectuals. It was a plea for a sense of political realism and the acceptance of the Odra and Nysa border in the name of peace and overcoming hostility (Wolff-Powęska 2010, 356).

The Polish bishops' message to German bishops from December 1965 was a plea for dialogue, forgiveness and reconciliation.[4] Appealing to the Evangelical truths of loving thy neighbour, faith in the possibility to touch and change human conscience, hope for change in the spirit of good will and reaching out to each other constituted a display of intellectual courage and moral determination. Christianity was the catalyst for forgiveness, although it was not an easy process. Groups of Germans (from the FRG and the GDR), meeting at the site of the Nazi concentration camp Auschwitz-Birkenau, were driven by the motto "through atonement to understanding and reconciliation" (Deselaers 1999, 49–54).[5]

A huge role in the processes of reconciliation was played by outstanding figures who could dare to make special gestures and meaningful symbols. On the German side, they were two statesmen who brought the process of reconciliation to the confession of guilt and forgiveness. One of them was Willy Brandt who, as West German Chancellor, visited Poland in December 1970 to normalize mutual relations and confessed the guilt of the German nation while kneeling at the foot of the Monument to the Heroes of the Ghetto Uprising. The other was President Roman Herzog who, on the fiftieth anniversary of the outbreak of the Warsaw Uprising on 1 August 1994, asked for forgiveness for everything the Germans inflicted on the Polish nation.

These acts of goodwill, boiling down to ritual "apologies", made it possible to close the book on a certain chapter in Polish-German relations. They were, indeed, a crowning achievement of a certain process of "contrition" which found its expression in German payments of damages to the victims of Nazism, scattered across the world.

Successive speeches of FRG presidents (Richard von Weizsäcker on the fortieth anniversary and Roman Herzog on the fiftieth anniversary of the war's end), the invitation for Polish foreign minister Władysław Bartoszewski to visit the Bundestag, where he delivered a speech as part of the celebrations marking the fiftieth anniversary of the war's end, the establishment of 27 January each year as the Day of Remembrance for Victims of Nazism to mark the liberation of the Auschwitz concentration camp – these are symbolic and meaningful acts of political will on the German side that changed the feelings of the Polish nation.

For many Germans, *The treaty on the basis for normalization of relations between the PRP and the FRG* from 7 December 1970 meant farewell to pipe dreams and grievances. It was a turning point in the approach of both countries to each other. Increasing people-to-people contacts, and also raising difficult topics, facilitated "changes through rapprochement". They involved learning about each other, altering negative emotions, predicting the consequences of opening up and breaking psychological barriers.

It took the democratization of Poland and the reunification of Germany to create the necessary framework for rapprochement in both countries. The Moscow *Treaty on the final settlement with respect to Germany* ("2 + 4") of 12

September 1990 included a clear reference to Germany's and Poland's competence to definitively confirm the existing border between them. Both countries did it in the treaty of 14 November 1990, stating that "the existing frontier between them is inviolable now and in future and [they] mutually pledge to respect unconditionally their sovereignty and territorial integrity" (Kukułka 1998, 199).

The last quarter of the century is treated as a period of filling Polish-German reconciliation with concrete content. This period can be even considered the most important in the history of both nations and states, because, thanks to favourable circumstances, they got their first ever chance to build a qualitatively new Polish-German neighbourhood. First and foremost, there was a change in the moral and psychological climate that forms the background to the natural space for making up the lost time. Partnership ties were developed, which meant respect for the subjective attributes of each side. Many organizations and associations were created, connecting various social structures – professional groups, cities, municipalities, universities, and schools.

The enthusiasm for normalization on the Polish side was, however, accompanied by scepticism and reluctance on the German side. After the "iron curtain" came down, the ignorance of Germans about the history of mutual relations, especially the course of the war and occupation in Poland and other areas of Eastern Europe, came to the surface. Related to it was the indifference of the majority of society towards the newly articulated claims by the Federation of Expellees (Erika Steinbach) and the Prussian Trust, which unnecessarily provoked anti-German sentiments on the Polish side. The Polish nationalist right-wing circles (including the Law and Justice) raised many voices of opposition to the affirmation or amnesia-and-attention policy of the Polish authorities towards Germany, which was a relation between a weak victim and a strong tormentor.[6]

The last quarter of the century showed that reconciliation between nations is burdened with memory, which in many cases amounts to negative emotions. It is an interesting sociological observation that forgiving is easier for those who were the victims than for those who were on the aggressor's side and also suffered personal costs. Here it mainly means a part of the community of expellees and their descendants who remain obstinate and focused on their own grievances, unwilling to enter into any dialogue with Poland and reconcile with the Poles.

The paradox of contemporary international relations in Europe is that the continent's strongest power is a country responsible for the greatest crimes of the twentieth century, if not the greatest crimes ever. Germany has gone through the processes of expiation and rehabilitation in its post-war history, and its political and cultural elites have adopted anti-martyrological attitudes. But the martyrological history keeps returning, because the Germans, like other nations, feel the psychological need to have their own history in a martyrological and heroic version. A related aspect is the syndrome of reversing the roles of perpetrators and victims. Since the Germans lost the war and draconian conditions were imposed on them, it means they deserve to be called victims. The phenomenon may constitute the greatest challenge since the normalization of Polish-German relations.

The difficult settling of historical accounts between Poland and Russia

There is a high asymmetry in Poland's treatment of Germany and Russia due to their settling of accounts with "the demons of history". The Poles have proved to be more willing to forgive the Germans than the Russians, even though the German occupation claimed far more victims in the Polish society than the Soviet occupation (Karnowski 2009).[7]

In the 1990s came a shift from a discussion on the crimes of Hitlerism to a discussion on the crimes of Stalinism, the emphasis clearly moved from "Oświęcim to Katyń". Among many reasons for such a state one needs to point out that the reckoning with the past in Polish-German relations began much earlier, already in the 1960s, while these issues remained frozen in relations with the Russians until the early 1990s. The Russians couldn't, didn't want to or didn't know how to account for their past. This was mainly due to the difference between the status of the loser and the winner.[8]

Poland and Russia differ in their views on the history of the twentieth century. Wartime injustices have been compounded by reminiscences of the ideological hostility from the time of the 1920 Polish-Bolshevik war as well as post-war enslavement, which meant the imposition of Stalinist models of political system. In addition to the Russian aggression of 17 September 1939 and the *gehenna* of deportations and expulsions to labour camps, the biggest trauma is the Katyń atrocity and the failure of the Red Army to help the Warsaw Uprising. It is common belief in Poland that the insurgency ended in disaster because of the betrayal of Stalin, who not only didn't lend any assistance but also refused landing permission for Allied aircraft carrying aid for the insurgents.

Under the terms of the Yalta conference, over which Poland had no influence whatsoever, the country was incorporated into the Soviet sphere of influence. Its liberation by the Red Army, therefore, meant enslavement. Full independence and, indeed, freedom were regained only after shaking off communism. The problem, therefore, involves not only attitudes towards the war and its aftermath. It involves the contemporary identity of the Poles, who are unable to see relations with Russia differently than just as pages of "common hostility", rather than "common brotherhood" from the time of war against fascism.

A chance to create conditions for Polish-Russian normalization and reconciliation came with treaty-based regulation of mutual diplomatic relations (the *Treaty between Poland and Russia on friendly and good-neighborly cooperation* of 22 May 1992), the withdrawal of Russian troops from Poland (the process was completed on 17 September 1993) and the safeguarding of strategic energy supplies for Poland (Stolarczyk 2013, 28–34). In the declarative sphere, the Polish side – which can be seen in successive *exposés* of Polish Prime Ministers in the 1990s, called for normalization and the establishment of partnership relations, but in practice the relations were affected by emotions and a growing moral arrogance. The policy towards Russia came to be determined by the idea of missionism and

Prometheanism, with advancing the West's democratic values in the post-Soviet area at their foundation. Poland, instead of being a "bridge" between Russia and the West, started acting as an outpost for Western Europe and the US in confrontation with Russia.

Historically speaking, the democratic Poland accuses Russia of failing to account for the Stalinist atrocities, including first and foremost the Katyń crime. The atrocity against Polish officers in Katyń and other sites of the former Soviet Union (*c.* 25,000 killed), committed by NKVD, has never been fully explained. First of all, due to lack of access to necessary documents, it has proved impossible to identify individual perpetrators. While both Mikhail Gorbachev and Boris Yeltsin revealed the truth about the Katyń atrocity, Russian officials have not expressed remorse like German politicians[9] on the principle that the new, reborn Russia does not bear responsibility for the atrocities of the totalitarian Stalinist regime. It stems from the conviction that Russians themselves were victims of the Stalinist dictatorship, and the Katyń crime was only one of many mass atrocities (Ziemkiewicz 2012, 96).[10] There is also an ongoing dispute about the legal qualification of the crime.

Objectively one has to admit that the Poles are "immersed" in history, which means they are among exceptionally unforgiving nations. In the words of Paul Ricoeur, they suffer from the "remembrance disease", they "immerse themselves with memory about the suffered injustices" (Drozdowicz 2001, 250). Meanwhile, reconciliation requires looking "forward", with respect for the partner, its dignity and freedom in dialogue. Looking at dialogue solely through the prism of one's own benefits is a road to nowhere.

In Polish-German reconciliation, an enormous role was played by Christian churches – the Evangelical and the Catholic church. Thus far, similar processes have not taken place in Polish-Russian relations. True, there was a spectacular visit of Patriarch Kirill I in Poland and the signing of the *Joint message to the peoples of Poland and Russia* on 17 August 2012, but it is clear to see that forgiveness is anything but easy. Without mature reflection on both sides, all the symbolic acts, public gestures and declarations do not bring the desired results. It appears the Catholic church in Poland holds on to its conservative stances too tightly, while the Orthodox church does not see itself in the role of apologizing for the sins of totalitarianism.

Both on the German and Russian side it is possible to find many figures linked to Poland by the will of reconciliation. But while the Poles and the Germans were able to turn such personalities as Jerzy Turowicz, Stanisław Stomma, Mieczysław Pszon or Krzysztof Kozłowski, and Willy Brandt, Richard von Weizsäcker, Karl Lehmann or Georg Sterzinsky into advocates for accommodation, things are much more difficult with the Russians. First of all, the resentment towards each other that prevails on both sides is so strong that no one has the courage or strength to resist existing attitudes. It has turned out that mutual political gestures from Boris Yeltsin or Tadeusz Mazowiecki have failed to create the right climate for seeking effective solutions. Similarly conciliatory initiatives from the churches have not changed the dynamics of the processes in place.

154   *Stanisław Bieleń and Krzysztof Śliwiński*

Moreover, there was a pluralism of views on the issue of relations with Poland on the West German side, expressed both in coalition governance (CDU/CSU-SPD i SPD-FDP) and policy diversity of major political parties. Public discourse around German national guilt spawned the idea of the necessity to reconcile and come to an understanding with the Polish neighbour. This is what is missing on the Russian side. The concentration of power around the presidential centre in the Kremlin and a virtual demise of the opposition do not give any chance to develop a flexible position on normalization of relations with Poland (Lisiakiewicz 2012, 91–116). What is more, Russia does not have an imperative of the kind the Federal Republic of Germany had. Then, the lack of normalization of relations with the GDR, Poland and Czechoslovakia threatened, at the time of detente, to isolate West Germany in the European and international arena. For Russia, on the other hand, unsettled relations with Poland do not constitute any obstacle to achieving its great power objectives. The lack of normal Polish-Russian relations is nothing more than a "local" matter and concerns only the two partners. Moreover, West Germany since Konrad Adenauer made it its objective to achieve reconciliation and rapprochement with France, which for Willy Brandt as well as Helmut Kohl constituted a challenge to give reconciliation with Poland a similar historical significance. An important thing was the coincidence of the desires of both sides (Góralski 2011).

In the case of Russia, its political authorities have, in fact, made some gestures, which could be considered as important acts in the process of bilateral reconciliation. They included Vladimir Putin's participation in the commemorations of the seventieth anniversary of the outbreak of World War II at Westerplatte and an article by Prime Minister of Russia published in "Gazeta Wyborcza", titled *Pages of history – the reason for mutual grievances or the basis for reconciliation and partnership?* (Putin 2008). Putin's visit with Polish Prime Minister Donald Tusk to Katyń on 7 April 2010 was aimed at convincing the Polish side of the Russian side's good intentions and will to move towards final reconciliation. The visits and meetings obviously could not replace tedious dialogue and seeking solutions at the negotiating table for such difficult issues as the legal qualification of the Katyń massacre by the Russian side as a crime not subject to statute of limitations, making the entire Katyń investigation file available to the Polish side by the Russian Military Prosecutor's Office,[11] the return of the archives looted by the Red Army, recognizing the Poles as an oppressed nation, or compensation payments to the Poles who did forced labour in the former Soviet Union (Grajewski 2010, 735). The Polish presidential plane crash in Smoleńsk on 10 April 2010 proved to be a critical point in the process of rapprochement. It appeared that the deep trauma of the Polish society and expressions of sympathy from the Russian side would foster progress in the processes of reconciliation. But it turned out another way. Diverging views on the causes of the disaster and mistakes made during the investigation caused a setback in Polish-Russian relations (Meller 2011).[12]

Psychological and emotional attitudes towards each other are an obstacle to normalization and reconciliation between the Poles and the Russians. They have their sources both in distant past and quite recent events, mentioned earlier. First of all, manipulations over examples of mutual guilt for the tragedies of the twentieth century are the order of the day. While the Polish side is categorical in its judgements and principled in passing arbitrary verdicts for Stalinist crimes, the Russian side goes back to earlier events, relativizing Stalin's atrocities. In the context of responsibility for the Katyń crime, the Russian side raises, for example the issue of the fate of Bolshevik prisoners who died in prison camps in Poland in 1919–1921. Regardless of the fact that the Polish side has published the results of scientific research on this topic (see works by Kaprus Zbigniew), pointing that the number of dead prisoners did not exceed 17,000, the Russians knowingly equate the meticulously planned Stalinist atrocity, committed on the orders of the highest authorities of the Soviet Union, with the tragic fate of prisoners who died of various causes, mostly due to an epidemic of typhoid and poor living conditions, inflating their number to tens of thousands.

The Polish opinion-making environment has been widely dominated by Russophobia, which comes not only from deep historical accumulations and psychological complexes but also daily education at home, in school, in the church and so forth. Russophobic sentiments, more or less exposed, surging in various historical periods, are unfortunately a permanent feature and attribute of traditionally understood Polishness. It is an element of national identity, a criterion for identifying the "true" patriotic attitude. Russophobia is a certain fashion, the legitimacy of which is not questioned by anyone. You just need to look around and listen to what friends, uncritical presenters and the so-called TV experts say about the "Russkis", transmitting invectives and insinuations to the public. The public message is characterized by the "pejorativization" of the names Russia and Russians, creation of their negative images, non-alternativeness of perception and labelling as the embodiment of evil. It is accompanied by deliberate equating of anti-Sovietism with anti-Russianness, and the demonization of Vladimir Putin as the father of all woes (as the enemy of democracy, human rights and tolerance) is the hallmark of this caricatural political and media culture.[13]

Most Poles mentally remain hostages to archaic, stereotypical, often surreal and extremely simplified representations of Russia. It is striking that few in Poland care about reversing these negative trends, harmful to Poland's international image. Little is done to eliminate the obsessions, fears and phobias which make it difficult to look at Russia as a normal country, which has the right to define its own interests, even if they collide with Polish interests.

In light of the Russophobia that flourishes in Poland, what is needed is a new impulse for a therapy of memory, to free it from harmful obsessions and fear of Russia. One attempt to quasi-diplomatically support Polish-Russian reconciliation was the establishment of the Polish-Russian Group for Difficult Issues in 2002 and its reactivation in 2008. Artiom Malgin from the Russian side believes the overriding value of the consultative work of Russian and Polish historians is respect and mutual understanding in interpreting historical events, while not giving in to political pressures (Malgin 2010, 698). It is not certain, however, whether historians from both sides will succeed in turning attention away from the past and focusing on the future. For now, no one wonders how to build the foundations for peaceful coexistence of future generations through mutual forgiveness (Ricoeur 2006). Each party's insistence on their version of historical truth and demands for moral (and material) satisfaction block progress on the road to normalization and reconciliation.

While the democratic transformation in Poland helped to overcome negative attitudes towards the Germans, it proved a bitter lesson that freedom and democracy do not make normalization with undemocratic Russia any easier. On the contrary, a tendency can be seen that political manipulations over memory and accounts of suffering lead to regress rather than progress in complicated Polish-Russian relations. Divergent assessments of the Soviet era – associated by the Poles with hegemony and dependence and by the Russians with imperial power and a feeling of stability – will long continue to divide both parties and influence their historical policies. Overpersistence in the search for the perpetrators and justice for the wrongs suffered from the Soviet Union leads to the creation of new prejudices and confrontations on the Polish side. And on the Russian side it triggers a defensive reflex in the form of instrumentalization of history. The tradition of imperial haughtiness and the arrogance of Russian elites feed anti-Polish sentiments. Poland is attributed the role of a limitrophe state seeking to isolate Russia in the international arena (Бухарин2011). This criticism is driven by actions with anti-Russian overtones, such as the US anti-missile shield project or Warsaw's support for opposition activities in Ukraine.

Poland lacks in-depth reflection over the experiences of other nations in the field of reconciliation and normalization. The example of German-French relations draws the interest of no one but international relations experts (see works of Parzymies, Szeptycki and Lakomy). Similarly, the positive results of German-Russian or German-Israeli reconciliation go unnoticed. Conciliation models are not popularized, and hostility towards the Russians is treated as a normal thing in social and political life. This state of affairs is best reflected by the mass media, which regardless of their ideological provenience are racing to outdo each other in slanders, insinuations, witch hunts and the desire to discredit the other side.

Currently, we face a deficit of great political personalities, politicians who would be able to go against the dominant fashions. There are no moral authorities and courageous politicians who would restore the faith in the independence of thinking about close, neighbourly relations with Russia. Poland needs a courageous political leader who is able to assert national interests, make the broad masses realize that reconciliation with the Russian nation, like just reconciliation with the German nation, is an elementary requirement of Polish *raison d'etat*.

In relations with Russia, it is necessary to take advantage of the positive experiences from Polish-German cooperation, for example in the field of youth exchange. Where state institutions fail, it is worth embracing civil associations and non-political activities. An enormous role in this respect falls on the churches, just like it was in the case of Polish-German reconciliation. No battle over history leads to victory. We should rather listen patiently to the interpretations of our partners and cherish the memory of good in the face of the memory of evil

(Bingen 2010, 221–243). The point also is not to instil the historical trauma and obsessions in the next generations.

It appears it is the United States who could do the most for Polish-Russian reconciliation by changing its strategy towards Russia. It would resemble the 1960s when the West began to show interest in improving relations with the East (e.g. Pierre Harmel's NATO report from 14 December 1967), which had great impact on bringing the Bonn Republic's Eastern policy to its senses. Poland finds itself in the role of a state willingly acting as a public, sometimes infantile exponent of US interests. If the administration in Washington recognized the long-term value in forging positive relations with Russia, Poland would lose the motivation and scope to act as a spoiler. But if, according to American scenarios, it is supposed to continue to act as a "bolt" ("a continental barrier") against Russia, rather than a catalyst for rapprochement, there is no possibility of any Polish-Russian rapprochement in the foreseeable future. The pro-American nature of Polish political elites is the "cornerstone" of the foreign policy of the Third Republic, so there is a persistent conflict between the affiliations with America and improved relations with Russia.

As previous experience shows, the so-called Europeanization of Polish policy has had little impact on normalization and reconciliation with Russia. While it can be suspected that the European Union modifies the behaviour of governments in Warsaw, it is yet to translate into progress in Polish-Russian relations. Poland, in turn, has a chance to increase its credibility as a rational and influential team player, provided, however, that it calls for accord rather than discord with Russia. Only pushing its positive narration or vision of relations with Russia within the European Union guarantees that Poland's position is reckoned with. Any fear-mongering about Russia falls on barren ground in the European Union. That's because many Western countries are anxious for Russia to join the club of rich and stable countries, as then it will pose no threats of which the Poles constantly remind them.

In the process of normalization with Russia, it is worth pursuing the so-called small steps policy. It can be facilitated by using the experiences of Poland's relations with the Kaliningrad Oblast. Visa-free, "small" border traffic with the Russian exclave shows that both sides are reaping benefits, taking their chance to learn each other better and eliminate the artificially sustained misconceptions. In light of the increasing trade volume between Poland and Russia it is clear that entrepreneurs from both sides can create a pragmatic framework for cooperation despite the media and politicians. The experiences of Polish-German reconciliation could be used in this process, for example participation of regional communities, cities and local governments, expanding cooperation between regions and non-governmental organizations in the fields of education, culture and sport, agriculture, communications and telecommunications, in the areas of transport and environment protection. But the issue of reconciliation is a sensitive and delicate one; therefore, it is necessary to be very careful in employing the "third" factor (Bieleń 2012, 5–27).

158 *Stanisław Bieleń and Krzysztof Śliwiński*

The dramatic events in Ukraine and the Russian intervention in Crimea in February 2014 have shown once again, after the 2008 Georgian war, how strong the demand is for a hostile and aggressive Russia. A wave of hysterical comments has swept across the Polish nation, making it all but impossible for the man in the street to understand the essence of the ongoing situation. First and foremost, both the media and politicians are using extremely emotional, negative evaluative rhetoric, as a result of the groupthink syndrome, focusing attention on "Moscow's aggression", in isolation from the context and prior events. Rational reasoning struggles to reach the public, while common sense and restraint in response are at a premium.

Meanwhile, the Polish political life has been dominated by war rhetoric against Russia. Such rhetoric best serves Russophobic propaganda but does not bring any positive political effects in the long run. Anti-Russian emotions are a bad advisor to effective diplomacy. The crisis will end someday, because such is the nature of crises and Poland will remain Russia's neighbour and needs to think about its own interests. More realism and less moralism would come in handy.

Poland's asset is its experience with peaceful systemic transformation. The achievements of the "round table" should be a role model and not be seen as a piece of furniture from the rubbish heap of history. It's a shame, therefore, that the Polish side has failed to bring the Ukrainians round to national consensus and compromise, which could – like in Poland – lead to a gradual delegitimization of the old regime without causing panic in the Russian-speaking part of Ukraine and triggering a violent reaction from the Kremlin.

* * *

Lasting reconciliation with Germany and a return to normality in relations with Russia are in Poland's best interest. Arguably, there is a need to build a programme of positive thinking about both neighbours, instead of highlighting differences in mutual expectations, ambitions and potential. Looking at the level of political discourse in Poland, one can have serious doubts as to whether anyone will draw any instructive and constructive lessons from previous erroneous diagnoses. Many Polish decision makers fail to realize that by persisting in a state of confrontation with Russia, they restrict Poland's long-term, effective, appreciated ability to act in the international arena in the ever more complicated world. Intransigence towards Russia has unfortunately become the hallmark of identity of some political parties (especially the Law and Justice) and a means of rallying the electorate. It does not bode well for the future of the process of mutual reconciliation.

Notes

1 It was a psychological truth that those who suffered then inflicted sufferings on others.
2 Under the Big Three arrangements at Yalta in February 1945, Poland lost its Eastern lands to the USSR and its territory was moved west, so the Germans living there had to leave their homes. This created a sense of injustice on both sides.

Polish-German and Polish-Russian reconc. 159

3 An important role was also played by Catholic Intelligence Clubs and individual Catholic bishops, intellectuals and scientists.
4 The message included the well-known words: *We forgive and ask for forgiveness.* They caused not only a political storm in Poland but first and foremost paved the way more for reconciliation.
5 Polish-German rapprochement was facilitated by the aid provided by the Maximilian-Kolbe-Werk Association in Freiburg to former concentration camp prisoners, the work of the International Youth Meeting Centre in Oświęcim and the International Youth Meeting Centre in Krzyżowa.
6 The speech by Jarosław Kaczyński in the parliamentary debate concerning a draft resolution on Germany's reparations to Poland. IV term, 82. session, second day, 25 August 2004.
7 In the assessment of the Institute of National Memory, about 150 thousand Polish citizens died at the hands of the Soviets from the outbreak of World War II to early 1950s.
8 The Russian side, citing the victor's right, emphasizes the effects of the war that is the liberation of Europe from the fascist reign by the Red Army at the extreme cost of 27 million fatalities. The victory over Nazi Germany is one of the foundations of Russian identity and takes on a near religious character.
9 Meaningful in its nature was the tribute was paid on 25 August 1993 by President Boris Yeltsin at the Katyń cross at Warsaw's Powązki cemetery to the murdered officers and non-commissioned officers from Soviet prisons in Kozielsk, Starobielsk and Ostaszków and the word простите (forgive us) uttered there.
10 "In Katyń, for each pit with bodies of murdered Poles, there are six or seven pits filled with bodies of Russians and representatives of other nations, more or less friendly to Russians."
11 In 2004, the Russian Military Prosecutor's Office closed the "Katyń investigation" that dragged on since 1990, without recognizing the Katyń atrocity as genocide.
12 The phenomenon of the so-called Smoleńsk religion is accompanied by a manic search for traitors and foreign agents, with the governing party, the president and the prime minister counted among them.
13 Challenging the authority of another country's leader essentially means interfering in its internal affairs, yet hardly anyone remembers about it in Poland when it comes to Russia. It is absurd to claim a moral right to determine who should rule Russia, what historical policy the Russians are entitled to and what national interests they can pursue in the international environment.

References

Bieleń, Stanisław. 2012. "Trialog niemiecko-polsko-rosyjski, czyli o idei trójkąta kaliningradzkiego." *Polski Przegląd Dyplomatyczny* 2: 5–27.
Bingen, Dieter. 2010. "Pojednanie, wybaczenie, normalizacja – polityka odprężenia w latach sześćdziesiątych i siedemdziesiątych XX wieku widziana z niemieckiej i polskiej perspektywy." In *Pojednanie i polityka. Polsko-niemieckie inicjatywy pojednania w latach sześćdziesiątych XX wieku a polityka odprężenia,* edited by Friedhelm Boll, Wiesław J. Wysocki and Klaus Ziemer, 221–243. Warszawie: Niemiecki Instytut Historyczny w Warszawie i Uniwersytet Kardynała Stefana Wyszyńskiego w Warszawie.
Бухарин, Сергей Н. and Николай Н. Ракитянский. 2011. Россия и Польша. Опыт политико-психологического исследования феномена лимитрофизации. Москва: Институт русской цивилизации.

160　*Stanisław Bieleń and Krzysztof Śliwiński*

Deselaers, Manfred. 1999. "Pojednanie miedzy narodami. Perspektywa niemiecka." In *Pojednanie początkiem nowego życia*, edited by Zdzisław Józef Kijas, 49–54. Kraków: Wydawnictwo Naukowe Polskiej Akademii Teologicznej w Krakowie.

Drozdowicz, Zbigniew, ed. 2001. *Pamięć i zapomnienie w Europie przełomu wieków*. Poznań: Wydawnictwo Fundacji Humaniora.

Góralski, Witold M., ed. 2011. *Przełom i wyzwanie. XX lat polsko-niemieckiego Traktatu o dobrym sąsiedztwie i przyjaznej współpracy 1991–2011*. Warszawa: Dom Wydawniczy ELIPSA.

Grajewski, Andrzej. 2010. "Polacy i Rosjanie. Wzajemna percepcja." In *Białe plamyczarne plamy. Sprawy trudne w relacjach polsko-rosyjskich (1918–2008)*, edited by Adam Daniel Rotfeld and Anatolij W. Torkunow, 735. Warszawa: Polski Instytut Spraw Międzynarodowych.

Harasimowicz, Andrzej. 2013. *Bezpieczeństwo Polski 1918–2004. Granice, system międzynarodowy, siła własna*. Warszawa: Centrum Europejskie Uniwersytetu Warszawskiego.

Hyodo, Nagao. 2007. *Mosty przyjaźni. Polska dusza i japońskie serce*. Płock: Książnica Płocka.

Karnowski, Michał. 2009. "Nowy bilans ofiar II wojny światowej opublikowany przez Instytut Pamięci Narodowej." *Dziennik.* http://www.fpnp.pl/edukacja/pracaprzymusowa.php.

Kukułka, Józef. 1998. *Traktaty sąsiedzkie Polski Odrodzonej*. Wrocław: Ossolineum.

Lisiakiewicz, Rafał. 2012. "Miejsce Polski w rosyjskiej polityce zagranicznej za prezydentury Władimira Putina (2000–2008)." *Polityka Wschodnia* 1: 91–116.

Malgin, Artiom. 2010. "Stosunki polityczne między Polską a Rosją po 1990 r." In *Białe plamy-czarne plamy. Sprawy trudne w relacjach polsko-rosyjskich (1918–2008)*, edited by Adam Daniel Rotfeld and Anatolij W. Torkunow, 698. Warszawa: Polski Instytut Spraw Międzynarodowych.

Meller, Arkadiusz, ed. 2011. *Antologia zbrodni smoleńskiej*. Warszawa: Biblioteka Konserwatyzm, 1.

"Putin's Letter to the Poles." *Gazeta Wyborcza*, 31 Aug. 2008. http://wyborcza.pl/1,768 42,6983945,List_Putina_do_Polakow___pelna_wersja.html.

Ricoeur, Paul. 2006. *Pamięć, historia, zapomnienie*. Translated by J. Margański. Kraków: Universitas.

Stolarczyk, Mieczysław. 2013. "Rosja w polityce zagranicznej Polski w okresie pozimnowojennym (aspekty polityczne)." *Studia Politicae Universitatis Siliesiensis* 11: 28–34.

Wolff-Powęska, Anna. 2010. "O aktualność dialogu i pojednania w stosunkach polsko-niemieckich." In *Pojednanie i polityka. Polsko-niemieckie inicjatywy pojednania w latach sześćdziesiątych XX wieku a polityka odprężenia*, edited by Friedhelm Boll, Wiesław J. Wysocki and Klaus Ziemer, 356. Warszawa: Wydawnictwo Neriton.

Wolff-Powęska, Anna. 2011. *Pamięć – brzemię i uwolnienie. Niemcy wobec nazistowskiej przeszłości (1945–2010)*. Poznań: Wydawnictwo Zysk i S-ka, 13.

Ziemkiewicz, Rafał. 2012. "Nieznośny absurd pojednania." In *Perspektywy pojednania polsko-rosyjskiego. Wizyta patriarchy Cyryla I w Polsce*, edited by Arkadiusz Meller and Joanna Rak, 96. Warszawa: Klub Zachowawczo-Monarchistyczny.

12 France and Algeria
Conflict, cooperation and conciliation

Phillip C. Naylor[1]

Introduction

The historical relationship between France and Algeria is contentious and complex. During the colonial period (1830–1962), France assimilated Algeria as three departments (*départements*) in 1848. Although administratively integrated, Algeria was a colony ruled by governor-generals, European settlers (*colons/pieds-noirs*), and their metropolitan allies. Exploited Muslims (*indigènes*) suffered tangible and intangible upheavals. Nationalism emerged in the 1920s leading to a brutal War of Liberation (1954–1962) and independence.

Initially post-colonial France and Algeria needed the other as each country defined or redefined national identity – an imagination or re-imagination of nationhood – an ontological praxis with, however, epistemological consequences, notably, the suppression of memory and history. When the past was periodically evoked, relations suffered but never severed. Despite recurrent "psychodramas" both countries also pursued strategic conciliation.[2] France and Algeria still need to remember, recognize, and reconcile their past with the present, but substantial, restorative progress has occurred.

Colonialism and conciliation

The Proclamation of 1 November 1954 introduced Algeria's Front de Libération Nationale (FLN) and announced the beginning of the War of Liberation. It particularly called for the abrogation of "all edicts, decrees and laws . . . denying the history, geography, language, religion and customs of the Algerian people". By calling for the "restoration of the . . . Algerian state within the framework of Islamic principles" and the "recognition of Algerian nationality", the FLN historicized its intention and denounced colonialism's repudiation of an Algerian past (see Mandouze 1962, 239–243). France needed to accept not only independence but also an Algerian history and identity. Thus, decolonization was an *existential* enterprise – the assertion of selfhood as well as nationhood.

In turn, Algeria profoundly affected France's *essentialist* self-imagination as a centuries-old global, independent power with a history of grandeur (greatness). Given its entrenched colonial position and administrative assimilation, the idea that "Algeria is France" became a powerful atavism and political determinant.

162 *Phillip Naylor*

Conflict and confiscation

Frantz Fanon (1925–1961) viewed colonialism as "violence in its natural state" (Fanon 1968, 61). It was also pervasive: "expropriation, spoliation, raids, objective murder, are matched by the sacking of cultural patterns, or at least condition such sacking. The social panorama is destructured; values are flaunted, crushed, emptied" (Fanon 1969, 33; see also Hannoum 2010). Military operations against the *indigènes* featured the resistance of Abd al-Qadir in central and western Algeria in the 1830s and 1840s and, particularly, "genocidal" atrocities, for example the Awlad [Ouled] Riah's asphyxiation at Dahra in 1845) (see Gallois 2013, 158–171). Brutality characterized the "peaceful penetration" of the Sahara (Brower 2009, 81–84). The French suppressed a major revolt in 1871.

Land expropriations followed Muslim military defeats. Without a sustainable primary sector compounded by a practically non-existent secondary sector, many Muslims immigrated to France. By the time the War of Liberation commenced, there were nearly 300,000 Algerian workers living there (L'évolution 1954, 6).

Conciliation and colonial reform initiatives

Colonialism impeded conciliation between colonialists and colonized. Nevertheless, officers in the Bureaux arabes (established in 1841) endeavoured to mediate relations between tribes and settlers. President Louis-Napoleon freed Abd al-Qadir in October 1852 from prison and established an enduring friendship. As Napoleon III (after December 1852), he hoped to temper colonial abuses and favoured the designs of utopian socialists like Ismaÿl Urbain, who viewed Algeria as a social laboratory. In his famous 6 February 1863 letter to the governor-general, Napoleon III stated, "Algeria is not a colony proper, but an Arab Kingdom." Furthermore, he declared that "the *indigènes* like the *colons* have equal right to my protection" (Abi-Mershed 2010, 174). Although well intentioned, the Sénatus-Consulte of 1865, which sought to protect the property of the colonized, actually expedited expropriation.

The Senate (Ferry) Report of 1892 was critical of conditions in Algeria, but the settlers' political allies inhibited amelioration. During World War I, Algerians' service and sacrifice deeply moved Premier Georges Clemenceau. He presented a series of reforms gathered under the Jonnart Law of 1919. *Indigènes* received more representation in councils, but the reforms hardly threatened settler domination. The Blum-Viollette Bill of 1936 offered French citizenship to 21,000 to 25,000 assimilated *indigènes* without their loss of Muslim legal status; however, the legislation never reached the National Assembly's floor. Under Charles de Gaulle's Ordinance of 7 March 1944, 60,000 Muslims received citizenship and increased *indigène* representation in assemblies. By that time nationalists, notably Ferhat Abbas, called for an autonomous Algeria as articulated in the Manifeste du Peuple Algérien (March 1943). In a rare moment of elite unity, Abbas organized the Amis du Manifeste et de la Liberté (AML) with Messali Hadj, a proponent of independence, as its leader.

Then a seminal and tragic event occurred in May 1945. During a parade celebrating Allied victory in Europe in Sétif, placards appeared calling for independence. Shots rang out, and security forces rampaged.[3] The Sétif violence (and that at Guelma and Khechafa) radicalized younger nationalists. The passage of the Organic Statute for Algeria in 1947, touted as a reform to increase Muslim political participation, resulted in fixed elections. Increasingly dissatisfied with Messali, the younger elite formed the FLN in 1954.

On individual levels there was conciliation, if not amity, between *pieds-noirs* and *indigènes*. Algerian writers, for example Mouloud Feraoun (1913–1962) and Kateb Yacine (1929–1989), were close to Albert Camus (1913–1960) and the poet Jean Sénac (1926–1973). They particularly admired Camus's reportage of Kabylia's misery in the 1930s (Camus 2013, 37–84). However, they criticized him for ignoring or objectifying Muslims in his novels (see Le Sueur 2001). Malek Bennabi (1905–1973), a renowned Algerian intellectual, admired his French besides Muslim teachers. He found French and Muslim civilizations to be personally besides intellectually compatible (Bennabi 1965, 1970). Thus, there were dialogues, but colonialism impeded conciliation, especially after revolutionary war broke out.

The war of liberation and conciliation

The War of Liberation continued the existential struggle of the colonized. Slimane Chikh wrote: "the colonized in taking up arms creates himself, because he creates his own history and forges his own destiny in becoming a *historical subject*" (Chikh 1981, 218). The prospect of losing Algeria also affected France's essentialist imagination of itself. Governor-General Jacques Soustelle equated: "to abandon Algeria, is to condemn France to decadence" (Soustelle 1957, 69). Fearing that the Fourth Republic aimed to decolonize Algeria, the politicized Army revolted in Algeria and Charles de Gaulle resumed power. Arriving in Algeria in June 1958, de Gaulle uttered: "*Je vous ai compris*" (I have understood you), a statement that to many masked his intentions. De Gaulle fundamentally sought to preserve some kind of French presence.

Conciliatory initiatives

While attempting to suppress the revolution, infamously using torture to gather intelligence, the French government concurrently pursued impressive economic and social reforms and programmes. Although self-interested, French investment also sought conciliation. Jacques Soustelle inaugurated the Sections Administratives Spécialisées (SAS) (reminiscent of the Bureaux arabes) that established centres throughout Algeria to teach and train Algerians. Nevertheless, stationed soldiers also occasionally tortured captured prisoners. Teachers were imported to instruct the burgeoning numbers of students finally attending school. The *Perspectives décennales* (February 1958) envisioned a completely changed economy with a dynamic secondary sector still linked to France, fuelled by recent

164 *Phillip Naylor*

natural gas and petroleum discoveries in the Sahara. De Gaulle's Constantine Plan (October 1958) complemented the *Perspectives décennales*. The government inaugurated the Office Algérien de la Main-d'Oeuvre (OFAMO) in 1956 and the Fonds d'Action Sociale (FAS) in 1958 to serve (and monitor) the emigrant labour community (see Lyons 2013).

On individual levels, Albert Camus urged moderation and a "civil truce" (Camus 2013, 140–159). Archbishop Léon-Étienne Duval sympathized with Algerians (see Duval 1984). French intellectuals, for example Jean-Paul Sartre, Jacques Berque, Simone de Beauvoir, Francis Jeanson, and Henri-Irenée Marrou, supported Algerian independence (see Le Sueur 2001).

Charles de Gaulle refashions the relationship

De Gaulle needed to conciliate to secure a French presence. When referring to the Constantine Plan, he perceived it as a means "to preserve and develop ties which exist between the Algerian and French communities . . . in spite of grief that both sides have unfortunately experienced" (de Gaulle 1964, 117–118). France intended to stay engaged:

> The ambition of the Constantine Plan . . . is not to ensure the revenues of an assisted Algeria, but to make Algeria a modern country, modern for all its inhabitants living in every part . . . in symbiosis with France.
>
> (Délégation 1960, 61)

De Gaulle endured a *pied-noir* insurrection in January 1960 and a *putsch* by generals in April 1961. By that time, de Gaulle aimed to decolonize Algeria.

The Evian accords

The Evian Accords framed the post-colonial relationship: "the relations between the two countries will be founded, in mutual respect of their independence, on the reciprocal exchange of benefits and the interests of the two parties" (Ambassade 1962, 7). France secured a post-colonial presence – Saharan hydrocarbon installations and military bases, including atomic testing sites. Paris also promised to continue massive economic and social aid. On the other hand, *pied-noir* flight vitiated meticulous protective stipulations. The accords stipulated an amnesty, but *harkis*, Algerian soldiers aligned with France, particularly suffered severe retributions. From the Algerian nationalists' perspective, France's perpetuated presence qualified independence and necessitated "post-colonial decolonization" promising confrontation along with cooperation and conciliation.

Cooperation(/conciliation) and the post-colonial relationship

On 1 July 1962, Algerians voted for independence "in cooperation with France". Despite the imperative of post-colonial decolonization to complete liberation, cooperation (French aid) was vital. In turn, conciliation with Algeria also served France's interests.

France inaugurates cooperation

Cooperation still correlated with French essentialist values of grandeur and independence. To Foreign Minister Maurice Couve de Murville cooperation was "the means to pursue the civilizing work and development conducted by the colonial power" (Couve de Murville 1971, 450). When de Gaulle listed his accomplishments as president, he included "cooperation replacing colonialism" (de Gaulle 1970, 4:404). Thousands of *coopérants* (teachers and trainers) helped create a positive, penitent image of France while in service in Algeria. Nicole Grimaud perceived cooperation as expiation and a means to restore French moral authority. Cooperation addressed a "bad conscience" and was a "moral obligation". It also was a way "to compensate the . . . painful loss of Algeria" (Grimaud 1984, 40). By pursuing a generous cooperation with Algeria and ensuring privileged relations with the newly independent state, France hoped to renovate its international image especially with developing nations. Secretary of State for Algerian Affairs Jean de Broglie aptly viewed Algeria as the "narrow door" to the Third World, a bilateral means to multilateral ends (*L'Année* 1965, 326; *LM*, 7 November 1964). Cooperation with conciliation protected French interests in Algeria, but it was not framed as reconciliation. France and Algeria preferred to forget the past for the present.

Algeria responds to cooperation

The FLN's Tripoli Programme (1962) and Algiers Charter (1964) projected a socialist Algeria and targeted the Evian Accords. Prime Minister then President Ahmed Ben Bella repeatedly called for the accords' "revision". Concurrently, the government nationalized abandoned land and property, planned "Algerianization" by "Arabizing" education and challenged French and international companies in the Sahara by organizing SONATRACH, a national hydrocarbons enterprise. In June 1965, Colonel Houari Boumedienne deposed Ben Bella but continued his policies. Boumedienne was determined to build a state and remove the French post-colonial presence.

A month after the coup, France and Algeria concluded the Algiers Accords. By this agreement, France retained its oil concessions, but Algeria received higher royalties. In addition, France and Algeria set up an Association Coopérative (ASCOOP), a partnership between SONATRACH and what would be ERAP (a reorganized French national oil corporation). Sensitive to Algeria's desire to industrialize, France agreed to fund an Organisme de Coopération Industrielle (OCI). This innovative agreement exemplified conciliation as well as bilateral cooperation.

By the time hydrocarbons negotiations resumed in 1969, France and Algeria were no longer as strategically dependent upon the other, for example France had pulled out from military bases and all atomic testing sites and Algeria diversified

166 *Phillip Naylor*

economic partners (notably El Paso Gas Corporation). Algeria nationalized the hydrocarbons sector in February 1971 – the decisive post-colonial decolonization. To Boumedienne, this meant the final revision of "the colonial pact drawn up at Evian". He stated:

> Let France get used to the fact of our national sovereignty and all problems, big and small, can be settled. The common interests of the two countries are numerous and evident. They are dictated by history, geography, and the economy.
>
> (*CSM*, 8 May 1971)

Although the nationalization strained relations, by the end of the year, SONATRACH and the French oil companies concluded agreements that made them minority partners. France also continued cooperation.

The relancement *and* redressement *of relations*

Both countries aspired for normalization after the hydrocarbons nationalization but too many variables uniquely distinguished the relationship. In July 1973 Foreign Minister Abdelaziz Bouteflika arrived in Paris and signalled a conciliatory *relancement* (re-launching) to improve relations, which was highlighted by President Valéry Giscard d'Estaing's visit to Algeria in April 1975.

Upon his arrival, the French president declared: "historic France salutes independent Algeria" (Naylor 2000, 112). The statement offended Algerians since it suggested that Algeria did not have a history. It illustrated an incipient metaphysical shift in the relationship from political ontology – being and nationhood (i.e. the assertion of post-colonial national identity) – to political epistemology – knowledge, memory, and historicism. The latter became increasingly important, for example Algeria demanded the repatriation of archives, a recovery of history. The government produced the National Charter in 1976 reaffirming Algeria's identity and historical heritage. The promise of the *relancement* dissipated as France failed to address the trade imbalance with a significant hydrocarbon purchase. Furthermore, Giscard displayed his partiality towards Morocco regarding Western Sahara.

Elected president in 1981, François Mitterrand, a former minister of the interior during the war, pursued a conciliatory *redressement* (redress) of the relationship for personal as well as political reasons. His visit to Algiers in 1981 led to a flurry of agreements in 1982 highlighted by a natural gas accord in February that evoked the Algiers Accords of 1965 by which France paid a higher price in order to help finance Algeria's development. The French redefined cooperation as "co-development". The relationship remained at a relatively high level, but a confluence of crises led to Algeria's destabilization, its fierce *fitna* or civil strife.

Algeria's fitna *and France*

The 1990s, known as Algeria's "dark decade", claimed approximately 175,000 lives. Despite ideological reservations regarding the deposal of President Chadli

France and Algeria 167

Benjedid and the termination of parliamentary elections in January 1992, France supported the Algerian government during these years, especially in financial circles (e.g. the Paris Club) by rescheduling foreign debt. Nevertheless, it also favoured opposition parties' Sant'Egidio National Contract and Platform (January 1995) that aspired to end the escalating violence. Paris's ambivalence frustrated Algiers. Nonetheless, France welcomed Algeria's qualified "re-democratization", for example the November 1995 election of Liamine Zeroual as president. The *fitna*'s violence also included bombings in France (1995–1996). Extremists in Algeria murdered French conciliatory voices including Cistercian monks and Bishop Pierre Claverie of Oran (1996) (Naylor 2010, 735–742). Horrendous violence attracted greater international attention. François Mitterrand supported a European Union investigation (January 1998), which the Algerian government reluctantly accommodated. The United Nations also dispatched a delegation (August).

Abdelaziz Bouteflika's election as president led to amnesties in 1999 (Civil Concord Referendum) and in 2005 (Charter for Peace and National Reconciliation). Both documents expressed a "forgive and forget" tone.[4] Meanwhile, the overwhelming power of the state forced Islamist insurgents to find refuge in remote areas, limiting them to intermittent operations.

Recovering history and memory

Intimated as early as 1975 during Giscard d'Estaing's visit, there was a shift from political ontology to historical epistemology. Issues regarding memory and knowledge began to rise in the late 1970s into the 1980s. For Algeria, the upheaval known as the Berber Spring of 1980 exalted Berber culture and history, thereby challenging Arabization and the identification of Algeria as simply an Arab state. The government rehabilitated Belkacem Krim (assassinated by Algerian agents in 1970) and Ramdane Abane (executed by elite rivals in 1958). The "enriched" (revised) National Charter of 1986 included a section on history and included the nationalist contributions of Ferhat Abbas and Messali Hadj, previously unmentionable names.

The publication of Benjamin Stora (1992) emphasized the obfuscation of the war by both French and Algerian governments. *Pieds-noirs* produced scores of works – many of which were nostalgic. The *harkis* who survived subsequently became the "forgotten of France", despite books and efforts of Bachaga Boualam (1963) and other activists. Field officers Maurice Challe (1968) and Jacques Massu (1971) produced memoirs of the war. Yves Courrière (1968–1971) and Alistair Horne (2006) offered surveys. Nevertheless, on the governmental and political level, both sides were most interested in addressing immediate interests rather than the distressing past. It was only in 1999 when the French Parliament classified "the events in Algeria" as a war, which President Bouteflika commended (*LM*, June 2000).

During the trial (1997–1998) of Maurice Papon (charged with crimes against humanity for the deportation of Jews during the Second World War), documentation dating from the period when he was prefect of police in Paris (1958–1967)

168 *Phillip Naylor*

described the brutal police suppression of the 17 October 1961 Algerian emigrant workers' march in protest of curfew laws and in support of independence. Researchers revealed the extent of the violence and estimated that scores to hundreds were killed in what was actually a police riot (see Cole 2006; House and MacMaster 2006). In 2001, Mayor Betrand Delanoë placed a plaque at the pont Saint-Michel in memory of the workers, many of whom drowned in the Seine River. President François Hollande also paid particular tribute to the workers in 2012.

Louisette Ighilahriz, an Algerian militant, detailed her imprisonment during the War of Liberation (*LM*, 20 June 2001) and later published a memoir (Ighilariz 2001). She implicated General Jacques Massu and Col. Marcel Bigeard, the latter one of the most decorated soldiers in the Army, by declaring that the officers were present when she was tortured. By the time of Massu's death in 2002, the general regretted the use of torture. He did not remember Ighilahriz. Although refuting Ighilahriz's claims, Bigeard admitted that torture was used in the Algerian War.

General Paul Aussaresses's war memoir also appeared (2001), which caused a sensation. This book recounted torture and revealed that Larbi M'hidi, a prominent FLN leader, was not a suicide, as French authorities claimed, but was hanged. Recalcitrant rather than repentant, the remorseless book shocked France by its callous candour. Although protected by amnesties, he was fined and President Chirac stripped his Legion of Honour status.

The refondement *of relations*

These roiling memoirs did not deter President Jacques Chirac's determination to upgrade the bilateral relationship – a *refondement* (refounding). He aspired to have a friendship agreement with Algeria, modelled on the Franco-German treaty of 1963 to achieve reconciliation. Before visiting Algeria in March 2003, Chirac stated that the war was a "painful moment in our common history that we must not and cannot ignore". He added: "it is time now to move forward . . . and build with Algeria a strong, trustful and impartial relationship" (*Guardian*, 3 March 2003). Both presidents initialled the "Algiers Declaration", calling for a partnership and greater cooperation "without 'forgetting the past'" (*NYT*, 3 March 2003). France promoted the "Year of Algeria", featuring cultural events throughout 2003 as a means to enhance the signing of a friendship treaty. Ambassador Hubert Colin de la Verdière visited Sétif on 27 February 2005 and referred to the violence of 1945 as an "inexcusable tragedy", which was reiterated days later by Foreign Minister Michel Barnier (*EW*, 8 May 2005). This was the first time that the French officially recognized that tragedy.

Nevertheless, on 23 February, conservatives (including from Chirac's Union pour un Mouvement Populare; UMP) inserted controversial wording into a National Assembly bill calling for educators to "recognize in particular the positive character of the French presence overseas, notably in North Africa". History teachers disapproved, claiming that state wanted to dictate an "official history" (*CSM*, 4 January 2006). In December, Chirac stated: "laws are not meant to write history. . . . The writing of history is for historians." He perceived that France "has known moments of light and darker moments. It is a legacy that we must fully assume . . . respecting the memory of everyone" (*CSM*, 4 January 2006). Meanwhile, Bouteflika demanded in turn an apology for French "acts" during colonialism and the War of Liberation "in order for new and wider prospects of friendship and cooperation" (AFP, 11 March 2005). Although Chirac finally abrogated the wording in the bill, the legislation undermined the possibility of a friendship treaty.

His successor, Nicolas Sarkozy, visited Algeria in July and December 2007. His discourse was conciliatory but not apologetic. He called for a bilateral "more lucid and objective look at the past" (*EW*, 10 July 2007). Recognizing the colonial system as "profoundly unjust" (*LM*, 5 December 2007), he stated: "I did not come to deny the past but to tell you that the future is more important." He added: "the mistakes and crimes of the past were unpardonable" (*LM*, 6 December 2007). In April 2008, Ambassador Bernard Bajolet referred to the violence at Sétif, Guelma, and Kherrata as "appalling massacres" and "murderous madness" (*LM*, 27 April 2008). While it could be argued that Sarkozy's discourse aimed at convincing Bouteflika to participate in his vaunted Mediterranean Union, his conciliation also contributed to hydrocarbons contracts (regarding importation of natural gas and the construction of a "cracker" by SONATRACH and Total to produce ethylene and other by-products[5]) and a nuclear agreement.

Sarkozy's successor, François Hollande, practically apologized for colonialism when he visited Algeria in December 2012. He declared: "during 132 years, Algeria was subjected to a profoundly unjust and brutal system." He identified that system as "colonialism" and added: "I recognize here the suffering that colonialism inflicted on the Algerian people." Hollande also asserted: "we respect memory, all memories. To recognize, to establish the truth is an obligation [that] links Algerians and French. That is why it is necessary that historians have access to archives" (*LM*, 22 December 2012).

Historiography and reconciliation

Hollande's call for conscientious historiography echoed appeals already made by Bouteflika and Sarkozy. Significant histories followed (Stora 1992; Pervillé 2002; Harbi and Stora 2004). Furthermore, archives continue to open in France and Algeria.

Nevertheless, Algeria's dominant narrative regarding the war and colonialism remains ideological and political rather than historical with significant consequences. Guy Pervillé (2002, 8) explained:

> The official version . . . glorified the heroism and suffering of the martyrs of independence, but also the rupture with France and use of violence against the French and their supporters. Critical history was marginalized or proscribed. This is why the same scenario of terrorism and of repression was replayed since 1992 by armed Islamists and by the Algerian military command.

170   Phillip Naylor

Algerian governments have used this narrow view of the past as a means of legitimizing their authority. The Revolution served as a matrix.

The French did not have an "official version", despite the suggestive National Assembly wording of February 2005. Nevertheless, "their collective memory is torn between multiple contradictory and conflictive group memories: those defeated . . . (career soldiers, "pieds-noirs", "harkis"), active supporters (militants of the anti-colonialist Left or Algerian nationalists) or those who more or less . . . accepted [decolonization]" (Pervillé 2002, 9).

Collaboration between French and Algerians in conferences and publications is especially encouraging (see Manceron and Remouan 1993; Harbi and Stora 2004; Bouchène, Peyroulou, Tengour and Thénault 2012; Erlingsen-Creste and Zerouki 2012). Pervillé concluded that historiographical and political reconciliation could occur only if France and Algeria address the past together (Pervillé 2002, 323).

The consequences of an apology

During the uproar of the Ighilahriz-Aussaresses period, 56 per cent of the French who participated in a poll published by *Libération* favoured requesting forgiveness from Algeria (Pervillé 2002, 323). If France offered an apology, there would be a domestic backlash since it would be interpreted as a repudiation of the imperial past. But as Benjamin Stora stated: "France has to accept that it is not head of an empire any more. . . . We have to get over it" (*CSM*, 4 January 2006). An apology would free French policy and undercut Algerians who want to criminalize French colonialism. Nevertheless, there is a difference being confessional and genuinely contrite.

The Algerian government may not want an apology, since it would lose bilateral leverage. If France apologized, the focus would shift to Algeria and the FLN during the War of Liberation, for example chronic intraelite strife; the atrocities perpetrated against *pieds-noirs* and *harkis*. Furthermore, an apology could evoke the government's unexplained actions during the civil strife of the 1990s (Algerians protested the Charter for Peace and National Reconciliation's amnesty and irresolution regarding the "disappeared".). A truth and reconciliation proceeding is out of the question as long as the oligarchic *Pouvoir* (the powers that be) exercises authority. Indeed, the Algerian statesman Redha Malek asserted that history cannot be written without "freedom and a critical spirit" – that is democracy (*EW*, 5 July 2007).

Conclusion

Azouz Begag, a French-Algerian anthropologist, novelist, and ex-minister stated: "France, which needs to find itself and come together, cannot move forward into the future without facing its past with courage" (*CSM*, 4 January 2006). This applies to Algeria too. Each country must first reconcile its memories with itself – a critical (and courageous) introspection, a self-reconciliation including reflecting upon inconvenient painful histories. Thus, interiority is crucially important

France and Algeria   171

before engaging exteriority – that is the other. Furthermore, each country must not only remember but also learn how to remember, which means critically considering memory and history. Memory can heal, but it first must be remembered and conscientiously and honestly historicized. Memory must be collective and inclusive rather than selective and exclusive.[6]

At this time, perhaps the best that can be hoped for regarding the bilateral reconciliation is "ambivalent forgiveness". Michalinos Zembylas explains that "*ambivalent forgiveness* refers to the experience of both positive and negative feelings towards forgiving (or not) someone. . . . The construct of ambivalent forgiveness emphasizes that forgiveness can exist alongside lingering resentment" (Zembylas 2012, 23). This "play" engaging forgiveness while recognizing resentment (i.e. without forgetting the past) may be the best way, albeit a stage, towards achieving a more consensual, comprehensive bilateral reconciliation. While Algeria rightly views itself as victim and France as perpetrator of atrocities, actually French and Algerians were both perpetrators and victims in the colonial and post-colonial periods. Curiously, while Algerian discourse repeatedly demanded apology, it deferred forgiveness. Currently, shared security concerns (threats) in North Africa and Europe compel French-Algerian conciliation and may edge it towards reconciliation.

What Camus wrote decades ago still resonates regarding the bilateral relationship:

> It is good for a nation to be strong enough in its traditions and honorable enough to find the courage to denounce its own errors, but it must not forget the reasons it may still have to think well of itself. It is in any case dangerous to ask it to confess sole responsibility and resign itself to perpetual penance.
>
> (Camus 2013, 32)

French and Algerians must be willing to engage their past and express themselves freely with themselves and with each other, that is harmonize history internally and externally. This continues to challenge each country as the past is often evoked (e.g. compensation for Algerians affected by French nuclear testing in the Sahara). Conciliation will continue for a variety of strategic reasons – political, economic, social – but reconciliation can occur only when French and Algerians individually and collectively resolve to remember and reconcile memory with history, forgetting with forgiving. Furthermore, forwarding conciliation towards reconciliation does not have to be exclusively achieved by political actors and gestures. For example Boualam Sansal and Kamel Daoud (writers), Cheb Khaled and Rachid Taha (musicians), and Rachid Bouchareb and Lyes Salem (film directors) appeal to French as well as Algerian audiences.

Despite festering wounds and agonizing psychodramas, the relationship has hopefully, if tentatively, entered a new stage – a *ressourcement*, an anguishing but liberating "healing" – instilled with a new consciousness that is not only repentant but also redemptive.

172 *Phillip Naylor*

Notes

1 Two lectures at Marquette University informed and inspired this chapter: Rev. Bryan Massengale's "Race and Reconciliation" [February 2014] and Michalinos Zembylas's presentation on "Ambivalent Forgiveness" [April 2013]. I particularly appreciated funding providing by Hong Kong Baptist University and Marquette University's College of Arts & Sciences, Center for Peacemaking, and the Office of International Education.
2 Conciliation refers to gaining goodwill and favour or to placate. Reconciliation brings people together after a disagreement, to *settle* a quarrel, to harmonize. Conciliation and reconciliation are intrinsically dialogical.
3 The Tubert Report claimed that 103 Europeans died and between 1,020 and 1,300 Muslims fell. It is generally believed that between 5,000 and 10,000 Muslims died and perhaps 15,000 and 20,000, even possibly 45,000 given settler retributions (Naylor 2015, 463).
4 Paul Ricoeur warned (referring to Vichy): "the pardon of amnesty has taken on the value of amnesia" (Ricoeur 2004, 451).
5 The unfulfilled cracker initiative ended in 2014. Sarkozy encouraged partnerships between SONATRACH and French companies, for example Total, Suez and Gaz de France.
6 The Internet is also contributing to historicism (see Denhez n.d.).

References

Abi-Mershed, Osama. 2010. *Apostles of Modernity: Saint-Simonians & the Civilizing Mission in Algeria.* Stanford, CA: Stanford University Press.
Agence France-Presse (AFP).
Ambassade de France. 1962. *Texts of Declarations Drawn up in Common Agreement at Evian, March 19,1962 by the Delegations of the French Republic and the Algerian National Liberation Front.* New York: Ambassade de France, Service de Presse et d'information.
L' Année politique, économique, sociale, et diplomatique en France, 1964. 1965. Paris: Presses Universitaires de France.
Aussaresses, Paul. 2001. *Services spéciaux, Algérie, 1955–1957: Mon témoignage sur le torture.* Paris: Perrin.
Bennabi, Malek (Mālik bn Nabī). 1965. *Mémoires d'un témoin du siècle: L'enfant.* Vol. 1. Algiers: Éditions Nationales Algériennes.
———. 1970. *Mukhakarāt shāhid al-qarn: al-Ṭalib.* Vol. 2. Beirut: Dār al-Fikr.
Boualam, (Bachaga) Benaissa Said. 1963. *Les harkis au service de la France.* Paris: France-Empire.
Bouchène, Abderrahmane, Jean-Pierre Peyroulou, Ouanassa Siari Tengour and Sylvie Thénault, eds. 2012. *Histoire de l'Algérie à la période coloniale (1830-1962).* Paris: Éditions La Découverte/Algiers: Éditions Barzakh.
Brower, Benjamin Claude. 2009. *A Desert Named Peace: The Violence of France's Empire in the Algerian Sahara, 1844–1902.* New York: Columbia University Press.
Camus, Albert. 2013. *Algerian Chronicles.* Translated by Arthur Goldhammer. Cambridge, MA: Belknap Press of Harvard University Press.
Challe, Maurice. 1968. *Notre révolte.* Paris: Presses de la Cité. *Christian Science Monitor (CSM).*
Chikh, Slimane. 1981. *L'Algérie en armes, ou le temps des certitudes.* Paris: Economica.

Cole, Joshua. 2006. "Entering History: The Memory of Police Violence in Paris, October 1961." In *Algeria & France, 1800–2000: Identity, Memory, Nostalgia*, edited by Patricia M.E. Lorcin, 117–134. Syracuse, NY: Syracuse University Press.

Courrière, Yves. 1968–71. *La guerre de l'Algérie*. 4 vols. Paris: Fayard.

Couve de Murville, Maurice. 1971. *Une politique étrangère, 1958–1969*. Paris: Librairie Plon.

De Gaulle, Charles. 1964. *Major Addresses, Statements, and Press Conferences, May 19, 1958–January 31, 1964*. New York: French Embassy, Press and Information Division.

———. 1970. *Discours et messages*, vol. 4. Paris: Plon.

Délégation générale du gouvernement en Algérie, Direction du Plan et des Études économiques. 1960. *Plan de Constantine, 1959–1963: rapport général*. Algiers: L'imprimerie officielle.

Denhez, Olivier. n.d. "Les mémoires de la guerre d'Algérie: une mise en point." http://histgeo.discipline.ac-lille.fr/lycee/mise-en-oeuvre/mise-en-oeuvre-terminale/presentations-aux-collegues/les-memoires-de-la-guerre-d2019algerie-une-mise-au-point.

Duval, Léon-Étienne. 1984. *Le cardinal Duval: "évêque en Algérie."* Interviews with Marie-Christine Ray. Paris: Le Centurion.

Erlingsen-Creste, Hélène and Mohamed Zerouiki. 2012. *Nos pères ennemis: morts pour la France et l'Algérie, 1958–1959*. Toulouse: Éditions Privat.

Fanon, Frantz. 1968. *The Wretched of the Earth*. Translated by Constance Farrington. New York: Grove Press.

———. 1969. *Toward the African Revolution (Political Essays)*. Translated by Haadon Chevalier. New York: Grove Press.

Gallois, William. 2013. *A History of Violence in the Early Algerian Colony*. New York: Palgrave Macmillan.

Grimaud, Nicole. 1984. *La politique extérieure de l'Algérie*. Paris: Karthala.

Hannoum, Abdelmajid. 2010. *Violent Modernity: France in Algeria*. Cambridge, MA: Harvard Center for Middle Eastern Studies.

Harbi, Mohammed and Benjamin Stora, eds. 2004. *La guerre d'Algérie, 1954–2004: La fin de l'amnésie*. Paris: Robert Laffont.

Horne, Alistair. 2006. *A Savage War of Peace: Algeria, 1954–1962*, Rev. ed. New York: New York Review of Books.

House, Jim and Neil MacMaster. 2006. *Paris 1961: Algerians, State Terror, and Memory*. Oxford: Oxford University Press.

Ighilariz, Louisette. 2001. *L'Algérienne*. Paris: Fayard/Calmann Lévy.

Le Monde (*LM*).

Le Sueur, James D. 2001. *Uncivil War: Intellectuals and Identity Politics during the Decolonization of Algeria*. Philadelphia, PA: University of Pennsylvania Press.

"L'évolution économique (deuxième partie): questions sociales et culturelles." 1954. *Notes et études documentaires* (Documentation Française), no. 1.963.

Lyons, Amelia. 2013. *The Civilizing Mission in the Metropole: Algerian Families and the French Welfrare State During Decolonization*. Stanford: Stanford University Press.

Manceron, Gilles and Hassan Remouan. 1993. *D'une rive à l'autre: la guerre d'Algérie de la mémoire à l'histoire*. Paris: Syros.

174　*Phillip Naylor*

Mandouze, André, ed. 1962. *La révolution algérienne par les textes.* Paris: Maspéro.

Massu, Jacques. 1971. *La vraie bataille d'Alger.* Paris: Plon.

Naylor, Phillip C. 2000. *France and Algeria: A History of Decolonization and Transformation.* Gainesville, FL: University Press of Florida.

———. 2010. "Bishop Pierre Claverie and the Risks of Religious Reconciliation." *Catholic Historical Review* 96(4), October 2010: 720–742.

———. 2015. *Historical Dictionary of Algeria,* 4th ed. Lanham, MD: Rowman & Littlefield.

Pervillé, Guy. 2002. *Pour une histoire de la guerre d'Algérie, 1954–1962.* Paris: Éditions Picard.

Ricoeur, Paul. 2004. *Memory, History, Forgetting.* Translated by Kathleen Blamey and David Pellauer. Chicago: University of Chicago Press.

Soustelle, Jacques. 1957. *Le drame algérien et la décadence française: réponse à Raymond Aron.* Paris: Plon.

Stora, Benjamin. 1992. *La gangrène et l'oubli: la mémoire de la guerre de l'Algérie.* Paris: Editions la Découverte.

Watan-El (EW).

Zembylas, Michalinos. 2012. "Teaching about/for Ambivalent Forgiveness in Troubled Societies." *Ethics and Education,* 7, no. 1 (March): 19–32.

Index

Abanc, Ramdanc 167
Abbas, Ferhat 167
Abd al-Qadir 162
Abe, Shinzo 54, 65n2, 97
absolute critique 88–9
Adenauer, Konrad Hermann Joseph
  30–1, 33, 48, 154
Agulhon, Maurice 36
Algeria 6, 7, 8; colonialism and
  conciliation in 161–3; cooperation
  and post-colonial relationship with
  France 164–7; dark decade 166–7;
  Evian Accords 164; French apology
  to 169–70; historiography and
  reconciliation in 169–70; recovering
  history and memory in 167–70; War
  of Liberation 161, 162, 163–4
American Black Power movement 140
amity symbolism in Franco-German
  relations: beyond realist and idealist
  readings of 32–5; emergence of 30–2;
  reconciliation entrepreneurs and
  35–8; ritualization in 37–8
Analects 74–5, 75–6
Anderson, Benedict 43
anti-Zionism 46
apartheid *see* South Africa
apologies, state 5, 41, 54–5, 60–2,
  65n3, 138, 143–5, 150, 169, 170
artists as reconciliation teachers 116
ASEAN regionalization 108
Assefa, Hizkias 99
Assmann, Aleida 4
Aussaresses, Paul 168
Australia 144, 145; awareness of
  indigenous rights in 138, 145–6;
  see also New Zealand

Bajolet, Bernard 169
Ban Ki-moon 97
Bartoszewski, Władysław 149, 150
Baylis, Joseph 33
Beauvoir, Simone de 164
Begag, Azouz 170
Begcard, Marcel 168
Benjedid, Chadli 166–7
Bennabi, Malck 163
Bensberger Circle 48
Bensberger Memorandum 45, 149
Berber Spring 167
Berque, Jacques 164
Bjork, James 44–5
Black Sash, South Africa 18
blood revenge 70–3, 75, 78; *see also*
  Ruist traditions
Blum-Viollette Bill of 1936 162
Boesack, Allan 19
Boltanski, Luc 35
Boualam, Bachaga 167
Bouchareb, Rachid 171
Bougherara, Nassima 33
Boulding, K. E. 99
Boumedienne, Houari 166
Bouteflika, Abdelaziz 166,
  167, 169
Brandt, Willy 1, 54, 113, 116, 153,
  154; example of repentance 60–2;
  Warsaw Ghetto Monument and 5,
  41, 46, 150
Brecke, Peter 9n4, 45–6
Bringing Them Home 142–3
Broglie, Jean de 165
Brounéus, K. 100
Brubaker, Rogers 42
Buddhism: Zen 87; *see also* zange

176 *Index*

Budweisers into Czechs 43
Buffet, Cyril 33
Byrnes, Giselle 3, 8

Cambodia 102, 106
Camus, Albert 163, 164, 171
Challe, Maurice 167
Chiang Ching-kuo 125
Chiang Kai-shek 125
Chikane, Frank 19
China: challenges of teaching
international reconciliation in
110–19; "Chineseness" and 8,
123–4; lack of self-interrogative
depth in literature 9n3; military
parades 97; perspectives on
nationalism and Taiwan/Hong
Kong 132–3; relations with Japan
8, 97, 98, 103; Ruist traditions
of revenge 69–79; scope and
justifications of vengeance in Chinese
literary contexts 70–2; vengefulness
in cultural settings of 69–70; xiezui
55–65, 65n5, 66n8–11; *see also* East
Asia; Hong Kong; Sino-Japanese
relations; Taiwan
Chirac, Jacques 32, 168–9
Chung, Martin 6–7
Clark, Helen 144–5
Claveric of Oran, Pierre 167
Clemenceau, Georges 162
co-confession 7, 64–5
Cold War era relations 48–9, 49n5,
102, 122
confession 62–4
Confucius 55–6, 57, 73; *see also*
Master Kong
Cook, James 139, 141
cooperation 164–6
Courrière, Yves 167
Couvre de Murville, Maurice 165
Crimea 158

Dahl, Elizabeth 4
Daoud, Kamel 171
Defrance, Corine 33
de Gaulle, Charles 31, 33, 37, 38, 162,
163, 164, 165
Delanoë, Bertrand 168
Delori, Mathias 6
Deng Xiaoping 129
Detainees Parents Support
Committee 18

Doctrine of Repentance 62
Duara, Prasenjit 133

East Asia 97, 107–8; challenges of
teaching international reconciliation
in 110–19; geopolitics and memory
politics in 100–1; power transitions
in 101–3; reconciliation dynamics in
105–7; reconciliation theories and
98–100; trauma politics in 103–5;
US hegemony in 102; *see also* China;
Japan; Sino-Japanese relations
Elysée Treaty of 1963 6, 31, 32, 33, 37
entrepreneurs, reconciliation 35–8
Evian Accords 164

Fanon, Frantz 162
Fan Sui 59, 63
Feraroun, Mouloud 163
filial vengeance 72–4, 79–80n7
forgiveness model of reconciliation 46–7
France 7; apology to Algeria 169, 170;
beyond realist and idealist readings
of symbolism in relations between
Germany and 32–5; colonialism
and conciliation in Algeria 161–3;
cooperation and post-colonial
relationship with Algeria 164–7;
emergence of amity symbolism with
Germany 30–2; Evian Accords 164;
occupation administration during
World War II 38n1; relations with
Algeria 6, 8, 161–71; relations with
Germany 5, 6, 29–38; ritualization
in reconciliation with Germany
37–8; shared martyrdom of World
War I 34; symbolic resources used
by reconciliation entrepreneurs in
35–8
Frieberg, Annika 6, 116

Galtung, Johan 99
Gauck, Joachim 29
Gellner, Ernest 43
Gemba, Koichiro 106
geopolitics and memory politics 100–1,
107, 167–71
Germany 7; beyond realist and idealist
readings of symbolism in relations
between France and 32–5; Cold
War era 48–9, 49n5; emergence of
amity symbolism with France 30–2;
forgiveness model of reconciliation

and 46–7, 60–1; nationalizing projects in borderlands 44–5, 49n1; occupation of Poland during World War II 42; relations with France 5, 6, 29–38; relations with Poland 5, 8, 41–9, 149–51, 156–7; ritualization in reconciliation with France 37–8; shared martyrdom of World War I 34; symbolic resources used by reconciliation entrepreneurs in 35–8; teaching reconciliation in 112–13; Warsaw Ghetto Monument and 5, 41, 60, 150
Geyer, Michael 44
Gibney, Mark 139
Giscard-d'Estaing, Valéry 34, 166, 167
Goldstone Commission 17
Graczyk, Roman 47
Grand Overview 70–1
Grimaud, Nicole 165
Guam 102
Guan Fu 56, 60

Hadj, Messali 162, 167
hagiographic literature 34
Hague, William 113
Han Han 133
Hani, Chris 16
Harbi, Mohammed 116
Harmel, Pierre 157
Hauser, Béatrice 33
Hayner, Priscilla B. 138
He, Yinan 4, 54, 99, 100
Hegel, Georg W. F. 88
Hennclowa, Józefa 47
Heo, Seunghoon Emilia 9, 9n2, 107
Herzog, Roman 150
hierarchical trespasses 6–7
histoire croisée 44
historians as reconciliation teachers 116
historiography and reconciliation 169–70
Hitler, Adolf 37
Hobsbawm, Eric 43
Hollande, François 29, 38, 168, 169–70
Hong Kong 7, 8; current Chinese perspectives on 132–3; education and identity discourse in 130–1; historical background 128; recent trends in public opinion 131–2; reunification with China 122; rise of "Hongkongese" consciousness in 129–30; *see also* China
Hornc, Alistair 167
Horvat, A. 106
Howard-Hassman, Rhoda E. 49n6
Huáng Zongxi 77
Hu Jintao 130
Hunter, Alan 7–8

idealist readings of symbolism 32–5
Ighilahriz, Louisette 168
inherited animosities 8
Inkatha Freedom Party, South Africa 15, 16
Iwabuchi, Tatsuji, 65

Japan 9n2; challenges of teaching international reconciliation in 110–19; relations with China 8, 97, 98, 103; relations with Korea 9; role in World War II 7; zange and 7, 84–93; *see also* East Asia; Sino-Japanese relations; Tanabe, Hajime
Jarausch, Konrad 44
Jeanson, Francis 164
Joseph, Helen 19
Judeo-Christian traditions 62–4, 76, 116
Judson, Pieter 49n2

Kacowicz, A. 99
Kant, Immanuel 88
Katyn 116
Khaled, Cheb 171
King, Jeremy 43
Kisielewski, Stefan 149
Kogon, Eugen 61
Kohl, Helmut 29, 36, 154
Kohn, Hans 43
Kong, Master 72–3, 74, 75–6, 79; *see also* Confucius
Korea 7, 9, 9n2, 101; reconciliation theories and 98–100; relations between North and South 102; teaching reconciliation in 110, 113; *see also* East Asia; Sino-Japanese relations
Kozłowski, Krzysztof 153
Krim, Belkacem 167
Kupchan, C. 99

178 *Index*

Laos 102
leadership in reconciliation process
  18–19
Lederach, John Paul 4, 98
Lee Myung-bak 113
Lee Teng-hui 125, 126
Lefranc, Sandrine 34
Legge, James 73–4
Lehmann, Karl 153
Levet, Jean-Louis 116
Lian Po 58
Li Lóngxiàn 71, 74
Lin, Gang 9n3
Lin Xiang Ru 58
Lipscher, Winfried 48
Lithuania 48
Liu, Zaifu 9n3
Liú Zongzhou 77–8, 79, 80n13–14
Lombardo, Anthony 49n6
Long, William 9n4, 45–6
Lui, Tai-lok 131
Lunheng 56
Luthuli, Albert 19
Lu Zahogong 57

Ma, Eric Kit-wai 131
Maimonides 54, 62, 63
Malgin, Artiom 155
Manceron, Gilles 116
Mandela, Nelson 16, 18–19, 20
Maori people of New Zealand
  141–3, 146
Marianne allegory 36–7
Marrou, Henri-Irenée 164
Massu, Jacques 167
Matthews, Gordon 131
Ma Ying-jeou 127–8
Mazowiecki, Tadeusz 153
McGuinness, Martin 113
Memorandum of the Bensberg Circle
  149–50
memory and reconciliation 100–1,
  167–71
Mèngzi 74–5
Ménudier, Henry 33
Merkel, Angela 38, 113
metanoetics 83; *see also* zange
M'hidi, Larbi 168
Míng Rú xuéàn 77
Minow, Martha 139
Min Yue 59
missionism 152
Mitter, Rana 123

Mitterrand, François 29, 36, 166, 167
Morgenthau, H. 33
Mpetha, Oscar 19

Nanjing Massacre 97
national mythmaking 5
Naude, Beyers 19
Naylor, Phillip 2, 3, 8
New Zealand 7, 8; awareness of
  indigenous rights in 138, 145–6;
  child separation policies in 142–3;
  Mabo case 142; Maori of 141–4,
  146; native title in 140–1; processes
  addressing indigenous rights in
  138–9; state apology to Chinese
  community 144; state apology to
  Maori people 143–4; state apology
  to Samoa 144–5; Treaty of Waitangi
  141–2; Waitangi Tribunal 143–4;
  white settlers in 139–40; *see also*
  Australia
Niemöller, Martin 149
Nishida, Kitaro 90
Nobles, Melissa 138
Nora, Pierre 36
Norway 113
Northern Ireland 138

Obama, Barack 97, 102
obstacles to reconciliation 2–3
Okri, Ben 22
other-power 7, 86–8

Papon, Maurice 167
Park Geun-hye 113
Pepper, S. 129
Pervillé, Guy 169
Pétain, Philippe 37
Pfeil, Ulrich 33
Pfister, Lauren 7
Philippines, the 102
Philosophy as Metanoetics (*Zangedo toshite
  no tetsugaku*) 83, 84
Poland 7, 113; burden of historical
  injustices against 148–9; Cold
  War era 48–9, 49n5; European
  Union and 157; forgiveness model
  of reconciliation and 46–7, 60–1;
  nationalizing projects in borderlands
  44–5, 49n1; occupied by Germany
  during World War II 42; relations
  with Germany 6, 7, 8, 41–9, 149–51,
  156–7; relations with Russia 152–8;

religions and reconciliation 45, 47, 48, 149–50; Russophobia in 155–6; Warsaw Ghetto Monument 6, 41, 46, 60–2
politics: geo 100–1, 107; identity 122–35; memory 100–1, 167–71; trauma 103–5
power transitions 101–3
Preure, Mourad 116
Prometheanism 153
Pszon, Mieczysław 153
Putin, Vladimir 154

Ramaphosa, Cyril 19
Ratzinger, Joseph 149
realist readings of symbolism 32–5
reconciliation 1–2; confession and 62–4; definitions, obstacles, opportunities and the will for 2–3; dynamics in East Asia 105–7; entrepreneurs 35–8; forgiveness model of 46–7, 60–1; geopolitics and memory politics in 100–1, 167–71; historiography and 169–70; identity politics and 122–35; imperfection of 99; leadership in 18–19; memory and 100–1, 167–71; methodology and historiography for studying 3–5; nation building and 20–2; religion and 45, 47, 48, 62–4, 149; repentance and 83–93; state apologies and 5, 41, 54–5, 60–2, 65n3, 138, 143–5, 150; symbolism and 19, 29–30; teaching 110–19; theories and East Asia 98–100; xiezui 55–62, 65n5, 66n8–11; zange 7, 84–93
Reconciliation After Violent Conflict: A Handbook 9
Record of the Rites, The 72, 74–5, 76, 79
religion and reconciliation 45, 47, 48, 116, 149–50; confession in 62–4; repentance in 64; *see also* zange
religious actors as reconciliation teachers 116
Remouan, Hassan 116
repentance 64; self-power and other-power in 86–8; zange and 84–93
revenge, Ruist traditions of 69–79 *see also* Ruist traditions
ritualization in symbolism 37–8
Rock, S. R. 100
Rosoux, Valérie 33, 34–5

Ruist traditions 69, 78–9; ambivalence in response to vengeful action as dilemma in 74–5; identifying problem of vengefulness in Chinese cultural settings and 69–70; justifications of filial vengence 72–4; reconsidering teachings from Liú Zongzhou in overcoming 77–8; reconsidering teachings from *the analects* in overcoming 75–6; scope and justifications in Chinese literary contexts 70–2
Russia 7, 8, 48, 152–8; actions in Ukraine and Crimea 158; *see also* Soviet Union, the

Salem, Lyes 171
Samoa 144–5
Sangnier, Marc 36
Sansal, Boualam 171
Sarkin, Jeremy 6
Sarkozy, Nicolas 169
Sartre, Jean-Paul 164
Schröder, Gerhard 32
Schuman, Robert 30
self-inflicted void 2
self-power 86–8
Sénac, Jean 163
shared martyrdom 34
Shattered Past: Reconstructing German Histories 44
shichou 3
Shiji 55, 56, 60, 65n5, 66n7
Shin Pure Land Buddhism 83, 86–7; *see also* Tanabe, Hajime
Sinkkonen 133
Sino-Japanese relations 54–5; Brandt's Kniefall as model for xiezui in 60–2; confession as alternative system of post-wrongdoing expression in 62–4; state apologies and 54–5; xiezui in 55–62; *see also* East Asia
Sisulu, Albertina 19
Skibowski, Klaus Otto 48
Smith, Anthony D. 43
Snyder, Timothy 43
Soustelle, Jacques 163
South Africa 4, 5–6, 25–6; Inkatha Freedom Party 15, 16; interim Constitution 16; languages of 22; leaders in transition and reconciliation 18–19; nation building and reconciliation process 20–2; new

180   *Index*

Constitution 21–2; reconciliation journey 17–19; success with reconciliation process 15–17; Truth and Reconciliation Commission 4, 5, 9n4, 16, 17–18, 20, 22–5, 138

Soviet Union, the 104, 149, 152–8; *see also* Russia

Stalin, Josef 104, 152

Steinbach, Erika 151

Sterzinsky, Georg 153

Stomma, Stanisław 149, 153

Stora, Benjamin 116, 167, 170

Struve, Lynn 78

Sunflower, The 116

Sun Yat-sen 125

Susman, Helen 19

symbolism in reconciliation process: beyond realist and idealist readings of 32–5; emergence of amity 30–2; in Franco-German relations 29–30; in South Africa 19

Taha, Rachid 171

Taiwan 7, 8; commonalities with China 122; current Chinese perspectives on 132–3; historical background 124; identity politics and mainland relations under Ma Ying-jeou 127–8; nativism and educational politics 125–6; official identity discourse in Martial Law era 124–5

Tambo, O. R. 19

Tanabe, Hajime 7, 83–4; on death of reason 88–9; ethical implications of philosophy of 89–91; on meaning of zange 84–6; on self-power and other-power 86–8

teaching reconciliation 110–11; contributing to reconciliation 111–12; in Europe compared to Asia 112–13; hope for Asia 117–19; *two to tango* approach 115–17; and what makes us believe what we believe 113–14

Thévenot, Laurent 35

Three People's Principles 125, 126

Thum, Gregor 43

trauma politics 103–5

Treaty of Waitangi 141–2

Treaty of Waitangi Act 142

Truth and Reconciliation Commission, South African 4, 5, 9n4, 16, 17–18, 20, 22–5, 138

Truth of Postwar History and Politicians Crushed by the US 103

Tung Chee-hwa 130, 134

Turowicz, Jerzy 153

Tusk, Donald 154

Tutu, Desmond 1, 4, 9, 19

two to tango approach to teaching reconciliation 115–17

Ukeru, Magosaki 103

Ukraine 158

United States, the 102, 157

Urbain, Ismaÿl 162

Veblen, Thorstein 123

Versöhnung 3

Verwoerd, Hendrik 19

Vickers, Edward 8

Vietnam War 102

Wada, Andrzej 116

Wałesa, Lech 149

Walsh, Dermott 7

Walt, S. M. 100

Waltz, K. N. 100

Wang, Z. 101

Wáng Li 70–2, 74

Wang Ming-ke 126

Wáng Yángmíng 77–8, 79, 90

War and Reconciliation: Reason and Emotion in Conflict Resolution 45

Warsaw Ghetto Monument 5, 41, 46, 60–2, 150

Weissman, M. 107

Weizsäcker, Richard von 150, 153

Werner, Michael 44

Wiesenthal, Simon 116

will to reconcile 2–3

Wolff-Powęska, Anna 149

World War I: peace/reconciliation trees 36; as shared martyrdom 34

World War II: French voluntary combatants in the Nazi SS during 37, 39n3; *histoire croisée* 44; mass genocide in Poland during 148; Tanabe Hajime on 83–4, 88; Warsaw Ghetto Monument and 5, 41, 46, 60–2, 150; *see also* France; Germany; Poland

Wyszyński, Stefan 47

xiezui 55–60, 65n5, 66n8–11; Brandt's Kniefall as model of 60–2; limitations of 64–5
Xi Jinping 97
Xu Jia 59, 63

Yacine, Kateb 163
Yang Jiechi 106
Yeltsin, Boris 153
Yonah, Rabbeinu 63
Young, James 2

Zahra, Tara 45
zange 7; death of reason and 88–9; ethical implications of 89–91; meaning of 84–6; self-power and other-power in 86–8
Zembylas, Michalinos 171
Zen Buddhism 87
Zeroual, Liaminc 167
Zhu Rongji 54
Ziebura, G. 32
Zimmerman, Bénédicte 44